Domestic Abuse and Child Contact

This book presents papers from an International Symposium on Contact Disputes and Allegations of Domestic Violence: Identifying Best Practices, held in London in May 2017.

The editors invited a group of international experts to explain the approaches taken in their jurisdictions to allegations of domestic violence in child contact cases, with a view to identifying international best practices in such cases. The book includes contributions from England and Wales, Scotland, Ireland, Canada, Sweden and Spain, as well as information presented at the symposium from New Zealand and Australia. The chapters include attention to particular issues such as specialist domestic violence courts, judicial training and hearing children's voices. Collectively, the chapters identify a set of common problems experienced across all of the jurisdictions, including an overwhelming emphasis on the value of children's ongoing contact with non-resident parents and the consequent minimisation of domestic violence and the muting of the voices of children who do not wish to have contact with abusive parents. Best practices in taking domestic violence seriously and providing adequate protection from further abuse for children and non-abusive parents were less in evidence. However, the concluding chapter draws together details of several initiatives and approaches which offer promising ways forward.

The chapters in this book were originally published as a special issue of the *Journal of Social Welfare and Family Law.*

Rosemary Hunter FAcSS is Professor of Law and Socio-Legal Studies at the University of Kent.

Adrienne Barnett is Senior Lecturer in Law at Brunel University London.

Felicity Kaganas is Professor of Law at Brunel University London.

Shazia Choudhry is Professor of Law at Queen Mary University of London.

Domestic Abuse and Child Contact

International Experience

Edited by
Rosemary Hunter, Adrienne Barnett, Felicity Kaganas and Shazia Choudhry

Routledge
Taylor & Francis Group
LONDON AND NEW YORK

First published 2021
by Routledge
2 Park Square, Milton Park, Abingdon, Oxon, OX14 4RN

and by Routledge
52 Vanderbilt Avenue, New York, NY 10017

Routledge is an imprint of the Taylor & Francis Group, an informa business

British Library Cataloguing-in-Publication Data
A catalogue record for this book is available from the British Library

ISBN13: 978-0-367-64538-0

Typeset in Minion Pro
by codeMantra

Publisher's Note
The publisher accepts responsibility for any inconsistencies that may have arisen during the conversion of this book from journal articles to book chapters, namely the inclusion of journal terminology.

Disclaimer
Every effort has been made to contact copyright holders for their permission to reprint material in this book. The publishers would be grateful to hear from any copyright holder who is not here acknowledged and will undertake to rectify any errors or omissions in future editions of this book.

Contents

Citation Information

The chapters in this book were originally published in the *Journal of Social Welfare and Family Law*, volume 40, issue 4 (2018). When citing this material, please use the original page numbering for each article, as follows:

Introduction

Introduction: contact and domestic abuse
Rosemary Hunter, Adrienne Barnett and Felicity Kaganas
Journal of Social Welfare and Family Law, volume 40, issue 4 (2018) pp. 401–425

Chapter 1

National self-image as an obstacle to ensuring children's rights in the context of domestic violence and family law – the case of Sweden
Linnéa Bruno
Journal of Social Welfare and Family Law, volume 40, issue 4 (2018) pp. 426–440

Chapter 2

Contact disputes and allegations of gender violence in Spain
Teresa Picontó-Novales
Journal of Social Welfare and Family Law, volume 40, issue 4 (2018) pp. 441–458

Chapter 3

A voice or a choice? Children's views on participating in decisions about post-separation contact with domestically abusive fathers
Stephanie Holt
Journal of Social Welfare and Family Law, volume 40, issue 4 (2018) pp. 459–476

Chapter 4

The approach in Scotland to child contact disputes involving allegations of domestic abuse
Kirsteen M Mackay
Journal of Social Welfare and Family Law, volume 40, issue 4 (2018) pp. 477–495

Chapter 5

Enhancing judicial skills in domestic violence cases: the development, implementation, and preliminary evaluation of a model US programme
Peter G Jaffe, Claire V Crooks, Maureen Reid, Jennifer White, Danielle Pugh-Markie and Linda Baker
Journal of Social Welfare and Family Law, volume 40, issue 4 (2018) pp. 496–514

Chapter 6

Specialised domestic violence courts in Canada and the United States: Key factors in prioritising safety for women and children
Jennifer Koshan
Journal of Social Welfare and Family Law, volume 40, issue 4 (2018) pp. 515–532

Chapter 7

Specialist domestic violence courts for child arrangement cases: safer courtrooms and safer outcomes?
Mandy Burton
Journal of Social Welfare and Family Law, volume 40, issue 4 (2018) pp. 533–547

Conclusion

Conclusion: international best practices
Rosemary Hunter and Shazia Choudhry
Journal of Social Welfare and Family Law, volume 40, issue 4 (2018) pp. 548–562

Contributors

Linda Baker Faculty of Education, Western University, London, Canada.

Adrienne Barnett Brunel Law School, Brunel University, London, UK.

Linnéa Bruno Department of Child and Youth Studies, Stockholm University, Sweden.

Mandy Burton Law School, University of Leicester, UK.

Shazia Choudhry School of Law, Queen Mary University of London, UK.

Claire V Crooks Faculty of Education, Western University, London, Canada.

Stephanie Holt School of Social Work & Social Policy, Trinity College Dublin, Ireland.

Rosemary Hunter Kent Law School, University of Kent, UK.

Peter G Jaffe Faculty of Education, Western University, London, Canada.

Felicity Kaganas Brunel Law School, Brunel University, London, UK.

Jennifer Koshan Faculty of Law, University of Calgary, Canada.

Kirsteen M Mackay Faculty of Business and Law, Open University, UK.

Teresa Picontó-Novales Facultad de derecho, Universidad de Zaragoza, Spain.

Danielle Pugh-Markie Center for Court Innovation, New York, USA.

Maureen Reid Faculty of Education, Western University, London, Canada.

Jennifer White Futures without Violence, San Francisco, USA.

Introduction: contact and domestic abuse

Rosemary Hunter, Adrienne Barnett and Felicity Kaganas

ABSTRACT

This article introduces the special issue of the *Journal of Social Welfare and Family Law* on contact disputes and allegations of domestic abuse. It first describes the aims and findings of the International Symposium on Contact Disputes and Allegations of Domestic Violence – Identifying Best Practices at which the papers in the special issue were originally presented. It then outlines the position in England and Wales regarding allegations of domestic abuse in child arrangements cases, highlighting the difference between the 'law in the books' and the 'law in action'. Thirdly, it discusses the research evidence on another prominent international approach to domestic abuse allegations – legislative presumptions against custody or unsupervised visitation/contact for abusive parents. The experience of presumptions in the USA and New Zealand suggests that a similar gap between 'law in the books' and 'law in action' exists, together with potential problems of legislative drafting. Finally, the article outlines the contributions of the other papers in the special issue to our understanding of international approaches to ensuring safety for children and resident parents in family proceedings where allegations of domestic abuse are raised.

The international symposium on contact disputes and allegations of domestic violence – identifying best practices

Post-separation arrangements for children where domestic abuse[1] is a feature of parental relationships is an area of law and practice that has troubled women's groups and feminist scholars, including the editors of this special issue, for many years. In England and Wales domestic abuse was virtually ignored in legal and family law professional practice relating to post-separation child contact, jeopardising the safety and well-being of children and victim parents, until the landmark case of *Re L, V, M, H (Contact: Domestic Violence)* [2001] Fam 260, when the Court of Appeal laid down guidelines for courts in such cases. Since then, we have seen a 'cycle of failure' – demonstrable failure to apply the *Re L* guidelines, new practice provisions designed to strengthen the guidelines, continuing concerns about implementation of the new provisions prompting further reforms, followed by renewed concerns about implementation.

This led the editors of this special issue to ponder how we could escape the cycle of failure and, in particular, how real and sustained cultural change in legal and professional practices and perceptions could be achieved. It was apparent from international research and literature that other jurisdictions experienced similar issues in family law to those encountered in England and Wales. Rather than focusing on our domestic failings, we wondered what we could learn from the way in which those other jurisdictions managed such cases.

The result of these questions was an International Symposium held on 4–5 May 2017 at the Inner Temple in London. Sponsored by The Honourable Society of the Inner Temple, Queen Mary University of London and Brunel University London, the aim of the Symposium was to identify best practices for dealing with allegations of domestic abuse in family law proceedings concerning post-separation arrangements for children. Experts in the field from Australia, New Zealand, Sweden, Spain, the USA, Canada, England and Wales, Scotland and Ireland were invited to present papers about the measures adopted in their jurisdictions to address this issue and to evaluate how those measures were working in practice. We were particularly interested to hear about the success or otherwise of specific approaches including presumptions against unsupervised contact with perpetrators of domestic abuse (New Zealand, the USA), legislation prioritising child safety concerns (Australia, Sweden), the explicit framing of domestic abuse as gender violence/violence against women and of children as direct victims of gender violence (Spain), specialist domestic violence courts (the USA, Canada, England and Wales), judicial education (Canada, the USA) and strategies of listening to children affected by abuse (Scotland, Ireland). Our interest was also determinedly socio-legal. Speakers were asked to address not just what their laws or other measures provided for, but how they operated in practice, and what factors helped or hindered their effective implementation. Representatives of key stakeholder groups in England and Wales, including the judiciary, policy makers, government agencies, women's groups, and academics, attended and participated in the international dialogue about what works to prioritise safety and minimise harm for children and adult victims of abuse in private family law cases, and how models adopted elsewhere might translate (or not) into the local context. This special issue presents most of the papers from the Symposium, providing a rich compilation of international experience on contact and domestic abuse. Where, for one reason or another, Symposium participants were not able to write up their paper, we have included key information from their jurisdictions and presentations in this Introduction and in the Concluding article.

While we had expected to identify a range of 'good practice' models from overseas which might prompt a rethink of the approach taken in England and Wales, it is fair to say that the main message of the Symposium was not of the existence of a wealth of better options, but of widely shared common problems, which persist across a range of different legislative and practice configurations. While this suggests that the unsatisfactory state of affairs in England and Wales is by no means unique – and indeed may not be as internationally lagging as we had expected and can be seen to have some virtues in that context – it does mean that there are not many positive alternatives available to be drawn upon for future practice development. Nevertheless, a handful of approaches discussed at the Symposium stood out as offering at least a potential way forward. The two major obstacles to the effective implementation of *any* measures designed to ensure safety from domestic abuse which emerged clearly from the presentations and discussions are a pro-contact culture in the family justice system and, related to this, the under-resourcing of services and systems to support children, affected parents and perpetrator parents, and to promote judicial and practitioner expertise in understanding and addressing issues of abuse. If these characteristics are present, other initiatives aiming to foster safety are likely to be undermined. Three approaches which can help to achieve change in the underpinning culture and related resourcing are the adoption of a human rights framework for determining contact disputes involving allegations of domestic abuse, the adoption of trauma-informed practice by family justice systems and actors, and the development of integrated services which seek to address issues of domestic abuse in a holistic way, focusing on the needs of the family as a whole rather than solely on the legal matter raised in an application for contact or a protective injunction. These three approaches are the subject of the final article in this special issue.

The Symposium opened with an account of the current situation concerning domestic abuse allegations in child arrangement proceedings in England and Wales, for the benefit of our international audience. This was followed by an analysis of the evidence from the USA and New Zealand on presumptions against contact. We now turn to a discussion of these two issues, before introducing the subsequent articles in this special issue.

Child arrangements and domestic abuse – the state of play in England and Wales

Despite persistent evidence over the last 20 years that domestic abuse is minimised by family courts and professionals dealing with post-separation arrangements for children, and that (mostly) mothers and children may be exposed to unsafe contact arrangements, little real progress has been made. Drawing on the available research evidence and recent case law, we suggest reasons why the framework for dealing with allegations of domestic abuse in child arrangements proceedings is problematic and why the current approach may not be working effectively.

Background

Family law cases involving litigation between divorcing or separating couples over post-separation arrangements for their children are known as 'child arrangements cases' in England and Wales. This replaces the previous statutory language of 'custody' and 'access', and subsequently 'residence' and 'contact'. 'Child arrangements orders' are defined as orders 'regulating arrangements relating to...with whom [and when] a child is to live, spend time or otherwise have contact...with any person' (s 8 Children Act 1989). Section 1 of the Children Act 1989 provides that, when a court is considering making an order, the child's welfare must be the paramount consideration. Courts are further guided by the 'welfare checklist' set out in s 1(3) of the Children Act 1989, which requires courts to 'have regard in particular' to a range of factors including the child's wishes and feelings, their characteristics and needs, the capability of the parents in meeting those needs, and any harm which the child has suffered or is at risk of suffering.

Since the late 1970s family policy and legal decision-making and professional practice in parenting proceedings has been shaped by the strong assumption that children need contact with non-resident fathers for their emotional, psychological and developmental health, leading to what has been described as a de facto 'presumption of contact' (Bailey-Harris, Barron, & Pearce, 1999; Hunt & Macleod, 2008). The higher courts have repeatedly emphasised that 'cogent' or 'compelling' reasons are required to refuse contact and that courts should not 'give up' on endeavouring to ensure that contact happens.[2] This construction of the welfare principle, together with the perception that 'conflict' and contested court hearings are 'bad' for children, has led to a strong imperative by judges and legal and child welfare professionals to encourage agreement for contact (Bailey-Harris, Davis, Barron, & Pearce, 1998; Hunter & Barnett, 2013). Mothers who oppose or seek to restrict contact have been seen as 'implacably hostile', i.e. selfish, manipulative, irrational or unreasonable (Harrison, 2008; Kaganas & Day Sclater, 2004) or, more recently, as potentially 'alienating' their children against their fathers (Eaton, Jarmain, & Lustigman, 2016).

Despite the strength of the 'presumption of contact' and the rarity of refusals of contact orders (less than 0.3% in 2011) (Ministry of Justice, 2012), fathers' rights groups pressed for a presumption of shared care, asserting that courts were unreasonably excluding fathers from children's lives. The Family Justice Review in 2011 recommended against any presumption (Family Justice Review, 2011, p. 23). Contrary to this recommendation, in April 2014 the government amended s 1 of the Children Act 1989 to include a presumption that 'unless the contrary is shown…involvement of [a] parent in the life of the child concerned will further the child's welfare' so long as that parent can be involved in the child's life in a way that does not put the child at risk of suffering harm.

The cycle of failure: child arrangements/contact and domestic violence

UK Government strategies to end violence against women and girls focus on criminal prosecutions, education, and support for victims of violence (HM Government, 2014, 2016). In addition, local authorities take the protection of children from exposure to domestic violence to be a central part of their child protection role (Local Government Association, Cafcass, & Women's Aid, 2006). However, domestic violence policies in England and Wales rarely address the area of private family law. Marianne Hester has observed that the 'differences in culture, practice and discourse' between professionals working in criminal justice, child protection and family law proceedings is so striking that they could be said to occupy three different planets (Hester, 2011).

Yet a large proportion of child arrangements/contact cases in England and Wales take place within a context of domestic abuse (at least 50% – see, e.g. Cafcass & Women's Aid, 2017; Harding & Newnham, 2015; HMICA, 2005; Hunt & Macleod, 2008; Perry & Rainey, 2007). Despite this prevalence and the well-documented effects of domestic abuse on victims and children, courts and professionals in England and Wales virtually ignored the issue of domestic abuse when considering applications for residence or contact. The pioneering study by Marianne Hester and Lorraine Radford in 1996 revealed that the perceived importance for children of maintaining contact with non-resident fathers led courts and professionals to minimise domestic violence and to focus on persuading mothers to agree to contact rather than on fathers' behaviour, with the result that very few of the contact arrangements agreed or ordered in cases involving domestic violence were ultimately safe (Hester & Radford, 1996; see also Anderson, 1997; Barnett, 2000; Kaganas & Piper, 1999).

As a result of the research by Hester and Radford and pressure from women's groups, the Children Act Sub-Committee of the Lord Chancellor's Advisory Board on Family Law (CASC) published 'good practice' guidelines for the judiciary setting out the approach which ought to be taken when domestic violence was put forward as a reason for denying or limiting parental contact (Lord Chancellor's Advisory Board, 2001). At the same time, the Court of Appeal heard the combined appeals of *Re L, V, M, H (Contact: Domestic Violence)* [2001] Fam 260. Drawing on a report to the court by expert child psychologists, Drs Sturge and Glaser (2000), the court acknowledged that domestic violence involves a 'significant failure in parenting' and laid down guidelines for courts and professionals in contact cases where allegations of domestic violence are made, based on those developed by CASC. These include the requirement to hold a fact-finding hearing on disputed allegations of domestic violence and the imperative to ensure that the risk of harm is minimised and the safety of the child and resident parent is secured before, during and after contact.

Subsequent research indicated that the *Re L* and CASC guidelines were largely ignored and their application was inconsistent and 'patchy' because courts and professionals continued to prioritise contact over children's and resident parents' safety. Domestic violence continued to be minimised by courts and professionals and women who raised allegations of domestic violence continued to be viewed with suspicion, disbelieved and treated as obstructive. Fact-finding hearings were inconsistently and rarely held, and even in cases of proven domestic violence, applications for direct contact were very rarely refused; the most common final outcomes were for direct, unsupervised contact (Aris & Harrison, 2007; DCA and DfES, 2004; HM Inspectorate of Court Administration, 2005; Humphreys & Harrison, 2003; Hunt & Macleod, 2008; Perry & Rainey, 2007; Trinder, Connolly, Kellet, & Thoday, 2004; Trinder, Firth, & Jenks, 2009).

Following the publication by Women's Aid of a report about 29 children who were killed in England and Wales between 1994 and 2004 as a result of contact arrangements (Saunders, 2004), the Family Justice Council (FJC) issued a report which called for a 'cultural change...with a move away from "contact is always the appropriate way forward" to "contact that is safe and positive for the child is always the appropriate way forward"' (Craig, 2007, p. 27). The FJC recommended that a Practice Direction should be issued embodying the CASC and *Re L* guidelines and its own recommendations. In response, a Practice Direction was issued by the President of the Family Division in May 2008 which was revised in 2009 and subsequently incorporated into the Family Procedure Rules 2010 as Practice Direction 12J (PD12J). PD12J now establishes the framework to be followed by courts and professionals in child arrangements cases where allegations of domestic abuse are raised.

The history of PD12J since its introduction bears a striking resemblance to the history leading up to it. Research following its introduction showed that PD12J was not being implemented as intended. Although there were some variations in practices and approaches, judges and professionals tended to see only recent, serious physical violence as being relevant to the issue of contact (Barnett, 2014, 2016; Coy, Perks, Scott, & Tweedale, 2012; Hunter & Barnett, 2013; Thiara & Gill, 2012). Hunter and Barnett (2013) found a marked difference between 'legalistic' understandings of domestic abuse, focused on discrete incidents of physical violence (largely held by family lawyers and the judiciary), and social science understandings, which recognise its power and control dynamics. Judges and professionals continued to view women's complaints about domestic violence with suspicion, perceiving them to be a delaying tactic and/or designed to disrupt the other party's relationship with the child (Barnett, 2015; Coy et al., 2012; Hunter & Barnett, 2013). Risk was not always adequately assessed because the nature of the abuse was misunderstood (Trinder, Hunt, Macleod, Pearce, & Woodward, 2013), and the risk and welfare assessment provisions of PD12J were not applied properly or at all. Direct contact was invariably agreed or ordered and refusals of contact orders continued to decline (Barnett, 2014, 2016; Coy et al., 2012; Hunter & Barnett, 2013). The most likely type of contact ordered would be supervised or supported, although resort was often had to informal means of supervision by family or friends because of the limited availability of contact services (Hunter & Barnett, 2013). Hunter and Barnett (2013) concluded, therefore, that the 'cultural shift' called for by the FJC remained incomplete.

PD12J was revised in April 2014 to bring its provisions and terminology into line with other amendments to child arrangements proceedings that came into effect at that time. The amendments included inserting a new, broader definition of 'domestic violence' focusing on coercive control, implementing some of Hunter and Barnett's recommendations in order to improve protection for children and victim parents, and attempting to make the process more user-friendly for litigants in person (LIPs).

In 2016 Women's Aid published *Nineteen Child Homicides*, which updated its earlier report and documented the deaths of a further 19 children killed by their fathers in the context of contact arrangements between 2005 and 2015. At the same time, Women's Aid launched its Child First campaign 'to stop avoidable child deaths as a result of unsafe child contact with dangerous perpetrators of domestic violence' (Women's Aid, 2016). A Parliamentary Briefing Paper by the All-Party Parliamentary Group on Domestic Violence (2016) and a House of Commons debate on domestic abuse, child contact and the family courts held on 15 September 2016, both highlighted serious concerns about the treatment and experiences of victims of domestic abuse in family courts and made further recommendations for reform. In November 2016 Mr Justice Cobb, having reviewed PD12J at the request of the President of the Family Division, produced a report with proposed revisions to PD12J (Cobb, 2016). The final, revised (and current) version of PD12J came into effect on 2 October 2017, having been somewhat watered down from Mr Justice Cobb's original draft. PD12J 2017 reinforces the mandatory nature of many of its provisions, clarifies its broad concern with all forms of domestic abuse, and requires courts to record in their orders certain information demonstrating that its provisions have been followed. Whether the latest revisions will overcome the dominant 'contact at all costs' approach and the other obstacles to achieving a real cultural shift discussed below, remains to be seen.

In theory: the procedure for addressing allegations of abuse

PD12J sets out in considerable detail a four-stage procedure that courts are supposed to follow when allegations of abuse are raised as an issue in child arrangements proceedings.

First, the issue of abuse needs to be brought to the court's attention. This is not entirely left to the parties. In all child arrangements proceedings the court's child welfare service – known as Cafcass (the Children and Family Court Advisory and Support Service) – will undertake initial safeguarding checks with police and local authorities, and separately with the parties, to identify any prior criminal or social services actions or concerns relating to domestic or child abuse. The results of safeguarding checks are supposed to be available to the court at the first hearing, termed the

First Hearing Dispute Resolution Appointment (FHDRA). If the results of the safeguarding checks are not available at the FHDRA 'and no other reliable safeguarding information is available, the court must adjourn the FHDRA until the results of safeguarding checks are available' and should not generally make any interim child arrangements order in the absence of safeguarding information (PD12J, para. 12).

Secondly, if there are contested allegations of domestic abuse which are relevant to any child arrangements order the court may make, the court must determine as soon as possible whether it is necessary to conduct a fact-finding hearing to adjudicate on the disputed allegations, in order to provide a factual basis for the subsequent welfare determination, including the assessment of risk (para. 16). Where disputed allegations of domestic abuse are undetermined, PD12J prescribes that the court should not make an interim child arrangements order unless it is satisfied that it is in the interests of the child to do so and the order would not expose the child or the non-abusive parent to an 'unmanageable' risk of harm (para. 25).

Thirdly, once it is established that domestic abuse has been perpetrated (whether as a result of findings of fact, admissions or otherwise), the court must consider whether to order any expert assessment of any party or the child (including a safety and risk assessment), and whether any party should engage in any intervention (such as participation in a Domestic Violence Perpetrator Programme (DVPP)) as a precondition to any child arrangements order (paras. 33–34). The assessment is often undertaken by a Cafcass officer, but other experts may be instructed.

Finally, a determination should be made of what arrangements will be in the child's welfare. In making this determination, the court must take into account the abuse found to have occurred, any risk assessment, any harm the child and the resident parent has suffered or is at risk of suffering, a range of factors derived from the original Sturge and Glaser report (Sturge & Glaser, 2000) (including the motivation of the abusive parent in seeking contact and their likely behaviour during contact), the other factors in the welfare checklist, and the need to ensure that future arrangements will be in the best interests of the child, will not expose the child to an 'unmanageable' risk of harm, and will not expose the resident parent to further domestic abuse (paras. 35–37).

Additionally, in recognition of the fact that a high proportion of child arrangements orders are made by consent, PD12J requires the court to scrutinise proposed consent orders to ensure they accord with the welfare of the child (para. 6). In this respect, it tries to ensure that courts have sufficient information available to them about (potential) issues of abuse to enable them to determine whether proposed agreements are likely to be safe.

This process, on paper, seems to focus attention appropriately on determining the existence and effects of domestic abuse and to prioritise the safety of children and their non-abusive parents. However, when it comes to implementation, ongoing problems have been encountered at every stage.

In practice: barriers to implementation

The assumption in favour of contact

PD12J operates in the context of the very strong assumption – now reinforced by the legislative presumption – that contact is always in children's best interests. This includes the notion that contact is always better than no contact, that direct contact is always better than indirect contact, and that unrestricted contact is the ideal to be worked towards. The onus is very firmly on the party seeking to deny or limit contact, and a very high level of risk must be established before contact will be considered potentially harmful. This position is reinforced by case law from the Court of Appeal, which has been at pains to promote contact and so, in many cases, has downgraded and minimised anything other than severe, recent physical violence. In domestic abuse-contact cases reported in 2014–16, the Court of Appeal allowed five out of seven appeals. In all of these cases, a fact-finding exercise had been undertaken at which trial judges made findings of abusive behaviour and refused to order direct contact, but the appeal court overturned their decisions (Barnett, 2017). Mr Justice Cobb's original amendments to PD12J provided that the statutory presumption of contact contained in s 1(2A) of the Children Act 1989 should not apply '[w]here the involvement of a parent in a child's life would put the child or other parent at risk of suffering harm arising from domestic violence or abuse' (Cobb, 2016, p. 12). But this was omitted from the final draft which only requires courts to 'consider carefully whether the statutory presumption applies' when domestic abuse is alleged or admitted (para. 7) – a missed opportunity to mitigate the strong pro-contact culture.

Pressures to settle

As discussed above, parents in dispute over post-separation arrangements for their children are pressured from every angle to settle rather than pursue their dispute in court. The government expects parents to take responsibility for their own private disputes rather than relying on public resources to resolve them,. and reinforced this message in 2013 by withdrawing legal aid for family court proceedings (other than for those victims of abuse who can produce specified evidence of the abuse) while strongly promoting the alternative avenue of mediation (Legal Aid, Sentencing and Punishment of Offenders Act 2012). There is compelling evidence that cases involving domestic abuse are inappropriately accepted into and 'settled' in mediation (Barlow, Hunter, Smithson, & Ewing, 2017). And parties to cases that do go to court are still encouraged by the court and lawyers to reach agreement (Barnett, 2016).

While PD12J exhorts courts to scrutinise proposed consent orders to ensure that they do not expose children and non-abusive parents to the risk of harm, its provisions continue to be undermined by the strong pro-settlement culture and lack of resources to adjudicate in most or even a sizeable proportion of cases involving issues of domestic abuse (Hunter & Barnett, 2013). A recent study by Cafcass and Women's Aid (2017) found that the vast majority of interim and final orders, including in cases where allegations of domestic abuse were raised, were made by consent.

When is abuse considered relevant?

Hunter and Barnett (2013) documented a range of views among judges and lawyers as to when allegations of violence would be considered 'relevant' to the question of contact (see also Barnett, 2015; Coy et al., 2012). In particular there remained a widely-held belief that violent men could be 'good enough' fathers, that violence against the mother did not necessarily have any impact on the children, that 'historic' violence which had occurred earlier in the relationship, when children were too young to remember, or which had been succeeded by apparently 'successful' contact could be disregarded, or that only severe physical violence directed at or in the presence of the children was relevant.

As noted above, the 2014 revisions to PD12J broadened the definition of domestic abuse to emphasise coercive and controlling behaviour, and also reinforced the fact that children may suffer psychological or emotional harm from living with violence and abuse and may also be harmed indirectly 'where the domestic abuse impairs the parenting capacity of either or both of their parents' (para. 4). Nevertheless, recent case law shows some judges continuing to dismiss 'historic' violence and focusing solely on physical violence. For example, in *Re V (A Child) (Inadequate Reasons for Findings of Fact)* [2015] EWCA Civ 274, McFarlane LJ emphasised the fact that all but one of the allegations took place prior to the child's birth or when he was still an infant despite an ongoing pattern of coercive and controlling behaviour. For this reason, he said:

> most, if not all, of the allegations were not in fact relevant to whether or not young T in 2012/2013, who had been having contact with his father, including staying contact, at whatever regularity, could carry on having contact to this father in the future. [37]

Yet Cafcass and Women's Aid point out that 'contact taking place before proceedings and [by] consent may not always equate to an "agreement" about contact and may instead be indicative of a context of coercion or fear' (Cafcass & Women's Aid, 2017, p. 3). Similarly, in *Re K (Children)* [2016] EWCA Civ 99 the trial judge dismissed as irrelevant an incident of physical violence that took place five years earlier on the basis that there was 'no evidence of recent physical violence between father and mother' (at [13]), failing to contextualise the earlier violence within his findings of continuing controlling, aggressive behaviour. When allegations considered insufficiently serious or recent are 'weeded out' and disregarded, the welfare determination then proceeds as if those allegations did not exist.

Other pressures not to hold a fact-finding hearing

The pre-2014 research suggested that fact-finding hearings were disfavoured because they introduced delays in the proceedings, increased 'acrimony' between the parties, used up scarce resources, and were, in any event, to little effect because findings of abuse carried relatively little weight in the welfare determination (Barnett, 2014, 2015; Hunter & Barnett, 2013). Thus, there was a tendency to avoid fact-finding hearings if possible, but scant evidence to suggest that allegations of abuse were dealt with at the final, welfare hearing. These pressures on court time and judicial resources have only intensified since 2014, coupled with a new procedural emphasis on judges managing cases tightly and concluding them expeditiously (Practice Direction 12B – the Child Arrangements Programme). This was seen recently, for example, in the case of *Re T* [2016] EWCA Civ 1210, in which, after lengthy delays, the trial judge discharged orders for a fact-finding hearing on the basis that proceeding with the hearing was no longer either necessary or proportionate. As the Court of Appeal pointed out, however, rather than moving to a composite hearing at which both the contested allegations of violence and the other welfare issues could be dealt with together, the judge had simply jettisoned the allegations and treated them as no longer relevant to the question of welfare, a decision that was held to be wrong in principle.

While there has been no systematic review of court files since the advent of PD12J to determine how often fact-finding hearings are held, a recent small-scale study by Cafcass and Women's Aid of 216 files found 62% contained allegations of domestic abuse but a fact-finding hearing was held in only five cases (2017, p. 10). Nor is there any evidence to suggest that contested allegations are routinely dealt with at composite hearings instead. PD12J 2017 provides detailed guidance as to how a court should determine whether it is necessary to engage in the fact-finding exercise, and requires courts to record in the order their reasons for determining that a fact-finding hearing is not necessary. The list of potential reasons, however, remains a long one.

The focus of fact-finding on 'incidents' of violence

Separate fact-finding hearings have their origins in child protection proceedings, where they were introduced to facilitate the process of determining whether the 'threshold criteria' for the court's intervention are met – that is, that the child has suffered or is at risk of suffering significant harm due to lack of reasonable parental care (Children Act 1989 s 31). Courts were encouraged to consider 'whether or not there were questions of fact within a case which needed to be determined at an early stage' (Wall, 2010, para. 11). Bracewell J in *Re S (Care Proceedings: Split Hearing)* [1996] 2 FLR 773, explained that cases suitable for such 'split hearings' 'would be likely to be cases in which there is a clear and stark issue [in dispute], such as sexual abuse or physical abuse' (at 775). From their inception, therefore, fact-finding hearings are a product of and are underpinned by a legalistic, incident-based approach to allegations of abuse.

The practice also developed of requiring the use of so-called Scott Schedules for fact-finding hearings, which are itemised tables setting out the dates and brief descriptions of the specific allegations the alleged victim seeks to prove, together with the alleged perpetrator's response. These schedules can have the effect of compelling victims to construct and articulate the abuse they have sustained in a disaggregated and decontextualised way. Furthermore, the pre-2014 research found that many judges, in an effort to contain the scope of fact-finding hearings, would limit the number of 'incidents' that could be included in the schedule, and anecdotal evidence suggests that this practice continues (Barnett, 2015; Hunter & Barnett, 2013). At best, then, findings would be made on a limited number of discrete incidents of physical violence, which meant that the full extent of the risk posed to the victim and child was minimised or invisible. The 2014 revisions to PD12J attempted to counter the incident-focus of fact-finding by specifically directing the court to consider 'what evidence is required in order to determine the existence of a pattern of coercive, controlling or threatening behaviour, violence or abuse' (para. 19).[3] Unfortunately, at a late stage of the drafting, an amendment was added so that the court is also required to consider whether 'the key facts in dispute can be contained in a ... Scott Schedule' (para. 19).

A further problem with fact-finding hearings is that the alleged victim has the burden of proving the abuse. So if the judge cannot decide which party is telling the truth, and there is no 'independent' evidence to assist, they can simply decide that the victim has not proved her case. In *Re V (Inadequate Reasons for Findings of Fact)* [2015] EWCA Civ 274, for example, the trial judge found that the mother had failed to prove that the father had bombarded her with threatening calls and messages. This, in turn, led the Court of Appeal to highlight the 'historical' nature of the findings that *were* made against the father, which was one of the reasons why his appeal was allowed. Victims' ability to prove the abuse they have sustained may also be impeded by the suspicion and disbelief with which women's allegations of abuse are met, and the inability of courts and professionals to understand the effects of abuse on women, whose coping strategies can include 'dissociating themselves from the violence, "forgetting" about abuse, retaining vague and sketchy memories of violent incidents, [and] minimising the seriousness of the violence' (Hunter, 2006, p. 742). This can be seen in the perception that mothers who are 'credible' in their testimony should be able to provide a coherent narrative. In *Re V (Inadequate Reasons for Findings of Fact)* McFarlane LJ unpicked the trial judge's findings against the father by comparing what the mother had said in her Scott Schedule against her oral evidence and that of her witnesses and in so doing, found inevitable inconsistencies and contradictions which undermined her credibility.

Skipping or truncating the risk assessment/intervention stage

The research studies and case law on PD12J also suggest that where domestic abuse is found to have occurred, there is then considerable pressure to move the case on – ideally to continue or restore contact – as quickly as possible (Hunter & Barnett, 2013; Trinder et al., 2013). For example, judges may dispense with expert risk assessments and make their own (minimising) assessment of the effect of the abuse and the degree of ongoing risk posed by the father (Women's Aid, 2016). In *Re W* [2012] EWCA Civ 528, the judge had made significant findings of sustained domestic abuse by the father at a fact-finding hearing but had then refused an application for a report by Cafcass and a psychological assessment of the father, stating that he was satisfied that the father had been ill but was now much better and that further assessment was therefore unnecessary. His decision that contact should proceed was overturned on appeal, with Black LJ making clear that the assessment of the father's mental state and the risk of further violence was a matter on which the judge required further professional assistance (see also *Re F (Children)* [2015] EWCA Civ 1315). Additionally, risk assessments may be obtained from unqualified sources, leading Women's Aid (2017) to recommend that PD12J be amended to require that in all cases where domestic abuse has occurred, the court should obtain a safety and risk assessment conducted by a specialist domestic abuse practitioner working for an appropriately accredited agency. This proposal was not adopted in the 2017 revision of PD12J, but in any event, any such assessment may fail to capture the entirety of the risk if findings have been made which reflect only a fraction of the whole dynamic of a coercive and controlling relationship. The recent case law indicates that the appellate courts focus almost solely on the risk of physical violence (in some cases only to the child). For example, in *Re M (Children)* [2013] EWCA Civ 1147 the Court of Appeal allowed the father's appeal because the trial judge failed 'to adequately address why the children's safety and the management of the mother's anxieties cannot be achieved under any circumstances of supervision' (per Macur LJ at [19]).

As far as interventions for perpetrators are concerned, Hunter and Barnett (2013) found that courts were disinclined to order fathers to undertake DVPPs because they took 'too long' to commence and to complete, a view shared by some family lawyers (Barnett, 2014). Anger management courses or parenting programmes might be preferred because they were more available and quicker, despite their acknowledged inefficacy in addressing the risk of future abuse (Iwi & Newman, 2015). The 2014 revisions to PD12J included specific acknowledgement that 'acceptance on a DVPP is subject to a suitability assessment by the service provider, and that completion of a DVPP will take time in order to achieve the aim of risk-reduction for the long-term benefit of the child and the parent with whom the child is living' (para. 34). As well as the low number of fact-finding hearings noted above, however, the Cafcass and Women's Aid study found only five referrals to DVPPs among their file sample (2017, p. 10).

Decision-making: the welfare stage

As discussed above, where domestic abuse is found to have occurred, PD12J requires courts and risk assessors to address the Sturge and Glaser (2000) factors now set out in paras. 36 and 37. The pre-2014 research found an inconsistent application of these factors by Cafcass officers and the lower courts (Barnett, 2014; Coy et al., 2012; Hunter & Barnett, 2013) and recent case law indicates a continuing failure to refer to or apply these provisions, despite the Court of Appeal repeatedly stressing that the discipline in these paragraphs offers the surest guide to correct decision-making. For example, in *Re P* [2015] EWCA Civ 466, the Court of Appeal overturned the orders for unsupervised contact made by the Recorder who had failed to obtain a risk assessment or to apply para. 36 to the established history of domestic abuse. In *Re F (Children)* [2015] EWCA Civ 1315 the Court of Appeal allowed the mother's appeal in a case where the trial judge completely ignored his own findings concerning the father's violence, and focused only on the father's application for a residence order (which he granted), not even considering the mother's contact application. The Court of Appeal were highly critical of the trial judge for failing to follow PD12J or to apply the welfare checklist.

However, there is considerable reluctance even by the appellate courts to hold fathers to account for their abuse or to require evidence that they have acknowledged its impact on their families and sought to make amends. In *Re K* [2016] EWCA Civ 99, the Court of Appeal castigated the guardian and the trial judge for requiring the father to apologise to the children and to the mother for his behaviour and demonstrate that he had changed, instead of commending them for what appears to have been a proper application of PD12J. Barnett found that it could be very difficult to persuade courts that a father seeking contact 'is motivated by anything other than a desire to see the children' (2014, p. 450). Participants in her study reported judges readily accepting expressions of contrition at face value and expressing sympathy for abusive fathers.

The pre-2014 research indicated that the typical response to findings of domestic abuse was a period of supported or supervised contact, with the expectation that this would eventually move on to unsupervised contact (Barnett, 2014, 2016; Hunter & Barnett, 2013). The more recent, small-scale Cafcass and Women's Aid (2017) study found that the most common order made when allegations of abuse are raised is for unsupervised direct contact (39%). Supervised or supported contact was ordered in 11% of such cases. Although Cafcass officers recommended either indirect or no contact in nearly a quarter of cases in which domestic abuse was alleged,[4] no direct contact was ordered in only 2%, with no order being made in 12% (and final disposal being unknown in 31%).

The quality of supervision was also an issue raised in the pre-2014 research, with some courts preferring supervision by family members to the use of child contact services, caused partly but not entirely by the limited availability of supervised contact centres (Hunter & Barnett, 2013). Responding to concerns raised by Women's Aid about this apparently ongoing problem, PD12J 2017 states that: 'Where a risk assessment has concluded that a parent poses a risk to a child or to the other parent, contact via a supported contact centre, or contact supported by a parent or relative, is not appropriate' (para. 38). What effect this provision will have, or whether it will be circumvented by consent orders and the lack of risk assessment, remains to be seen.

Litigants in person

The withdrawal of legal aid for private family law proceedings from April 2013 has resulted in a significant increase in litigants in person in the family courts (Ministry of Justice, 2017). The forensic and adversarial structure of raising allegations, fact-finding, risk assessment and welfare determination is particularly difficult for litigants in person (Trinder et al., 2014). This creates another disincentive to fact-finding, and further opportunities for issues of violence and abuse to be disregarded (Barnett, 2016). The 2014 amendments to PD12J suggest that a fact-finding hearing 'can be an inquisitorial (or investigative) process', and that 'the judge...should be prepared where necessary and appropriate to conduct the questioning of the witnesses on behalf of the parties, focusing on the key issues in the case' (para. 28). However, many judges remain reluctant to take on this role (Corbett & Summerfield, 2017). Women's Aid (2017) raised concerns about the prevalence of fathers acting in person and using the opportunity to perpetuate their abuse of mothers by directly cross-examining them in family court proceedings. Abusive cross-examination is barred in criminal trials for sexual assault, but not in family proceedings (House of Commons, 2017). Proposed legislation which would have introduced a very limited ban on direct cross-examination by alleged perpetrators of abuse in family courts was abandoned due to the June 2017 general election. Instead, Practice Direction 3AA to the Family Procedure Rules, which came into effect on 30 November 2017, simply requires courts to consider making directions about the way in which a 'vulnerable witness' (which includes victims of domestic abuse) may be cross-examined (para. 5.5).

In summary, while there is always room for improving the detail of PD12J, the problems discussed above suggest that simply attempting to fine-tune it is unlikely to achieve the cultural change called for by the Family Justice Council 10 years ago. The gap that exists between the law on paper and the law in action suggests that the barriers to a real shift in judicial and professional practice and perceptions need to be addressed at a more fundamental level.

Presumptions against contact

The trajectory in England and Wales could have been quite different had the Court of Appeal in *Re L* accepted Sturge and Glaser's (2000) recommendation that a finding of domestic abuse should have a clear consequence in raising a presumption against direct contact. After reviewing the effects of domestic abuse on children and setting out the risks created for children of direct contact with an abusive parent, Sturge and Glaser concluded:

> [T]here should be no assumption that contact to a previously or currently violent parent is in the child's interests; if anything, the assumption should be in the opposite direction and the case of the non-residential parent one of proving why he can offer something of such

> benefit not only to the child but also to the child's situation (i.e. act in a way that is supportive to the child's situation with his or her resident parent and able to be sensitive to and respond appropriately to the child's needs) that contact should be considered. We would go as far as to suggest...a position in which a [parent]...who has been found to have been domestically violent to the child's parent should need to show positive grounds as to why, despite this, contact is in the child's interests in order for an application to be even considered. There could be a requirement that that parent sets out how he proposes to help the child heal and recover from the damage done. (2000, p. 10)

Regrettably, the Court of Appeal rejected this recommendation, deciding that established domestic violence should not necessarily be a bar to contact and requiring instead that courts balance the evidence of domestic violence and its effects with the other factors in the welfare checklist, with the results outlined above. Other jurisdictions have enacted presumptions against direct contact. This section examines the operation of these presumptions and finds that they 'have met with very mixed results' (Lemon, 2001, p. 602).

The USA

Presumptions against the award of custody to perpetrators of domestic violence began to enter the statute books in the USA during the 1980s in response to the calls of domestic violence advocates to protect women and children from abuse. The first US national policy statement supporting such a presumption was House of Representatives Congressional Resolution 172 passed in 1990 which stated that 'credible evidence of physical abuse of a spouse should create a statutory presumption that it is detrimental to the child to be placed in the custody of the abusive spouse'.

In 1994, the National Council of Juvenile and Family Court Judges published the Model Code on Domestic and Family Violence (Lemon, 2001, p. 606). Section 401 states that where the court makes a determination that 'domestic or family violence has occurred', this 'raises a rebuttable presumption that it is detrimental to the child and not in the best interest of the child to be placed in sole custody, joint legal custody, or joint physical custody with the perpetrator of family violence'. The American Bar Association as well as the American Psychological Association recommended that states adopt statutory presumptions against custody for abusers and also urged that safeguards be put in place in relation to visitation; unsupervised contact should not be awarded unless the abuser has undergone treatment and can show he is no longer a threat (see Lemon, 2001, p. 607).

Garvin's (2016) review of the field found that over 40 US States have adopted statutory presumptions and/or other provisions to consider the impacts of domestic violence on children when determining custody. Twenty-four have enacted rebuttable presumptions based on the Model Code, most of which shift the burden of proof and/or guide judicial discretion. However the legislation varies. In some jurisdictions, the presumption refers to all types of custody. In others it operates only in disputes concerning joint custody. Definitions of domestic violence and the types of evidence required to trigger the presumption vary from State to State. The evidence required to rebut the presumption also varies. There is little consistency in the way States deal with counter-allegations of violence, and in States which have provisions favouring the 'friendly parent' or presumptions in favour of joint custody, the domestic violence provisions are undermined. Courts' application and interpretation of the presumptions has also limited their effectiveness.

Presumptions in favour of joint custody, friendly parent provisions and other risks

As Davis, Lizdas, Tibbetts, Murphy and Yauch point out, presumptions against custody in cases of domestic violence do not take effect unless the 'fact that domestic violence has occurred' is established. However presumptions in favour of joint custody 'simply start with a conclusion without any foundational showing whatsoever' (2010, p. 6). Unless the parent opposing joint custody has the wherewithal and the evidence to challenge the joint custody presumption, joint custody will be deemed to be in the best interests of the child (Davis et al., 2010, p. 7). Challenges to joint custody can also 'backfire' under friendly parent provisions embedded in State custody laws. 'Friendly parent' provisions require the court to consider each parent's willingness to support and encourage contact between the child and the other parent. A parent who challenges the joint custody presumption because of concerns about violence will be perceived to be hostile to contact and so fail to meet the friendly parent standard. 'Consequently, the rebuttal to the JPC presumption works *worst* when a child needs it *most*' (Davis et al., 2010, p. 11).

Even in the absence of friendly parent provisions, victims of abuse may not raise the issue for fear of retaliation, for fear of not being believed or for fear of losing their children in child protection proceedings (Davis et al., 2010, p. 17). Indeed a mother may lose custody because, as a victim of domestic violence, she may be considered less able to provide the emotionally and financially stable home favoured by US courts in applying the best interests of the child test (Conner, 2009; p. 197; Lamprecht, 2011; p. 363; Morrill, Dai, Dunn, Sung, & Smi, 2005; p. 1078).

Definitions of domestic violence

In order to activate the presumption against custody, there must be evidence or proof of domestic violence. Garvin observes that a 'common critique of statutes addressing domestic violence is that they rely on inadequate legal definitions, which tend to focus on violent acts and threats of physical violence' (2016, para. 11B). They do not cover emotional, sexual or financial abuse (Lemon, 2001, p. 615) or other forms of controlling behaviour or patterns of abuse (Conner, 2009, pp. 206–7). Critics have also pointed out that statutes tend to exclude all but recent incidents of violence and focus on discrete events, ignoring patterns of coercive control. For example, the presumption in the Florida legislation against shared parental responsibility is triggered only if a 'parent has been convicted of a misdemeanour of the first degree or higher involving domestic violence' or has been incarcerated (Florida Statutes Annotated s 61.13 4(c)(2)). 'Domestic violence' is defined only as physical or sexual assault, stalking, kidnapping or false imprisonment. So the focus is almost exclusively on serious physical violence leading to a conviction.

Evidence

Some States require that violence has occurred more than once. In others there must be a pattern or history of abuse or at least one serious incident. In terms of standards of proof, in some States, the statute merely provides that there must be a 'finding of domestic violence' or 'credible evidence of domestic violence' (Lemon, 2001, p. 615), while in others, as in Florida, there must be a criminal conviction.

The difficulties of proving domestic abuse – as something that occurs in private and is often unreported – are well known. In many cases, there is no evidence, or the only witness may be a child whom the mother and her lawyer are very reluctant to call into court (Conner, 2009, p. 184). Even reporting may not help, as 'Law enforcement involvement... does not guarantee proper documentation of injuries, property damage, or other evidence' (Conner, 2009, p. 184). In this context, requiring proof of multiple acts of abuse is particularly problematic (Conner, 2009, p. 199).

Rebutting the presumption against custody

Some States leave the requirements for rebuttal to the courts' discretion while others list specific factors that the court must consider in finding that the presumption has been rebutted. In California, for example, the court must consider:

> 1) whether the perpetrator has shown that it is in the best interest of the child to be in the custody of that parent; 2) successful completion of a batterer's program; 3) successful completion of a program for alcohol or drug abuse if found appropriate by the court; 4) compliance with court orders and with probation and parole conditions, if applicable; and 5) whether there has been any further violence. (California Family Code s 3044; cited in Lemon, 2001, p. 618)

As Garvin points out, however, completion of a 'batterer's' program does not necessarily render the abuser safe and the word 'successful' is open to interpretation (2016, para. 111A). In *Popovich v Newton* (No B194324, 2008 WL 116261, California Court of Appeal, 2nd District, 14 January 2008) the mother claimed that the father's completion of a batterer's program could not be described as successful since he continued to deny, minimise and persist with his abusive behaviour. This claim was rejected, the presumption was rebutted and the best interests requirement of contact with the non-resident parent prevailed.

Unintended consequences

States have had to adopt dominant aggressor provisions so as to avoid penalising victims who act in self defence, and to deal with false counter-accusations. Lemon refers to observations by an attorney that perpetrators were filing civil protective orders in order to benefit from the presumption against custody, casting the victim as a perpetrator. They were also strongly defending allegations of abuse in order to avoid the presumption being invoked against them (Lemon, 2001, pp. 635, 665).

Supervised contact as a panacea

Statutory presumptions in the US are largely confined to the award of custody. While the majority of States provide in various ways for supervised visitation for the protection of children (Young, 2005, p. 7 and see fn. 17), there are no presumptions against visitation *per se*; supervised contact, it seems, is assumed to be safe. By contrast, Sturge and Glaser (2000) did not see supervised contact as the panacea in cases of domestic abuse, but considered it was likely to be useful only to maintain safety, manage contact or support the child where change in the short term was likely (2000; pp. 12–13; see also Perry & Rainey, 2007). In particular, supervised contact does not protect children from the emotional harm of having to have contact with a parent who has previously traumatised them (Robertson et al., 2007, p. 98). As discussed below, heavy reliance on supervised contact in conjunction with the New Zealand presumption was one of the factors that made it unworkable.

Judicial interpretations of the legislation

The US literature is critical of judges who, in applying the presumptions, have shown little understanding of the dynamics of domestic violence and patterns of domination and control. For example, the North Dakota Supreme Court confirmed in *Tulintseff v Jacobsen* (615 NW 2d 129 (2000) at 134) that domestic violence not resulting in serious injury which was committed three or more years before the proceedings was too remote. In the Massachusetts case of *Custody of Zia* (50 Mass App Ct 237 (2000)) the court held that, despite two abuse protection orders and a pending charge of assault and battery, the mother's challenge to the judge's finding that '[t]here is no history of domestic violence perpetrated by or upon either party' was not persuasive. There was no history or pattern of domestic violence that would preclude an award of custody to the father (at 246). In *Brown* v *Brown* (867 P2d 477, Oklahoma Court of Appeal, 1993) there was evidence that the father once shoved the mother roughly up against a doorway, threatened her with violence when he suspected her of infidelity and broke the windows in another man's car because he believed, wrongly, that the wife was having an affair with him. The court said:

> we do not see in this behavior any sort of pattern of abuse; much less do we find any evidence which supports [the mother's] claim that [the father's] acts constitute 'ongoing domestic abuse'... We...construe the phrase 'ongoing domestic abuse' to mean abuse which is still occurring, or has occurred with sufficient frequency and recency to give rise to some expectation that it will continue or will recur, and thus will constitute a threat to any child of whom the abusive person is granted custody. As such, 'ongoing domestic abuse' is not merely one or two isolated instances of proscribed behaviour. (at [7]-[10])

Judges' failure to understand the dynamics of abuse also leads them to disbelieve victims' accounts, for example, if they do not recollect details, contradict themselves or appear nervous. By contrast, perpetrators are often manipulative and confident and their demeanour is interpreted as evidence of truthfulness (Conner, 2009, pp. 174, 177). In addition, according to Lamprecht, 'There is a long-standing judicial belief that women tend to exaggerate the violence that they have endured in order to manipulate the court into awarding them custody' (2011, p. 364).

Further, judges also appear to have been implicated in what commentators have described as a backlash against these presumptions. Lemon cites a report by an Arizona lawyer to the effect that judges were refusing to hear evidence of domestic violence and were giving strong preference to joint custody (2001, p. 660). Sometimes they would hear the evidence but then decide cases according to their assessment of the child's best interests, holding that best interests considerations rebutted the presumption (p. 661). Lemon also refers to a survey conducted in California that revealed resistance by some judges to applying the presumption, partly due to lack of time and resources but also because they disliked having their discretion curtailed. They considered joint custody almost always best, even in cases of domestic violence. They would also try to get parties to agree an outcome by repeatedly ordering them to try to mediate. The presumption was also seen to be having an effect on applications for restraining orders, with judges being increasingly reluctant to grant these and demanding corroboration of abuse (p. 664; see also Garvin, 2016).

Effects of a presumption

Despite all these problems, presumptions do appear to have some positive effects. Morrill et al. (2005) found that in States with a presumption, courts were more likely to award sole legal custody to mothers and less likely to award joint legal custody. However in States with competing legislation such as presumptions in favour of joint custody, those provisions prevailed and joint custody was the common outcome. The researchers also found that, although there was no difference in terms of the proportion of visitation applications granted, there was more likely to be structured or conditional visitation in States with a presumption. Nevertheless, the US experience demonstrates both limited understanding of domestic violence on the part of legislators (and hence unduly narrow drafting of presumptions as well as the existence of contradictory provisions), and judicial interpretation and application of the law in a way that makes the effect of presumptions even less protective. Most US academics writing on this subject recommend better training and education for judges and others working in the legal system. However Morrill et al. (2005) came to the conclusion that whether judges had attended domestic violence training made little difference to their decision-making, although the quality of that training could not be ascertained.

The New Zealand presumption against unsupervised contact

In 1994 Alan Bristol, a New Zealand father engaged in a custody battle with his ex-wife, killed himself and his three daughters. The subsequent inquiry by New Zealand's Chief Justice into the family court proceedings in the case suggested a need for law reform, and this opportunity was grasped by domestic violence campaigners to enact a version of the US Model Code provision in New Zealand (Robertson et al., 2007, p. 102). The Guardianship Act 1968 was amended in 1995 to include a presumption against the award of day to day care or unsupervised contact 'where a party is shown to have used violence against a child of the family or the other party in custody or access proceedings', 'unless the court is satisfied that the child would be safe during such care or contact' (Guardianship Act 1968 s 60(3)). The amendments also specified a set of risk assessment factors to be taken into account in determining whether the presumption was rebutted (s 61) and what should occur if allegations of violence were not proved but the court was nevertheless satisfied there was a real risk to the child's safety (s 60(6); later Care of Children Act 2004 ss 58–61; now repealed).

A 2006 review of experience with the presumption found that those working in the family justice system generally considered that it enhanced children's safety from the risk of family violence (Perry, 2006, 21). However, the presumption encountered a range of by now familiar problems in implementation. The legislative definition of 'violence' was confined to physical and sexual abuse, although in practice, judges were generally willing to take psychological abuse into account as well (Perry, 2006, pp. 6–7). The intention of the legislation was undermined by court orders for parties to attend counselling and mediation, resulting in 'consent' orders for contact, with women being advised by their lawyers to agree so as not to appear obstructive of contact (Robertson et al., 2007, pp.88–89, 97). Practical difficulties arose in that courts found themselves with limited information when making decisions about children's safety, since parents' written statements formed the only evidence in a high proportion of cases and these were often short on detail (Perry, 2006, p. 11). There were concerns about delays between the making of allegations of violence in an application for custody or a protection order, triggering a suspension of contact, and the making of final orders, with fathers being barred from seeing children for many months (Perry, 2006, p. 10). And the government's insistence that supervised contact centres should be run on a user pays basis resulted in under-resourcing and fewer and fewer providers willing to offer services (Perry, 2006, p.10). Consequently, families were often left to make their own supervision arrangements, and in many cases, supervision was undertaken by the custodial parent - precisely the situation the legislation had sought to avoid (Perry, 2006; p. 11; Robertson et al., 2007; p. 100). Moreover, in the face of judicial and contact parent objections to supervised contact, this came to be seen as a last resort when children's safety simply could not be otherwise assured (Perry, 2006, p.11), and as the worst case scenario, making it impossible for mothers to seek less than supervised contact (e.g. indirect or no contact) without being seen as hostile (Robertson et al., 2007, pp. 98–99).

The legislation was not well received by family court judges and judicial resistance included applying standards to determine safety which failed to follow the risk assessment checklist in s 61 (Robertson et al., 2007, pp. 110, 124). One respondent to Robertson et al.'s study summarised the judgment in which shared custody had been granted to her abusive ex-husband as follows: 'You're not with him now? He's not going to beat you. And has he ever beaten the child? No. He's not dangerous to her' (Robertson et al., 2007, p. 98). The backlash against the presumption was joined by the fathers' rights lobby, academics and policy-makers, who supported perceptions that the operation of the presumption tended to inflame conflict and make disputes more contentious, and that domestic violence allegations were used as a weapon in highly conflicted parenting disputes (Perry, 2006, pp. 12, 16–19). The presumption was finally repealed in a neoliberal reform of the Care of Children Act 2004 which came into force in 2014 and which, like the Legal Aid, Sentencing and Punishment of Offenders Act 2012 and Children and Families Act 2014 in England and Wales, was justified by concerns about adversarialism and delay and placed major emphasis on agreement out of court (see also Atkin, 2015). The new s 52 of the Care of Children Act 2004 contains a virtual presumption of contact in all cases, which some may argue has been implicit all along in the approach of the New Zealand family courts.

The following articles

The New Zealand experience suggests that even a well-drafted presumption may be subject to the same gap between law in the books and law in action as has been seen in the implementation of PD12J. The following articles explore a range of alternative approaches to allegations of domestic abuse in post-separation children's matters. The collection starts with Linnéa Bruno's analysis of how positive reforms in Sweden aimed at recognising women's bodily integrity, protecting children exposed to domestic abuse and prioritising children's wishes, have been undercut by political and professional discourses and understandings of domestic abuse manifested in a range of settings including the family courts. Drawing on the empirical research she undertook for her doctoral dissertation, *Times of trouble: Fathers' violence, the state and the separating family* (published in Swedish in 2016), Bruno explores the impact in custody proceedings of two social processes she identifies as endemic in Sweden: *familialisation* (the process through which kinship as a power structure is reproduced as seen, for example, in the promotion of shared custody and the positioning of children as objects) and *selective repression* (whereby responsibility for domestic violence is selectively distributed along racialised and gendered lines). Bruno's article explores how these processes result in abuse being actively *administered* rather than countered, in ways which contribute to its continuation.

A similar contradiction between progressive reforms and their implementation in practice is explored by Teresa Picontó Novales's study of the pioneering Spanish legislation which explicitly frames domestic abuse as gender violence/violence against women, together with further innovative measures enacted in 2015, which include attributing direct victim status to children living with domestic abuse and restrictions on contact and communication between fathers who have perpetrated gender violence and their children. However, Picontó Novales demonstrates how conservative judicial interpretation of these measures, underpinned by the greater priority given to the child's perceived 'need' for a relationship with the father over his abuse of the mother, means that real change is slow, with a minimal increase in the use of these new measures over the past two years.

The importance of listening to children is addressed by Stephanie Holt (Ireland) and Kirsteen Mackay (Scotland). Stephanie Holt observes that children's theoretical rights under Article 12 of the United Nations Convention on the Rights of the Child 1989 to participate in legal proceedings that affect them has struggled to achieve translation into practice in Ireland. Rather, universal assumptions of children's best interests result in children's competence to participate being questioned and their participation being restricted on grounds of age and maturity. Drawing on the narratives of children and young people involved in family court proceedings where domestic abuse was an issue, Holt concludes that when children's voices were listened to, contact arrangements were made safer and children were empowered.

Kirsteen Mackay considers the approach taken in Scotland to child contact cases in which there are allegations of domestic abuse. Sheriffs have a statutory duty to consider the need to protect a child from abuse and from the risk of abuse when making an order relating to parental rights and responsibilities (which includes child contact). Drawing on her analysis of court papers from 208 child contact disputes, surveys and interviews with sheriffs, professionals, former litigants and children, Mackay discusses the strengths and limitations of four key features of the case process in terms of protecting women and children – the availability of legal aid; the cautious process of successive child welfare hearings; the use of court appointed child welfare reporters to investigate all the circumstances of the child; and the statutory requirement that the child should be given an opportunity to express their views. Despite these measures, like Holt, Mackay finds that the assumption in Scottish case law that contact with non-resident parents will best promote the welfare of the child can work to undermine positive measures for seeking children's views, particularly where the impact of domestic abuse and children's fears are not taken seriously by professionals.

One way in which professional practices concerning domestic abuse may be improved is via enhanced training. The focus of the article by Jaffe et al. is on a particular judicial education initiative, 'Enhancing Judicial Skills in Domestic Violence Cases' (EJS), which was developed and implemented over the last 20 years in the United States by the National Council of Juvenile and Family Court Judges and Futures without Violence. Jaffe et al. present their findings of a preliminary evaluation of the programme based on the self-reports of 480 judges from diverse courts and jurisdictions across the US who had participated in a four-day workshop between 2006 and 2010. Overall, judges reported the programme to be engaging and effective, with most identifying specific benefits and behaviour changes in the areas of access to justice, judicial leadership, victim safety, and abuser accountability as a result of participating in the programme. Jaffe et al. observe, however, that ultimately the extent to which the programme is having an impact on the experiences of victims, perpetrators and children who come before the courts is unknown.

A further step from judicial education is the establishment of specialist domestic violence courts (SDVCs) for promoting the safety of children and resident parents in family cases where domestic abuse is an issue. Jennifer Koshan's article provides a wide-ranging and insightful review of SDVCs in the United States and Canada together with the more recent development (primarily in the United States) of integrated domestic violence courts (IDVCs). While there is much diversity in the jurisdiction of SDVCs, the most common type deal with criminal cases, while IDVCs have jurisdiction to hear criminal, family and civil protection matters in one setting. The article focuses on Koshan's qualitative study of the IDVC in Manhattan, New York, which she situates within existing evaluations of other IDVCs in the US and Toronto. She considers the advantages of one judge following the family through multiple proceedings, and conversely, disadvantages such as the high settlement rate of cases in IDVCs, in light of existing concerns about parties being pressurised to settle contact cases and about domestic abuse being minimised in such cases. It is clear from Koshan's article that more research is required on the specific impact of IDVCs on parenting disputes.

Mandy Burton provides critical insights into SDVCs in the criminal justice system in England and Wales, and the implications for such specialisation in the family justice system. She undertakes an in-depth examination of the one attempt in England and Wales at establishing an IDVC (in Croydon), and the reasons for its failure. Looking more generally at the evaluations reviewed by Koshan, Burton questions whether the empirical evidence makes a convincing case for developing IDVCs in England and Wales as a means of addressing child arrangement cases involving domestic abuse. She goes on to explore, as an alternative, the potential advantages of a model of specialisation within each of the criminal and family justice systems.

The concluding chapter summarises the most promising strategies raised at the symposium. Four programmes recently established in Australia take a trauma-informed, whole-of-family approach to meeting the legal and non-legal support needs of families affected by domestic abuse. Two of these operate outside the court setting in dispute resolution services, while two seek to address the needs of parties and their children holistically when they encounter the court system. The final strategy is a human rights approach to child arrangements cases. The European Convention on Human Rights is relevant to such cases not only via Article 8 (right to respect for family life: a qualified right), but also via Article 3 (right to freedom from torture and inhuman and degrading treatment: an unqualified right). A human rights approach would enable the rights of all family members to be taken into account, and would prioritise freedom from inhuman and degrading treatment for both children and their non-abusive parents. While the success of these approaches cannot be guaranteed, they do appear to offer the greatest prospects for building on the good practices and overcoming the problems identified in the foregoing articles.

Notes

1. Different jurisdictions use different terminology. The current preferred term in England and Wales is 'domestic abuse', but it has previously been 'domestic violence'. In Australia the term 'family violence' is preferred; in the USA it is still common to use the term 'battering', while Spanish legislation addresses 'gender violence'. These terms are used interchangeably in this Introduction and throughout the special issue, unless it is clear at any point that a distinction is being drawn between them. In each case, we and the other authors are referring to patterns of harmful, threatening, intimidating, coercive and controlling behaviours which are, in all of the societies discussed, overwhelmingly perpetrated by men against women and children.
2. See, eg, *Re S (Contact: Promoting Relationship with Absent Parent)* [2004] EWCA Civ 18; *Re M (Children)* [2009] EWCA Civ 1216; *Re J-M (A Child)* [2014] EWCA Civ 434; *Re T (A Child: Suspension of Contact: Section 91(14) CA 1989)* [2015] EWCA Civ 71.
3. PD12J 2017 retains this provision in slightly different wording: 'what evidence is required in order to determine the existence of coercive, controlling or threatening behaviour, or of any other form of domestic abuse' (para. 19).
4. The study did not report on findings of domestic abuse.

Disclosure statement

No potential conflict of interest was reported by the authors.

References

All-Party Parliamentary Group on Domestic Violence. (2016). *Domestic abuse, child contact and the family courts*. Retrieved from https://www.womensaid.org.uk/appg-reports/

Anderson, L. (1997). *Contact between children and violent fathers*. London: Rights of Women.

Aris, R., & Harrison, C. (2007). *Domestic violence and the supplemental information form*. London: Ministry of Justice.

Atkin, B. (2015). The revised family court system in New Zealand: Secret justice and privatisation. In M. Maclean, J. Eekelaar, & B. Bastard (Eds.), *Delivering family justice in the 21st century* (pp. 39–50). Oxford: Hart Publishing.

Bailey-Harris, R., Barron, J., & Pearce, J. (1999). From utility to rights? The presumption of contact in practice. *International Journal of Law, Policy and the Family*, *13*, 111–131.

Bailey-Harris, R., Davis, G., Barron, J., & Pearce, J. (1998). *Monitoring private law applications under the Children Act 1989: Report to the Nuffield Foundation*. Bristol: University of Bristol.

Barlow, A., Hunter, R., Smithson, J., & Ewing, J. (2017). *Mapping paths to family justice: Resolving family disputes in neoliberal times*. London: Palgrave Macmillan.

Barnett, A. (2000). Contact and domestic violence: The ideological divide. In J. Bridgeman & D. Monk (Eds.), *Feminist perspectives on family law* (pp. 129–150). London: Cavendish.

Barnett, A. (2014). Contact at all costs? Domestic violence and children's welfare. *Child and Family Law Quarterly*, *26*, 439–462.

Barnett, A. (2015). 'Like gold dust these days': Domestic violence fact-finding hearings in child contact cases. *Feminist Legal Studies*, *23*, 47–78.

Barnett, A. (2016). Family law without lawyers – A systems theory perspective. *Journal of Social Welfare and Family Law*, *39*, 223–245.

Barnett, A. (2017). 'Greater than the mere sum of its parts': Coercive control and the question of proof. *Child and Family Law Quarterly*, *29*, 379–400.

Cafcass & Women's Aid. (2017). *Allegations of domestic abuse in child contact cases*. Retrieved from Cafcass website: https://www.cafcass.gov.uk/news/2017/july/cafcass-and-women%E2%80%99s-aid-collaborate-on-domestic-abuse-research.aspx

Cobb, S. (2016) *Review of Practice Direction 12J FPR 2010 Child arrangement and contact orders: Domestic violence and harm – Report to the President of the Family Division*. Retrieved from Judiciary website: https://www.google.co.uk/url?sa=t&rct=j&q=&esrc=s&source=web&cd=1&ved=0ahUKEwih5NCT2LnYAhVDZFAKHXc8DYIQFggnMAA&url=https%3A%2F%2Fwww.judiciary.gov.uk%2Fwp-content%2Fuploads%2F2017%2F01%2FPD12J-child-arrangement-domestic-violence-and-harm-report-and-revision.pdf&usg=AOvVaw3GGfqkjjIFtgC6uxlGITl5

Conner, D. (2009). Abuse and discretion: Evaluating judicial discretion in custody cases involving violence against women. *American University Journal of Gender, Social Policy and Law*, *17*, 163–228.

Corbett, N. E., & Summerfield, A. (2017). *Alleged perpetrators of abuse as litigants in person in private family law: The cross-examination of vulnerable and intimidated witnesses*. London: Ministry of Justice.

Coy, M., Perks, K., Scott, E., & Tweedale, R. (2012). *Picking up the pieces: Domestic violence and child contact*. London: Rights of Women. Retrieved from: http://rightsofwomen.org.uk/wp-content/uploads/2014/10/Picking_Up_the_Pieces_Report-2012l.pdf

Craig, J. (2007). Everybody's business: Applications for contact orders by consent. *Family Law*, *37*, 26–30.

Davis, G., Lidzas, J., Tibbetts, S., Murphy, J., & Yauch, J. (2010). *The dangers of presumptive joint physical custody*. Minneapolis: The Battered Women's Justice Project. Retrieved from : http://www.bwjp.org/assets/documents/pdfs/dangers_presumptive_joint_physical_custody.pdf

Department of Constitutional Affairs, & Department for Education and Skills. (2004). *The Government's response to the Children Act Sub-Committee ('CASC') Report: 'Making contact work'*. London: DCA & DfES.

Eaton, D., Jarmain, S., & Lustigman, L. (2016). Parental alienation: Surely the time has come to effect change? *Family Law*, *46*, 581–583.

Family Justice Review. (2011). *Family Justice Review Final Report*. London: Ministry of Justice, Department for Education, Welsh Government.

Garvin, Z. (2016). The unintended consequences of rebuttable presumptions to determine child custody in domestic violence cases. *Family Law Quarterly*, *50*, 173–192.

Harding, M., & Newnham, A. (2015). *How do county courts share the care of children between parents? Full report*. Coventry: University of Warwick. Retrieved from Nuffield Foundation website: http://www.nuffieldfoundation.org/sites/default/files/files/Full%20report.pdf

Harrison, C. (2008). Implacably hostile or appropriately protective?: Women managing child contact in the context of domestic violence. *Violence Against Women*, *14*, 381–405.

Hester, M. (2011). The three planet model: Towards an understanding of contradictions in approaches to women and children's safety in contexts of domestic violence. *The British Journal of Social Work, 41*, 837–853.

Hester, M., & Radford, R. (1996). *Domestic violence and child contact arrangements in England and Denmark*. Bristol: The Policy Press.

HM Government. (2014). *A call to end violence against women and girls*. Retrieved from UK Government website: https://www.gov.uk/government/uploads/system/uploads/attachment_data/file/287758/VAWG_Action_Plan.pdf)

HM Government. (2016). *Ending violence against women and girls strategy 2016-2020*. Retrieved from UK Government website: https://www.gov.uk/government/publications/strategy-to-end-violence-against-women-and-girls-2016-to-2020

HM Inspectorate of Court Administration. (2005). *Domestic violence, safety and family proceedings: Thematic review of the handling of domestic violence issues by the Children and Family Court Advisory and Support Service (CAFCASS) and the administration of family courts in Her Majesty's Courts Service (HMCS)*. London: HMICA.

House of Commons. (2017). Domestic violence victims: Cross-examination. London: Hansard, Vol. 619. Retrieved from Hansard website: https://hansard.parliament.uk/Commons/2017-01-09/debates/8054FB6E-0CDD-4E9B-A6C3-393558156BBD/DomesticViolenceVictimsCross-Examination

Humphreys, C., & Harrison, C. (2003). Squaring the circle – Contact and domestic violence. *Family Law, 33*, 419–423.

Hunt, J., & Macleod, A. (2008). *Outcomes of applications to court for contact orders after parental separation or divorce*. London: Ministry of Justice.

Hunter, R., & Barnett, A. (2013). *Fact-finding hearings and the implementation of the President's Practice Direction: Residence and contact orders: Domestic violence and harm*. London: Family Justice Council. Retrieved from Kent Academic Repository website: https://kar.kent.ac.uk/35678/1/FFH%20report%20January%202013.pdf

Iwi, K., & Newman, C. (2015). *Engaging with perpetrators of domestic violence: Practical techniques for early intervention*. London and Philadelphia: Jessica Kingsley Publishers.

Kaganas, F., & Piper, C. (1999). Divorce and domestic violence. In S. Day Sclater & C. Piper (Eds.), *Undercurrents of divorce* (pp. 183–207). Aldershot: Ashgate.

Kaganas, F., & Day Sclater, S. (2004). Contact disputes: Narrative constructions of 'good' parents. *Feminist Legal Studies, 12*, 1–27.

Lamprecht, R. (2011). Advancing the best interests of the child: Why South Dakota should strengthen its rebuttable presumption against awarding custody to abusive parents. *South Dakota Law Review, 56*, 351–379.

Lemon, N. (2001). Statutes creating rebuttable presumptions against custody to batterers: How effective are they? *William Mitchell Law Review, 28*, 601–676.

Local Government Association, Cafcass, & Women's Aid. (2006). *Vision for services for children and young people affected by domestic violence*. London: Local Government Association.

Lord Chancellor's Advisory Board on Family Law, Children Act Sub-Committee. (2001). *Guidelines for good practice on parental contact in cases where there is domestic violence*. London: TSO.

Ministry of Justice. (2012). *Judicial and court statistics 2011*. Retrieved from UK Government website: https://www.gov.uk/government/uploads/system/uploads/attachment_data/file/217494/judicial-court-stats-2011.pdf

Ministry of Justice. (2017). *Family court statistics quarterly, England and Wales, January to March 2017*. Retrieved from UK Government website: https://www.gov.uk/government/statistics/family-court-statistics-quarterly-january-to-march-2017

Morrill, A., Dai, J., Dunn, S., Sung, I., & Smi, K. (2005). Child custody and visitation decisions when the father has perpetrated violence against the mother. *Violence Against Women, 11*, 1076–1107.

Perry, A. (2006). Safety first? Contact and family violence in New Zealand: An evaluation of the presumption against unsupervised contact. *Child and Family Law Quarterly, 18*, 1–21.

Perry, A., & Rainey, B. (2007). Supervised, supported and indirect contact orders: Research findings. *International Journal of Law, Policy and the Family*, *21*, 21–47.

Robertson, N., Busch, R., D'Souza, R., Lam Sheung, F., Anand, R., Balzer, R., & Paina, D. (2007). *Living at the cutting edge: Women's experiences of protection orders, Volume 2: What's to be done? A critical analysis of statutory and practice approaches to domestic violence*. Hamilton, NZ: University of Waikato.

Saunders, H. (2004). *Twenty-nine child homicides: Lessons still to be learnt on domestic violence and child protection*. Bristol: Women's Aid Federation of England.

Sturge, C., & Glaser, D. (2000). Contact and domestic violence – The experts' court report. *Family Law*, *30*, 615–629.

Thiara, R., & Gill, A. (2012). *Domestic violence, child contact, post-separation violence: Experiences of South Asian and African-Caribbean women and children*. London: NSPCC. Retrieved from NSPCC website: https://www.nspcc.org.uk/globalassets/documents/research-reports/domestic-violence-child-contact-post-separation-violence-report.pdf

Trinder, L., Connolly, J., Kellet, J., & Thoday, C. (2004). Families in contact disputes: A profile. *Family Law*, *34*, 877–881.

Trinder, L., Firth, A., & Jenks, C. (2009). *Opening closed doors: A micro analytic investigation of dispute resolution in child contact cases*. ESRC End of Award Report, RES-000-22-2646. Swindon: ESRC.

Trinder, L., Hunt, J., Macleod, A., Pearce, J., & Woodward, H. (2013). *Enforcing contact orders: Problem-solving or punishment?* Exeter: University of Exeter.

Trinder, L., Hunter, R., Hitchings, E., Miles, J., Moorhead, R., Smith, L., ... Pearce, J. (2014). *Litigants in person in private family law cases*. London: Ministry of Justice. Retrieved from UK Government webiste: https://www.gov.uk/government/uploads/system/uploads/attachment_data/file/380479/litigants-in-person-in-private-family-law-cases.pdf

Wall, N. (2010). *The President's guidance in relation to split hearings*. London: Judicial Office.

Women's Aid. (2016). *Nineteen child homicides: What must change so children are put first in child contact arrangements and the family courts*. Bristol: Women's Aid.

Women's Aid. (2017). *Child first: A call to action one year on*. Bristol: Women's Aid.

Young, S. (2004/2005). A presumption for supervised visitation in Texas: Understanding and strengthening family code section 153.004(e). *Texas Tech Law Review*, *37*, 327–355.

National self-image as an obstacle to ensuring children's rights in the context of domestic violence and family law – the case of Sweden

Linnéa Bruno

ABSTRACT

The aim of this paper is to highlight and discuss contradictions and challenges in the current policy and practice regarding fathers' violence towards mothers and children in the Swedish welfare state. In particular, professional discourses and understandings of domestic violence in disputes about contact, custody, residence and maintenance, following parental separation, are analysed. My research suggests that abusers find ways to manipulate professionals and get them unwittingly to enable their continued control of victimised mothers and children. One conclusion is that oppression is maintained through processes of familialisation and selective repression. These discursive practices reproduce intersectional inequalities and, in doing so, in many cases result in the administration rather than prevention of further violence.

Introduction

For some survivors of domestic abuse, the troubles end with separation – a new life begins. For many others, however, the troubles continue after separation. For some, physical and sexual violence may end, but stalking, harassment, financial abuse and conflicts regarding the children mean that the previous times of trouble transform into new ones (Brown, Frederico, Hewitt, & Sheehan, 2000; Ekbrand, 2006; Fleury, Sullivan, & Bybee, 2000; Radford & Hester, 2015). In my doctoral dissertation *Times of Trouble – Fathers' Violence, the State and the Separating Family* (published in Swedish in 2016) the times of trouble following a separation are analysed, contributing to a sociological understanding as to why violence so often persists when survivors have done what they could to escape from it. The thesis examined the handling of domestic violence in three domains of practice in the Swedish welfare state: 1) children's education in school and preschool; 2) family law proceedings concerning contact, custody, residence and maintenance; and 3) welfare benefits such as financial aid. In this article I focus on two salient social processes which were evident in all three domains and which facilitate the continuation of violence: *familialisation* and *selective repression*. These concepts are elaborated below. Selective repression, in turn, can be seen to follow two kinds of patterns which are discussed below under the headings *racialisation* and *gendered assignment of responsibility*.

Separation is a critical phase in an abusive relationship, especially so in cases where the perpetrator of violence and the abused party have children together (Enander, 2008; Featherstone & Peckover, 2007; Khaw & Hardesty, 2007; Radford & Hester, 2006). Within different domains of practice professionals have varying ways of formulating, or not formulating, violence as a problem, varying ways of understanding risk and exposure, and varying discourses. Variations in framing and handling domestic violence create contradictory outcomes and difficulties for victimised women and children (Eriksson, Bruno, & Näsman, 2013; Hester, 2011). For example, a mother may be told by a family law social worker that she has to promote a positive image of the father to the children, and let them see him – if not, she may lose custody. The child protection social worker involved in the same case may tell her she has to protect her children and not let them see their father – if she fails to protect, the children may be taken into care by the social services.

In Sweden, women run the greatest risk of being murdered when separating from a male partner. Many times, children are present. In a majority of cases, the mothers have, in various ways, looked for help – reported to the police, applied for a restraining order, shared information on violence with personnel in health care, at hospitals, or the social services. According to a review by National Board of Health and Welfare, of lethal violence committed by partners or ex-partners during 2016 and 2017, all victims had previous contact with relevant agencies and most cases could have been avoided had professionals acted more adequately (Socialstyrelsen, 2018)).

Most violent fathers have continued contact with their children after parental separation (Forssell, 2016; Forssell & Cater, 2015). A major Swedish evaluation of interventions for children who have experienced their mothers being physically abused by their fathers found that the single most important prerequisite for children to be able to benefit from the treatment was that contact with a perpetrator (either convicted or merely alleged as such) was not being forced upon them. This condition proved more decisive than the type of treatment being received by the children (Broberg et al., 2011). Hence, a court's decision might have considerable consequences for a child's opportunities for recovery, and the results speak against the current common practice of children being forced to have contact with someone they perceive to be a perpetrator of violence. Drawing from interviews with and psychometric data on 165 children and 165 mothers, researcher in social work Anna Forssell (2016), raises concerns about why and in whose best interest contact is maintained. All of the children in her sample had received treatment for being exposed to or directly subjected to violence from their fathers but 75 per cent of them had continued contact. Nearly half of the children in cases with indications of physical or sexual child abuse had unsupervised face-to-face contact. Further, the results confirm previous international studies on violent men's parenting which highlight self-centredness, expressions of entitlement to the children and/or mother and difficulties in viewing their actions from the child's perspective. In Sweden, the ideal father is active and engaged as a parent. Many children in Forssell's study described their fathers as disengaged, absent and lazy. By analogy with the concept of *relative poverty*, Cater and Forssell (2014) introduce the term *relative neglect* to conceptualise these children's situation. Furthermore, children who have been exposed to intimate partner violence, the authors emphasise, may have needs that exceed those of children in general, when it comes to safety and parenting skills.

Legal and political context

Sweden has the reputation of being a child-friendly and relatively gender equal society. Nevertheless, the family in Sweden was a lawless space until only a few generations ago and the father had the legal right to use violence for educational purposes towards his wife and children. The women's movement in the 1970s, supported by extensive research and a growing number of female politicians, was instrumental in putting women's rights to bodily integrity on the political agenda (Nordborg, 2005). Since the 1970s the government has emphasised welfare reforms enhancing women's financial independence through paid work, affordable child care and promoting gender-equal parental leave (Gunnarsson, 2013). In addition, reforms aiming at reducing men's violence have been initiated. Rape within marriage was criminalised in Sweden in 1965. In 1999 several reforms were taken on the basis of the government's report *Kvinnofrid – women's peace*. Sweden was the first country in the world to criminalise the purchase but not the selling of sex. Of great significance was the introduction of a new crime – *gross violation of integrity/a woman's integrity*. This takes into account the process of normalisation of violence in intimate relationships – it captures repeated acts against a partner or previous partner and violations designed to damage self-esteem. Each individual violation does not need to be severe, but as a repeated pattern they are, the legislator argued (Burman, 2010; Nordborg, 2005). Research suggests that the legal standing of victims of intimate partner violence has been improved by this legislation (Diesen & Diesen, 2013). Domestic violence, however, is still a major issue (FRA, 2014). Moreover, there are contradictions between the reforms of criminal law and those of family law, as will be discussed further below. Shared parenting after parental separation is also a political priority. Shared legal responsibility for children's custody is strongly recommended and, since 1998, can be awarded even against the explicit wish of one of the parents. As will be elaborated in this article, the policy efforts to promote parental co-operation after separation, including in cases with reported domestic violence, have negative consequences for victimised mothers and children (Bruno, 2015; Eriksson & Pringle, 2005). In the public debate, lack of gender equality has increasingly been associated with *racialised Other* men, constructed as a threat coming from abroad (Carbin, 2014; Keskinen, 2009; Towns, 2002). One of many examples of this, is when the violence of Swedish-born men against women born in Thailand is suggested, even in social medical research (Fernbrandt, 2013), to be related to the lack of gender equality in the victimised women's culture, rather than to the norms and values of the Swedish-born abusers. On the other hand, if the perpetrator is from Iraq, the same study seeks to find an explanation in the violence of his culture.

As with the question of the safety of women, child abuse has gradually been made into a social problem which requires political action. It was only in 1926 that the Swedish state was given legal rights to interfere in a family if a child was being mistreated or abused. The ban on corporal punishment of children from 1979 has had a norm shaping effect, as there has been a sharp decrease in child abuse (Diesen & Diesen, 2013). It is estimated that around 90 per cent of children were being physically abused a hundred years ago, compared to 10 per cent today. However it was not until 2014 that forced marriage and child marriage were criminalised.

Over the last decades, there has been an increased awareness of children's vulnerability in the context of family law proceedings, and also examples of legislative reforms aimed at increasing focus on the best interests of the child. Since 2006, Swedish family law stresses that special consideration is to be given to the risk of abuse when considering the best interests of the child. In addition, the child's need for contact with both parents, and the child's own wishes should be considered. Prior to this reform, the child's need for close contact with both parents was emphasised as the most important consideration. Also since 2006, children who are exposed to violence have the right to crime victim compensation from the state (Eriksson, 2011). However, the policy area is still characterised by intense discursive struggle (Burman, 2016; Eriksson et al., 2013). In her thesis, Gunilla Dahlkild-Öhman (2011) explores the scope for children's voices offered to children exposed to domestic violence, in court mandated investigations regarding custody, residence or contact. The legislation, she argues, is potentially transformative and radical since it may challenge established adult-child relations as well as gender relations. However, family law secretaries, the social workers specialised in family law who carry out these investigations, seem hesitant to talk to children about the violence as such.

The exposure of children to contact with abusive fathers and their limited possibilities for participation and protection do not necessarily change, even with the death of the mother. A recent governmental report (SOU 2017: 6, 2017) has confirmed that even when the father is convicted of the murder of the mother, he may still be given continued custody. In effect, this means that he has the right to decide from jail, for example, whether or not the children are to receive treatment in order to process their trauma and loss, or where they should go to school. Even being convicted of the murder of their mother does not necessarily disqualify him as legal custodian, according to current legislation. The report suggests this should change. But other suggestions in the same report have more problematic implications for victimised parents and children.

The main task of the report was to evaluate the 2006 custody reform and additionally to analyse the reasons behind the increase in the number of custody cases and consider whether there is a need for further regulations. Issues concerning domestic violence are downplayed in the text. The main aim of the 2006 reform was to strengthen the child's perspective and to give priority to the risk of abuse over contact and joint custody when considering the best interests of the child. The report suggests this may have contributed to more parents petitioning for sole custody. Moreover, parents increasingly focus on their difficulties cooperating rather than finding solutions, it is claimed. Therefore, the authors propose that courts should be able to award joint custody even if both parents oppose it. Yet increased emphasis on joint custody, irrespective of what has happened, and the possibility for the court to force parents to have frequent contact post separation, may aggravate the situation for victimised parents and children. Perhaps the most striking feature of the report, however, is its lack of support in research. The references to research are so few that the authors choose not even to include a list of references in this 600 page publication. It should be noticed, however, that the Swedish government has not yet made any propositions with reference to this report.

As an interesting contrasting example, I would highlight the more child-centred practice adopted in Norway. The Convention on the Rights of the Child is incorporated into domestic law, and children from the age of seven have the right to have their say in family law disputes. Moreover, the investigation must give further details about the child's own view on his or her situation. It is not uncomplicated, but it has been shown in a large study (Skjørten, 2013) that this has contributed to a shift from a focus on the parental couple in conflict to a focus on the situation of the individual child and her or his rights to participation. In addition, after decisions in family law proceedings are made, the judge together with a child psychologist is obliged to have a meeting with the child, and to give a face-to-face explanation of the decision. I find the Norwegian example interesting, as it shows how it may be possible to better implement the rights of children than what is being done in Sweden at present.

The study

The empirical base for my dissertation (Bruno, 2016) was all relevant cases from three strategically sampled district courts during 2010 and 2011. This yielded 196 disputed family law orders with indications of violence, involving a total of 224 children. I also reviewed 100 court records on welfare benefit appeals and conducted interviews with 22 teachers and other staff from 10 different schools and preschools, and with 8 victimised and divorced mothers. The thesis explored intersectional and institutional conditions for counteracting domestic violence in the Swedish welfare state, especially in the context of parental separation and family law proceedings. Professional discourses and practices were examined empirically in four sub-studies: two on school and pre-school, the third on obstacles to implementing children's rights in disputed contact cases, and the fourth on the handling of financial abuse in the context of parental separation in both welfare and in contact cases. The results have been published in English elsewhere (Bruno, 2015, 2017; Eriksson et al., 2013) and therefore the present article does not give a detailed account of the research methods used. The analytical focus throughout the four sub-studies was on how alleged and confirmed violent fathers and victimised children and mothers are positioned and their rights negotiated in the discursive practices of welfare professionals acting as representatives of the state.

Feminism, childhood studies and critical race studies

I am in agreement with those who, in their research on violence, emphasise gender and gendered processes as particularly relevant considerations (e.g. Hearn, 2012; Hester, 2011; Walby, 1990, 2013). Nevertheless, the results of the four sub-studies (Bruno, 2015, 2017; Eriksson et al., 2013) suggest that patriarchy, gender inequality or male privilege are insufficient as an explanation as to why the troubling (stalking, harassment, abuse) persists after separation, and that other structuring categories also are important. The analysis takes a double view of children in line with the sociology of childhood, as both competent actors with a right to participation and vulnerable subjects in relation to adults and with rights to protection and provision (Eriksson & Näsman, 2008; Fernqvist, 2011). The key concept of *familialisation* was coined by the Finnish childhood sociologist Leena Alanen (1994) in order to describe the tendency to naturalise the subjugation of children in the family, this being the child's only natural platform to access resources.

In addition, insights from critical race studies have contributed to the analysis. In this field of research, for example, it is suggested that Sweden is characterised by a hegemonic whiteness. As a consequence, passing as a white person makes it easier to be accepted as a Swede, while being born in Sweden with Swedish born parents may still result in racial discrimination and being perceived as an immigrant due to name or appearance. Whiteness – as an unmarked normative position – thus seems central for the construction of Swedish identity (Hubinette & Lundström, 2014). The concept of *selective repression* is related to this perspective. By this concept, I refer to the way in which representations of violence as a problem vary with the position of victims and perpetrators in relation to social categorisations and inequalities – in effect a selective disciplining of both perpetrators and of those who have been abused. A further theme in the analysis is the way in which different modes of the exertion of power (economic, discursive, legal-political and through violence) cut across the domains (areas of policy and practice) empirically investigated in the study. In so doing, these different modes of exertion of power can mutually support each other in maintaining (but also theoretically destabilising) inequalities, in this case related to age, gender, kinship, ethnicity, race and, to some extent, class. Hence I agree, for example, with Floya Anthias (2001, 2012)) who disputes the assumption (derived from the Marxist tradition) that some dimensions of inequality are more discursive/cultural while others are more economic/ material.

Familialisation

The dissertation shows how processes of familialisation can strengthen adult power, parent power and gender power simultaneously when children are positioned as objects or as incompetent subjects in cases with reports of control and violence, and that this can occur within all examined domains. The question of responsibility for care and parenting capacity is marginalised within the domain of custody, residence and contact, as most cases focus on the issue of cooperation between the separated couple, and the problem is represented as a conflict of interests between two equal parties (cf. Ingrids, 2014). A focus on the position of children, however, is important in order to put the complex of problems into perspective and to avoid reproducing simplified and stereotypical presentations of victim and perpetrator. Children can be emotionally ambivalent towards a violent parent and do not always wish for the relationship to end (Cater, 2004; Eriksson & Näsman, 2008). High levels of reports of domestic violence and children's vulnerability in this context call for risk assessment by the courts. As shown in my analysis of district court orders, comments on risk assessment were lacking in more than half of the cases which included reports of violence (Bruno, 2015). However, to assume that the wishes of the mother are always beneficial to the child would also be a form of familialisation, and this is not a conclusion which I draw from my research. Whenever the requests of the mother are framed as coinciding with those of the child without giving the child an opportunity to share his or her perspective and seriously considering the child's wishes, this also entails a denial of the individual situation of the child, as well as their rights, especially those regarding participation. A parent who is denied court-ordered contact with his or her child can apply for contact to be arranged through enforcement – and ultimately by police intervention (Röbäck &

Höjer, 2009). The parent can also have the other parent sued and fined for obstructing the contact. A child who misses his or her parent, however, has no rights to demand contact or to any compensation if a parent time and again fails to show up when contact is scheduled according to court orders (cf. Nordborg, 2005).

Different forms of power can have different significance in the different domains. Within the domain of Education, judicial power in the form of court orders may not be effective. The fact that there are court orders stipulating that there should be no contact with one parent does not guarantee that preschool or school staff will act in accordance with the orders and thereby protect the child. This does not necessarily mean that the staff disagree with the orders; they may rather be motivated by a fear of the abusive parent's violence. However, there are also cases where staff consider it perfectly reasonable to act against court orders and leave a child with the abusive parent – having the openly stated ambition not to interfere in the 'conflict' between the parents, and equating this with professionalism. I interpret this pattern as an expression of familialisation which does not consider the individual situation and rights of the child, but instead positions the child as an object for the adults' conflict of interests. In these instances, discursive power has greater significance than violence, judicial or economic power. However, in a school system which increasingly interacts with parents as customers, economic power and economic considerations are not irrelevant. Examples of this were found in interviews with teachers who claimed to have been instructed by their Principal to ignore their concerns regarding a child's situation. A school might choose to turn a blind eye to the exposure of a child to violence, making it an economic priority not to get into conflict with the parents in order to be able to keep them as happy customers.

Children are not involved in economic production and if they are given any attention at all in this sphere it is as an economic burden for whom the parents must provide. However, the UN Convention on the Rights of the Child states that they have the right to have their needs taken into consideration and a right to participation in all matters that concern them (Fernqvist, 2011). While the last decade has seen a dramatic increase in the attention given to the position of children being exposed to physical violence from a parent (or another adult) (Eriksson, 2011) one of my conclusions is that there is complete silence regarding children's exposure to the financial abuse of one parent towards the other (Bruno, 2017). Parents have a shared financial responsibility for their children and the law presupposes that resources are available to everyone in the family. However, as is suggested in Bruno (2017), as well as other studies, this is far from certain. The opportunities for exercising financial abuse, not least during or following a separation, are considerable (Branigan, 2004; Patrick, Cook, & McKenzie, 2008; Sanders, 2015; Ulmestig & Eriksson, 2017).

Kinship and parental rights as the right to ownership

Familialisation is the process through which kinship as a power structure is reproduced. This can also help to explain the great scope for action a father can have within the domain of Education, even in those cases where a court order denies him the right to access. He claims, and is given, power as a man in relation to the mostly female staff, as an adult in relation to the child, and as a father to the exposed child in particular.

In the Legal domain, children have neither the right to bring a claim nor the right to personal legal representation, nor the right to have a say; rather, they are constructed as objects for the conflict of the parents and thus have the status of a kind of property. As has been shown by Anna Singer (2000), legal custody is unrelated to the actual responsibility to provide care, appearing more like the parent's right to ownership than the rights of the child to have someone who provides for their needs and ensures their rights. Biological fatherhood in particular is seen as valuable in itself and appears to offer great capacity for action, even for convicted perpetrators of violence. Through the promotion of shared custody, the governance of the state appears to aim at keeping the separated family together, at a very high price in cases involving violence (cf. Eriksson, 2005; Hautanen, 2005; Heide Ottossen, 2006).

Nevertheless, exceptions to this effort to keep families together can be seen. In my empirical data (Bruno, 2017), there are examples of fathers who, in their interaction with professionals, show an apparent lack of interest in their children, for example by making their contact with the children conditional on the demand that all travel expenses be paid for by the mother, or by not showing up on a number of occasions when contact has been scheduled. Separation is then completed and an end to the troubles is realised on the father's conditions. The second important exception is related to privileges of whiteness and racialisation, which is discussed in the following section. As seen, the subjugation of children is achieved through familialisation, and the individual situation of the child is not considered when the problem is represented as a conflict between the adults. Against the adults, however, a selective repression is carried out.

Selective repression

My research confirms Keith Pringle's suggestion (2010) that difficulties in confronting and countering racism in Sweden intersect with insufficient societal responses to men's violence against women and children. My dissertation points to the effects of both familialisation and racialisation in the practices of district courts within the Legal domain. Furthermore, I show how disciplinary strategies can be utilised within the domain of Education, not primarily against the person who is abusive and threatens the safety of children and staff, but rather towards those being exposed to the abuse. There appears to be a selective culturalisation of domestic violence, a selective assigning of responsibility and a selective disciplining of perpetrators and those who have been abused.

Racialisation

As noted above, the dominating pattern of familialisation and legal regulation aimed at keeping the family together was potentially broken when fathers showed an all too apparent lack of interest in their children in their contact with professionals (Bruno, 2017). In addition, my research showed an exemption from the steer towards keeping separated families together to be typical in those cases where the father had a non-Nordic name (Bruno, 2015). In cases with indications of violence, it was four times more common for fathers with non-Nordic names not to be given visiting rights. I also found several cases where non-Nordic fathers were not given rights of access, or given only limited rights, without there being any reports of violence at all (Bruno, 2015). The expressed wishes of the child, or the court's idea of the child's true wishes, were decisive in these cases. Here, the cases where fathers with Nordic names were given complete access to the child, in spite of there being explicit reports of severe violence, and in spite of the wishes of the child not to have contact, stand out in remarkable contrast. Thus, it seems to be the nuclear family perceived as Swedish/Nordic that is to be kept together at all costs, not racialised Other families (cf. Eriksson, 2006). Kinship is thus also shaped by race (as a power structure) in the discursive practices of professionals.

The positions of victims and abusers are constructed in relation to each other, but can be weighed differently depending on the context. One of my conclusions (Bruno, 2015) was that the discursive practices regarding violence in parental separation are determined by the position of the perpetrator, not that of the victim. It is, in other words, not because the courts are more eager to protect children with non-Nordic names that they tend to emphasise the rights to protection and participation of these children in particular, and refer to the Convention on the Rights of the Child and so on in these cases, even if it might appear so at first sight. Rather, my interpretation of the findings is that it is the image of the *patriarchal Other* (Eriksson, 2006) which influences professional practice, in many cases probably subconsciously. This interpretation is supported by the fact that no other research indicates any particular concern to defend children with foreign backgrounds. Rather the contrary can be noted in, for example, the treatment of refugee children by the state or in relation to age determinations for unaccompanied refugee children before the granting of a residence permit (Hedlund, 2017; Wernesjö, 2014). There are, however, in interviews and court orders, very few examples of suspicion being openly cast on fathers with reference to their foreign (or non-Nordic) background. Thus, the patriarchal Other is invisible as a rationale for the activation of discourses of care and/or participation for children (Eriksson & Näsman, 2008). I interpret the activation of these discourses as mainly rhetorical. Instead, whiteness can be seen as the unmarked normative position (Hübinette & Lundström, 2014) which, together with adult privilege and male privilege, shapes family law disputes involving allegations of violence.

Gendered assignment of responsibility

In research on violence, and not least on sexual violence, victim blaming is an established concept. Those who give voice to problems are depicted as the site and cause of these same problems. There is extensive literature on how the gendered positions of victims and perpetrators are constructed in relation to each other in different discourses and practices, such as in criminal law, popular culture, youths discussing rape, the individual interpretations of events made by perpetrators and abused parties, and so on (see e.g. Alinia, 2013; Burman, 2010, 2016; Enander, 2008). In my research, the primary focus of examination was not on the complex and often ambivalent psychological processes of the positioning of oneself and others in relation to images of perpetrators and victims, but rather the positionings and presentations made by professionals. Furthermore, my main focus was on children's positions rather than gendered conflict, while still acknowledging the importance of feminist theory in understanding discursive practices surrounding fathers' violence.

In her analysis of American political discourse on men's violence against women, Nancy Berns (2001) identifies two discursive strategies: degendering of violence and gendering the blame. She claims that domestic violence is generally portrayed as mutual and gender symmetric and, if it is admitted that most perpetrators are men, the cause of the violence is sought in women's provocative behaviour. Examples of these discursive strategies can certainly be found in my data. However, explicit blame for the violence is less notable than the recurring pattern of indirect assignment of responsibility. While women are to a limited extent held responsible for the causes of the violence, they are, in their capacity as primary or sole care givers (cf. Singer, 2000: givers of *actual* care), consistently assigned responsibility for the effects of the violence on their children. Thus, what we are specifically dealing with here is *mother blaming* (cf. Harrison, 2008; Lapierre, 2010; Radford & Hester, 2006). Research by Eriksson (2005) suggests that some family law secretaries openly presuppose that the mother will act as a buffer between a potentially dangerous father and his children. Furthermore, the recurring emphasis on cooperation between the parents, although superficially gender neutral, does have gendered effects in cases with indications of violence, by formulating the violence of one parent against the other and/or against the child as a conflict between equal parties. To conclude, assigning of responsibility appears as a selective process by which the professionals' use of disciplining or repressive measures varies with the gender and race of perpetrators and those who have been abused.

Conclusion and looking ahead

Why does the troubling (abuse, coercive control or violations of integrity) persist, even after the separation? In the Swedish welfare state, what stands in the way of implementing the law and prioritising victimised children's rights after a separation, when the father is the perpetrator? My research suggests that the social processes which (albeit to varying degrees) are undermining the work of protection from domestic violence are familialisation and selective repression. These processes are supported by certain institutional and intersectional conditions. The results reinforce the notion that violence is actively *administered* in ways which contribute to the continuation of abuse. It should be emphasised that what is being examined here is not the intentions of the professionals involved, but the patterns of effects which follow from their practices. Many professionals are genuinely dedicated, and their intentions are generally to work for the best interests of children and to improve the conditions for people in vulnerable life situations. Practices regarding violence have their institutional and discursive contexts, and organisational, professional and political conditions, but within these structures active subjects are operating with the option of choosing different discourses and alternative courses of action. In some cases, the possibilities are limited by formal conditions, such as legislation and mandates to take action. In other cases, it is more a matter of informal conditions, interpretations of the situation and of the professional task. In some cases, there is a fear of making mistakes, or of being exposed oneself.

Fathers' violence against children and mothers constitutes an exercise of power in several ways. Control can be achieved by means of threats and violence, but it can also be enhanced by judicial power (in this case interpretations and established practices of family law), economic power and discursive power. Discursive power is not unambiguous, and different discourses are competing for legitimacy.

The national self-image

As Pringle (2010) has argued, Esping-Andersen (1990) and other researchers of welfare give a misleading picture when, in their comparative analyses and typologies of welfare systems, they only take into account the way in which states prioritise reforms for increased economic equality – where Sweden shows greater ambition compared to, for example, Great Britain. If the focus instead is placed on how the state handles issues of bodily integrity, such as in relation to institutional racism and men's violence against women, another image of Sweden appears. In particular, Pringle (2010) problematises the silence around sexual abuse against children. Taking this line of reasoning a step further, one might say that the Swedish welfare system is still fairly effective in countering poverty and securing the most basic material needs of its citizens, unless economic violence is exercised in the family (including after its dissolution). If, on the other hand, we use the handling of violence as an indicator of welfare, it can actually be questioned if Sweden has any welfare system worth mentioning.

The prevalence of domestic violence and the obvious difficulties in combating this problem challenge the Swedish self-image of being a gender equal, modern state with its rule of law and monopoly of violence intact. Women's increased economic independence and their advancement into positions within academia, culture and politics during the last half-century is welcomed by many men, but it is provoking to others and leads some of these to exercise violence in order to regain control. The increasing number of family law disputes can partially be seen in the light of this, as well as the urge to assign racialised men a greater responsibility for violence through selective culturalisation – viewing violence as cultural in some cases but not in others, depending on the ethnicity, skin colour, religion, etc. of the perpetrator.

I suggest that the current practice of prioritising abusive fathers' relations with (or control over) their children, over the rights of these children, is supported by conservative ideals of intact families and the normative power of the father – kinship as the right of ownership and as a power order of particular importance. In addition to this there is, simultaneously, a consensus-oriented and hegemonic discourse of gender equality which focuses on quantity – equal representation, equal amount of time with the mother and the father. Policy efforts to promote parental co-operation and to hold parents jointly responsible for their children's well-being have unintended and negative consequences for children exposed to domestic violence. Most fathers in Sweden are not abusive, but those who are can, ironically, use public discourses on the best interest of the child and on gender equality in order to gain continuous access to those being abused (Eriksson, 2005). A banal nationalism and a strong political commitment to create equal and involved fathers both have the unintended consequences of undermining the protection of victimised children and mothers. Obviously, fathers generally being more child-centered today than a generation ago is a positive development. It is crucial however, that professionals are able to recognise the difference between engagement and control.

Implications for policy and practice

My results confirm previous studies which point to a discrepancy between official rhetoric and practices with regard to the safety of children and the safety of women. This discrepancy is expressed as a lack of implementation of children's rights to protection, participation and provision, as well as the state's responsibility to work towards ending men's violence against women as part of the adopted goal of gender equality (Burman, 2010; Eriksson, 2013; Röbäck & Höijer, 2009). The violations of integrity persists in many cases, in spite of the mothers leaving their perpetrators in order to seek the protection of society for themselves as well as for their children. Apart from being sociologically relevant, the implications of my results are also practical and political. Implementation of more coherent and prioritised policies to combat violence within all domains of practice appears crucial (cf. Hester, 2011).

For the abuse or troubling to cease, it is necessary for the system to function in all its parts. When a preschool leaves an exposed child with a parent without visitation rights, or when the social services forcibly take a child from school in front of their friends – children for whom teachers are trying to create a safe learning environment – or when the district court makes a decision contrary to the risk assessment of the social services and the recommendations of child psychologists, the efforts of some professionals to ensure the rights of children are rendered ineffectual, due to the undermining of children's rights caused by other professionals.

It is necessary for all legislators and relevant authorities to take on board the scale of the oppression and to realise how the bureaucracy can be used by perpetrators and how they can unknowingly be made to administer the violence instead of countering it. Increased competence and guidance for implementation of children's rights is needed. All relevant professionals should have mandatory training in these issues. Further, I believe children should have their own legal representation in family law disputes. It is important in cases with children who have experienced violence (directly or indirectly), and who wish to maintain contact with a parent who has used violence (typically the father), that this contact is arranged following a thorough assessment of risks and in a way that is safe for everyone involved. In my view, forced contact can in most cases not be considered in line with the best interests of the child. Children should not have to take any responsibility for decisions regarding contact, custody or residence. However, a child who expresses a clear opinion should be able to have a stronger influence on the decision than at present. Politically, the conclusion can be drawn that in order more effectively to combat and prevent men's violence in daily life, the state must reconsider its nationalistic priorities regarding what and who should be protected from whom and on what terms

Disclosure statement

No potential conflict of interest was reported by the author.

References

Alanen, L. (1994). Gender and generation: Feminism and the 'child question'. In J. Qvortrup, M. Bardy, G. Sgritta, & H. Wintersberger (Eds.), *Childhood matters. Social theory, practice and politics* (pp. 27–42). Aldershot: Ashgate.

Alinia, M. (2013). *Honour-related violence against women in iraqi kurdistan.* Basingstoke Hampshire: Palgrave Macmillan.

Anthias, F. (2001). The material and the symbolic in theorizing social stratification. *British Journal of Sociology, 52*, 367–390.

Anthias, F. (2012). Intersectional what? Social divisions, intersectionality and levels of analysis. *Ethnicities, 13*, 3–19.

Berns, N. (2001). Degendering the problem and gendering the blame: Political discourse on women and violence. *Gender and Society, 15*, 262–281.

Branigan, E. (2004). *'His money or our money?' Financial abuse of women in intimate partner relationships.* Coburg, VIC: Coburg Brunswick Community Legal and Financial Counselling Centre.

Broberg, A., Almqvist, K., Almqvist, L., Axberg, U., Cater, Å., Eriksson, M., . . . Sharifi, U. (2011). *Stöd till barn som bevittnat våld mot mamma. Resultat från en nationell utvärdering.* Göteborg: Psykologiska institutionen, Göteborgs universitet.

Brown, T., Frederico, M., Hewitt, L., & Sheehan, R. (2000). Revealing the existence of child abuse in the context of marital breakdown and custody and access disputes. *Child Abuse & Neglect, 24*, 849–859.

Bruno, L. (2015). Contact and evaluations of violence: An intersectional analysis of Swedish court orders. *International Journal of Law, Policy and the Family, 29*, 167–182.

Bruno, L. (2016). *Ofridstid. Fäders våld, staten och den separerande familjen* (Doctoral dissertation). Sociologiska institutionen, Uppsala universitet, Uppsala.

Bruno, L. (2017). Financial oppression and post-separation child positions in Sweden. *European Journal of Social Work, 20*, 1–11.

Burman, M. (2010). The ability of criminal law to produce gender equality: Judicial discourses in the Swedish criminal legal system. *Violence against Women, 16*, 173–188.

Burman, M. (2016). Fathers' rights in Swedish family law reform: Taking account of fathers' violence against mothers. *Canadian Journal of Women and the Law, 28*, 152–181.

Carbin, M. (2014) The requirement to speak: Victim stories in Swedish policies against honour-related violence. *Women's Studies International Forum, 46*, 107–114.

Cater, Å. (2004). *Negotiating normality and deviation – father's violence against mother from children's perspectives* (Doctoral dissertation). Studies in Social Work, Örebro University, Örebro.

Cater, Å., & Forssell, A. (2014). Descriptions of fathers' care by children exposed to intimate partner violence (IPV) – Relative neglect and children's needs. *Child and Family Social Work, 19*, 185–193.

Dahlkild-Öhman, G. (2011). *Att börja tala med barn om pappas våld mot mamma. Radikalt lärande i arbetet med vårdnad, boende och umgänge* (Doctoral dissertation). Sociologiska institutionen, Uppsala universitet, Uppsala.

Diesen, C., & Diesen, E. (2013). *Övergrepp mot kvinnor och barn: Den rättsliga hanteringen.* Norstedts Juridik: Stockholm.

Ekbrand, H. (2006). *Separationer och mäns våld mot kvinnor* (Doctoral dissertation). Studies in Sociology, 28, Göteborgs universitet, Göteborg.

Enander, V. (2008). *Women leaving violent men. Crossroads of emotions, cognition and action* (Doctoral dissertation). Institutionen för socialt arbete, Göteborgs universitet, Göteborg.

Eriksson, M. (2005). A visible or invisible child? Professionals' approaches to children whose father is violent towards their mother. In M. Eriksson, M. Hester, S. Keskinen, & K. Pringle (Eds.), *Tackling men's violence in families: Nordic issues and dilemmas* (pp. 119–136). Bristol: Policy Press.

Eriksson, M., & Pringle, K. (2005). Nordic issues and dilemmas: Introduction. In M. Eriksson, M. Hester, S. Keskinen, & K. Pringle (Eds.), *Tackling men's violence in families: Nordic issues and dilemmas* (pp. 2–11). Bristol: Policy Press.

Eriksson, M. (2006). Avvikande eller osynlig – Rasifierande praktiker i familjerättssekreterares hantering av fäders våld. In P. de Los Reyes (Ed.), *Om välfärdens gränser och det villkorade medborgarskapet (SOU 2006: 37)* (pp. 183–216). Stockholm: Fritzes.

Eriksson, M. (2011). Contact, shared parenting and violence: Children as witnesses of domestic violence in Sweden. *International Journal of Law, Policy and the Family, 25*, 165–183.

Eriksson, M. (2013). Tackling violence in intimacy: Interacting power relations and policy change. *Current Sociology, 61*(2), 171–189.

Eriksson, M., Bruno, L., & Näsman, E. (2013). *Domestic violence, family law and school: Children's rights to participation, protection and provision.* Basingstoke: Palgrave Macmillan.

Eriksson, M., & Näsman, E. (2008). Participation in family law proceedings for children whose father is violent to their mother. *Childhood, 15*, 259–275.

Esping-Andersen, G. (1990). *The three worlds of welfare capitalism.* Cambridge: Polity Press.

Featherstone, B., & Peckover, S. (2007). Letting them get away with it: Fathers, domestic violence and child welfare. *Critical Social Policy, 27*, 181–202.

Fernbrandt, C. (2013). *Violence against foreign-born women in Sweden* (Doctoral dissertation). Lund University, Lund.

Fernqvist, S. (2011). Redefining participation? On the positioning of children in Swedish welfare benefit appeals. *Childhood, 18*, 227–241.

Fleury, R. E., Sullivan, C. M., & Bybee, D. (2000). When ending the relationship does not end the violence: Women's experiences of violence by former partners. *Violence Against Women, 6*, 1363–1383.

Forssell, A. (2016). *Better safe than sorry? Quantitative and qualitative aspects of child-father relationship after parental separation in cases involving intimate partner violence* (Doctoral dissertation). Örebro University, Örebro.

Forssell, A. M., & Cater, Å. (2015). Patterns in child–Father contact after parental separation in a sample of child witnesses to intimate partner violence. *Journal of Family Violence, 30*, 339–349.

FRA (EU Agency for Fundamental Rights). (2014). *Violence against women: An EU-wide survey. Main results report.* Vienna: FRA

Gunnarsson, Å. (Ed.) (2013). *Tracing the women-friendly welfare state: Gendered politics of everyday life of Sweden.* Göteborg: Makadam.

Harrison, C. (2008). Implacably hostile or appropriately protective? Women managing child contact in the context of domestic violence. *Violence Against Women, 14*, 381–405.

Hautanen, T. (2005). Bypassing the relationship between fatherhood and violence in Finnish policy and research. In M. Eriksson, M. Hester, S. Keskinen, & K. Pringle (Eds.), *Tackling men's violence in families: Nordic issues and dilemmas* (pp. 67–82). Bristol: Policy Press.

Hearn, J. (2012). A multi-faceted power analysis of men's violence to known women: From hegemonic masculinity to the hegemony of men. *The Sociological Review, 60*, 589–610.

Hedlund, D. (2017). Constructions of credibility in decisions concerning unaccompanied minors. *International Journal of Migration, Health, and Social Care, 13*, 157–172.

Heide Ottossen, M. (2006). In the name of the father, the child and the holy genes: Constructions of the child's best interest in legal disputes over contact. *Acta Sociologica, 49*, 29–46.

Hester, M. (2011). The three planet model: Towards an understanding of contradictions in approaches to women and children's safety in contexts of domestic violence. *British Journal of Social Work, 41*, 837–853

Hübinette, T, & Lundström, C. (2014). Three phases of hegemonic whiteness: understanding racial temporalities in sweden. *Social Identities: Journal for The Study Of Race, Nation and Culture, 20*(6), 423-437. doi:10.1080/13504630.2015.1004827

Hübinette, T., & Lundström, C. (2014). Three phases of hegemonic whiteness: Understanding racial temporalities in Sweden. *Social Identities: Journal for the Study of Race, Nation and Culture, 20*, 423–437.

Ingrids, I. (2014). *Dilemmas in child custody disputes. The child's best interests in courtroom discourse* (Doctoral dissertation). Department of Child and Youth Studies, Stockholm University, Stockholm.

Keskinen, S. (2009). Honour related violence and Nordic nation building. In S. Keskinen, S. Tuouri, & D. Mulinari (Eds.), *Complying with colonialism: Gender, race and ethnicity in the Nordic region* (pp.257–272). Farnham: Asgate.

Khaw, L., & Hardesty, J. L. (2007). Theorizing the process of leaving: Turning points and trajectories in the stages of change model. *Family Relations*, *56*, 413–425.

Lapierre, S. (2010). More responsibilities, less control: Understanding the challenges and difficulties involved in mothering in the context of domestic violence. *British Journal of Social Work*, *40*, 1434–1451.

Nordborg, G. (2005). Children's peace? The possibility to protect children by means of criminal law and family law. In M. Eriksson, M. Hester, S. Keiskinen, & K. Pringle (Eds.), *Tackling men's violence in families: Nordic issues and dilemmas* (pp.101–118). Bristol: Policy Press.

Patrick, R., Cook, K., & McKenzie, H. (2008). Domestic violence and the exemption from seeking child support: Providing safety or legitimizing ongoing poverty and fear. *Social Policy and Administration*, *42*, 749–767.

Pringle, K. (2010). Swedish welfare responses to ethnicity: The case of children and their families. *European Journal of Social Work*, *13*, 19–34.

Radford, L., & Hester, M. (2015). More than a mirage? Safe contact for children and young people who have been exposed to domestic violence. In N. Stanley & C. Humphrey (Eds.), *Domestic violence and protecting children: New thinking and approaches* (pp. 112–129). London: Jessica Kingsley Publishers.

Radford, L., & Hester, M. (2006). *Mothering through domestic violence*. London: Jessica Kingsley Publishers.

Röbäck, K., & Höjer, I. (2009). Constructing children's views in the enforcement of contact orders. *International Journal of Children's Rights*, *17*, s. 663–680.

Sanders, S. K. (2015). Economic abuse in the lives of women abused by an intimate partner: A qualitative study. *Violence Against Women*, *21*, 3–29.

Singer, A. (2000). *Föräldraskap i rättslig belysning*. Uppsala: Iustus förlag.

Skjørten, K. (2013). Children's voices in Norwegian custody cases. *International Journal of Law, Policy and the Family*, *27*, 289–309.

Socialstyrelsen. (2018). Dödsfallsutredningar 2016–2017.

SOU 2017: 6. (2017). *Se barnet! Betänkande av 2014 års vårdnadsutredning*. Stockholm: Elanders Sverige AB.

Towns, A. (2002). Paradoxes of (in)equality: Something is rotten in the gender equal welfare state of Sweden. *Cooperation and Conflict*, *35*, 157–179.

Ulmestig, R., & Eriksson, M. (2017). Financial consequences of leaving violent men - Women survivors and the social assistance system in Sweden. *European Journal of Social Work*, *20*, 560–571.

Walby, S. (1990). *Theorizing patriarchy*. Oxford: Basil Blackwell.

Walby, S. (2013). Violence and society: Introduction to an emerging field of sociology. *Current Sociology*, *61*, 95–111.

Wernesjö, U. (2014). *Conditional belonging: Listening to unaccompanied young refugees' voices* (Doctoral disseration). Uppsala University, Uppsala.

Contact disputes and allegations of gender violence in Spain

Teresa Picontó-Novales

ABSTRACT
In Spain, progress is being made to restrict contact between aggressors and their children in cases of gender violence. However, visits and communication, even shared custody, are still granted by judges despite shared custody being prohibited by law in such cases since 2005. Under recent legal reforms, children are now considered primary victims of gender-based violence. However, even today, Spanish judges frequently allow contact and even grant shared custody to the aggressor. This is despite the fact that in cases of gender violence, there are usually measures in force that include restraining orders and prohibitions against communicating with the mother. In these cases, communication between the father and his children is effected through grandparents or at the so-called 'family meeting points' – neutral spaces supervised by professionals. Insufficient budgets and shortcomings in the management of these meeting points have led to many problems, including women being murdered by their partners after leaving one of these meeting places.

Introduction

Alexandra S was murdered by her ex-partner in front of her five-year-old son on Sunday 10 July 2016 on the doorstep of a Family Meeting Point in Zaragoza, Spain.

Alexandra S's death was premeditated. On the Monday before the crime the aggressor had sent a letter to the Court of Violence against Women[1] (*Juzgado de Violencia sobre la Mujer* – JVSM) no 2 of Zaragoza advising that his ex-partner had failed to comply with the decision of the court allowing him to see the child and he also alleged, among other things, that the child might not be receiving schooling. This ensured that the court would contact the mother and order her to comply with the regime of communication and visits. Furthermore, the aggressor also calculated that his ex-partner would be in Zaragoza, because a trial was to be held against him on the Monday for coercion – which she had reported – for which the office of the public prosecutor called for a one-year prison sentence.

On the day of the murder, Alexandra took her five-year-old son to the Family Meeting Point established to facilitate the contact arrangements, as there was a restraining order in place for her protection. Her ex-husband was to collect the child at the same place 20 minutes later. In theory, the times are calculated so that ex-partners do not meet, but the aggressor, knowing the routines of the service, was waiting for her arrival at the door. Alexandra S was stabbed in the neck and abdomen by her ex-husband on the doorstep of the Family Meeting Point in Conde Aranda Street in Zaragoza in the presence of her son. After 30 hours fighting for her life and having been subjected to two complicated surgical interventions, Alexandra died the following day in the ICU of the Hospital Clínico Lozano Blesa in Zaragoza.

This case raises several issues which are addressed in this article:

1. There was a precautionary measure in place against the aggressor consisting of a restraining order due to his abuse of the victim, obviously broken to commit the murder – as it had been broken before – which did not guarantee Alexandra S's safety. In Spain, the official line insists that in the majority of deaths of women victims of 'gender violence' there is no previous complaint or restraining order. In two of the crimes that occurred in Zaragoza in the months before this case, however, the victim had already denounced her aggressor, without this being sufficient to prevent her murder. These and other cases should lead to a reflection on the effectiveness of the prevention apparatus deployed since Spanish Organic Law 1/2004 came into force, particularly the protocols for risk assessment. Spanish Organic Law 1/2004 of 28 December deals with comprehensive preventive and protective measures against gender violence. 'Gender violence' is defined as 'violence or different types of inferred violence by men against women, when both are or have been a couple, due to the mere fact of being women and which constitutes the manifestation of historically unequal relations of power'. ('Domestic violence', by contrast, is that which occurs between other family members) (General Council of the Judiciary, 2016).
2. In spite of evidence of having committed a crime of gender violence and of the objective risk to the victim, the aggressor had been granted contact with his five-year-old son. Spanish courts generally do not consider that a restraining order automatically implies prohibition of contact. Although Article 92.7 of the Spanish Civil Code prohibits shared custody[2] in such cases, a regime of communication and visits (contact) is usually granted to aggressors. But the inescapable reality is that the deaths of many children (over 50%) occur when they are alone with the aggressor during contact or as a consequence of a shared custody regime.[3]
3. In cases in which there is a restraining order in place either as a precautionary measure or as a secondary punitive measure,[4] Family Meeting Points are often the only resource that makes it possible to deliver and collect children without the parents coming into contact. In addition, it is assumed that they should guarantee the safety of the victims. Obviously, this purpose has not been accomplished. There is a difference between the theoretical role and the reality of Family Meeting Points. They are said to be a 'lesser evil', but their operation far from safeguards victims of gender violence. Indeed, they are designed to respond to conflict situations in cases of break-up, but not to address cases of gender violence.
4. In spite of advances in this regard, the way in which the five-year-old child was rendered invisible in the media's treatment of the aggression against Alexandra S continues to surprise, despite the fact that the murder occurred 'in the presence of' or 'in front of' him. At most, it is stated that he was protected by being assigned to a

foster family. According to the latest legislative changes made in Spain (Organic Law 8/2015 of 22 July), this child is a *direct* victim of a crime of gender violence. However, children continue to be the forgotten ones in cases of gender violence. This in spite of the fact that in the four years from 2013 to 2016, 160 children lost their mothers as a result of a crime of gender violence (Fundación Mujeres, 2017). And very many more have witnessed acts of gender violence against their mothers, so making them also victims of violence and of the undoubted consequences for their development. One report on the subject contains the terrible question 'Who will take away my memories?' put by the son of a victim of fatal gender violence in a seminar with victims (Fundación Mujeres, 2017).

The case of Alexandra S and her son obliges us to reflect on judicial and institutional practice in relation to shared custody and contact in the context of gender violence. More specifically, this article analyses the arguments on which judicial decisions rest, which in some ways ignore gender violence when they establish orders about communications and visits for sons and daughters of fathers who have been convicted of crimes of gender violence or in respect of whom there is well-founded evidence of violence. They sometimes also ignore the legislative and jurisprudential changes which have taken place in this regard. In relation to these matters, there are many other issues to which only brief allusion can be made and which may demand specific attention beyond the limits of this article. These include the operation of Family Meeting Points and the need to continue to improve the protocols for risk assessment, both in the policing and forensic fields. Finally, the article will make some general reflections on the issues analysed and will put forward some proposals for best practices.

Gender violence as a basis for the prohibition of shared custody

Spain is advancing in restricting contact and communication with fathers in cases where there is gender violence, but a regime of communication and visits and even shared custody of sons and daughters continues to be granted in divorce or separation cases in the context of gender violence or when the aggressor has a conviction in this regard. The award of shared custody has been prohibited by the Spanish Civil Code since 2005 in these cases. Article 92.7 of the Civil Code, establishes that:

> Shared custody shall not apply when either of the parents is subject to a criminal process initiated due to making an attempt against the life, physical integrity, freedom, moral integrity or sexual freedom and integrity of the other spouse or the children who live with both. Neither will it apply when the Judge notes, from the arguments of the parties and the evidence presented, the existence of well-founded evidence of domestic violence.

According to this article, it is clear that under Spanish law it is a legal cause for exclusion from shared custody that 'either of the parents is subject to a criminal process initiated due to making an attempt against the life, physical or moral integrity or sexual freedom and integrity of the other parent or the children who live with both'. Specifically, the article refers to crimes under Articles 138, 147, 163, 173 and other minor offences of the Spanish Criminal Code, in which both the spouse and children who live with them can be injured parties.

Being 'subject to a criminal process' used to be equivalent to being 'charged' with a crime but, after the latest procedural reforms of 2015, it includes being 'investigated' or 'prosecuted' (Sole Article, section 21, of the Spanish Organic Law 13/2015). In this regard, there have been many decisions in judicial practice since 2005 in which alleged aggressors appear in family proceedings as 'charged' after the presentation of an accusation or complaint and subsequent inception of criminal proceedings. The presentation of the accusation should be sufficient for family judges to reject the possibility of shared custody.[5] For example, the Sentence of the Provincial Court (SAP) of Asturias no 4, of 15 February 2013, established that:

> Article 92 of the Civil Code expressly anticipates that shared custody will not apply when the judge notes the existence of well-founded evidence of gender violence. This is a logical demand as it would be difficult to achieve the interrelationship required between the two parents in joint care and custody, without prejudicing the child, whose interest is a priority, in cases like the present with continuing, confirmed conflict between litigants.

This jurisprudential approach has been taken by the majority of courts (Pinto, 2015) and, as can be seen, it regards gender violence as a determining factor for rejecting joint care. However, opposite interpretations of Article 92.7 of the Civil Code have also been given. As such, it has been considered insufficient for rejection of shared custody that the father is subject to (or even has been convicted in) gender violence proceedings, unless the criminal behaviour carries a risk to the children or to the other parent. In this regard, the SAP of Castellón no 2, of 24 October 2014, argues that:

> It is not sufficient that [criminal] proceedings are open due to alleged threats and psychological abuse, brought by the mother of the child against the latter's father.... [T] o be able to exclude one of the parents from living with the child, [it is necessary] that a reasoned legal ruling has been pronounced in which well-founded, rational evidence of criminality is recorded and which [shows] in accordance with the said evidence, [that] application of the cohabitation regime could represent an objective risk to the children or to the other parent. Nothing has been proven or reasoned to say that the said risk applies in the case before us.

With the same view, the Sentence of the Court of Violence against Women no 1 of Denia, of 13 December 2012, established:

> ...in the present case, although it is true that the father has been convicted of a crime of gender violence, this Court considers that, from the evidence examined, it has not been proven that an objective risk exists to the child or the plaintiff that counsels the exclusion of joint assignment of the regime of cohabitation. In the judgement of this Court, it is not sufficient that a parent is subject to criminal proceedings due to domestic or gender violence to deprive the said parent of the possibility of obtaining an individual or shared regime of cohabitation with their children, rather it is also necessary for their criminal conduct to entail a risk to the children or to the other parent, as the higher principle must always be borne in mind of the interest of the child as, otherwise, the punishment of the parent would result in harm to the children who would be deprived of a normalised relationship with one of his or her parents without objective cause for this.

Subsequently, the SAP of Alicante no 4, of 15 October 2013, confirmed the decision of the Court of Violence against Women of Denia which established a regime of shared care with alternating weeks, in spite of the fact that the father was the 'criminally responsible author of a crime of mild injuries in the field of gender violence'. There are many other decisions like these such as SAP of Granada no 5, of 5 December 2014, and SAP of Barcelona no 12, of 25 July 2014.

Also noteworthy is the argument of the SAP of La Coruña no 3, of 27 May 2015, confirming the decision granting shared custody, in spite of it having been proven that the father was subject to criminal proceedings due to a crime against the mother and the dire relationship between them. This decision established that:

> In the present case the facts could fit into prohibition no.7 of Article 92 of the Civil Code, as the father ... has been subject to criminal proceedings for a crime against the freedom of the mother, coercion, [but] it is necessary to remember ... that the poor relations between the parents cannot be a determining factor in failure to grant shared care and custody, as *although it is true that the father has a relationship of complete lack of respect for the mother, even abusive and dominant, that is not relevant to determining shared care and custody* (emphasis added).

That is to say, even recognising that, in this case, the facts could fall within Article 92.7 of the Civil Code, the prohibition this establishes was not applied (Águeda Rodríguez, 2016, p. 305). At their heart, although based on the supposed best interests of the child, these decisions are reproducing a widespread cliché in Spanish society: boys and girls 'need a Dad and a Mum'. This very deep-rooted mentality is a prime example of a traditional view of the family and also serves to discourage adoptions by homosexual families and to justify the idea that an abuser can be a good father (Gracia & Jiménez, 2016, p. 173).

In the face of these ideas, however, it appears that an understanding of the child's true interest is winning out little by little, which is what should take precedence in the final analysis. As such, the SAP of Santander no 2, of 30 March 2016, rectifies the Sentence of the Court of Violence against Women of Santander, of 19 October 2015, which initially attributed shared care and custody to both parents. The SAP, based on Article 92.7, reminds us that:

> the fact that conflict may exist between the parents is one thing, but it is quite another thing that the framework of relationships is voided by a conviction for an unjustifiable crime of gender violence that separates the father from the family environment and from communication with the mother, which will preclude the sharing of parental function in accordance with the interest of their two children. Consequently, and in spite of the psychosocial report, it is appropriate to grant care and custody of the children [only] to the mother.

In addition to the foregoing, the court also noted that, from a careful reading of the totality of Article 92.7, it will be a legal cause for exclusion from shared custody that 'the civil judge notes the existence of well-founded evidence of domestic violence' (or of gender violence after the 2004 reform). That is, even if there are no criminal proceedings open, the civil judge dealing with the separation, divorce or parent-child measures, in view of the allegations and evidence examined in the process, can note evidence of domestic or gender violence. Having been notified of this evidence, the civil judge is obliged to make a statement to be sent to the Duty Court of Instruction[6] notifying the criminal courts of a possible offence. In addition, if the violence notified is gender violence, not only must the judge not award shared custody, but he or she must decline jurisdiction in favour of the Court of Violence Against Women (Article 49.1 of the Code of Civil Procedure). If no criminal proceedings have been initiated in the Court of Violence Against Women, the parties must be summonsed to appear before the Prosecutor and the civil process will continue until the response of the Court of Violence against Women to the request for relinquishment of jurisdiction is received (Article 49.2 of the Code of Civil Procedure). Once jurisdiction is transferred, the Court of Violence Against Women will continue with the process and decide on both the civil and criminal issues.

Communication and visits in the context of gender violence

Article 92.7 of the Spanish Civil Code can and must under certain conditions be interpreted to extend to the exclusion or suspension of communication and visits with respect to the parent subject to criminal proceedings or where there is well-founded evidence of domestic or gender violence, especially taking into account the terms of Article 94 of the Spanish Civil Code. Article 94 establishes the right of contact to the parent who does not have the children living with them, but it also indicates that the Judge 'may limit or suspend [contact] if serious circumstances arise that so advise'.

Spanish courts have been reluctant not to grant the right of communication and visits to fathers who are aggressors. Civil precautionary measures imposed for the protection of victims of gender violence as a general rule affect occupation of the family home and the provision of child maintenance, but usually maintain shared care and custody and the regime of contact.

As Table 1 shows, care and custody is suspended in some cases (between 7.2% and 11.3% depending on the year). In far fewer cases is the regime of communication and visits suspended (between 6.3% and 3.9%) and in very few cases is parental authority[7] suspended (between 0.7% and 0.4%). Thus, barely 5% of protection orders or other civil precautionary measures on average suspend aggressors' rights to contact.

The data in Table 1 show the scarce application of Article 94 of the Civil Code in relation to Article 92.7 when suspending contact in the context of gender violence when there is a protection order and even convictions. This situation was condemned by the NGO Save the Children, which reported that in Spain, 'gender violence is not a

Table 1. Civil measures deriving from protection orders and other precautionary measures (2006–2016).

	2006	2008	2010	2012	2014	2016
Occupation of family home	5677	7019	5952	4497	4247	4689
	31.1%	29.7%	29.4%	27.8%	29.2%	28.4%
Alternating use of family home	161	184	169	97	65	59
	0.9%	0.8%	0.8%	0.6%	0.4%	0.4%
Suspension regime of visits	1101	1111	793	710	623	1035
	6.0%	4.7%	3.9%	4.4%	4.3%	6.3%
Suspension parental authority	119	89	79	79	62	121
	0.7%	0.4%	0.4%	0.5%	0.4%	0.7%
Suspension care and custody	2048	2514	1859	1576	1133	1496
	11.2%	10.6%	9.2%	9.7%	7.8%	9.1%
Provision of child maintenance	5953	7697	6851	5336	4966	5614
	32.6%	32.6%	33.8%	33.0%	34.2%	34.1%
Protection of children	118	231	304	191	275	281
	0.6%	1.0%	1.5%	1.2%	1.9%	1.7%
Others. Civil	3101	4779	4269	3688	3154	3190
	17.0%	20.2%	21.1%	22.8%	21.7%	19.4%
TOTAL CIVIL MEASURES	**18,278**	**23,624**	**20,276**	**16,174**	**14,525**	**16,485**

Source: Prepared by the author based on statistics from the Observatory on Domestic and Gender Violence of the General Council for the Judiciary

determining factor in the Sentences of lower courts on contact regimes' (Save the Children, 2011, pp. 62–63). It underlines that in decisions of Spanish judges to suspend contact, the father's addictions and unruly behaviour carry more weight than gender violence – except in the case of aggression committed directly against children.

Therefore, we find that the majority of judicial resolutions have adopted the regime of shared custody and contact, even in spite of the existence of a conviction of the father for the crime of gender violence. In these cases, the decision is justified by the argument that the child has not been a victim of violence as the effects of the trauma caused to the mother did not reach the child.

A paradigmatic case in this regard is the subject of an important Supreme Court decision, the Sentence of the First Chamber of 26 November 2015:

> In view of the regulations and jurisprudential doctrine set out, we must declare that contact of a father with his daughter, when the former has previously been convicted of ill-treatment of [his other daughter], must be extremely restrictive and the court should exercise great caution when determining what contact should occur, as the risk of harm is more than clear in relation to a child with scarce possibilities of defending themselves.

The Supreme Court's Sentence was pronounced in 2015, when the legislative landscape had changed substantially with the legal reforms to be analysed in the following section, although the regulations the Supreme Court took into account were those in force when the events occurred and the action was initiated. The fact that a Court of Violence against Women should grant a right to visits, even though limited, to an aggressor towards the mother and one of the two daughters, and try to justify this by reference to the best interests of the child and the maintenance of family ties, is surprising to say the least. And the fact that that decision was ratified by a Provincial Court shows that the impact of gender violence on children and young people is not made fully visible in Spanish society (Gómez Pardos, 2011), and neither are the risks that a regime of communication and visits can involve for children and their mothers becoming victims of gender violence.

In the case of the Spanish State, this reality was already condemned by the United Nations Committee on the Elimination of Discrimination against Women at its session no 61 (Calvo García, 2016). In this Report, the Committee expressed its concern at the number of cases of boys and girls murdered by 'violent fathers during the exercise of their visiting rights'. This concern was aggravated by the unjustified non-compliance of the Spanish State with the CEDAW decision of 16 July 2014 in which it condemned the State for failing to protect Ángela González and her daughter, who were murdered by their abuser in 2003 during an established contact visit. In spite of the victim's reporting her ex-husband on 30 occasions due to threats and aggressions, the father's visits and communications with the daughter were not interrupted (CEDAW/C/58/D/47/2012, Communication No. 47/2012). More specifically:

> . . .the authorities, legal and social services and the experts (psychologists) had the normalising of the relationship between the father and daughter as their main objective, in spite of the reservations expressed by these two services about the father's behaviour. . . All these elements reflect a pattern of action that arises from a stereotypical view of contact rights, which in the case in question granted clear advantages to the father in spite of his abusive behaviour and minimised the situation of mother and daughter as victims of violence, placing them in a vulnerable situation (section 9.4).

Furthermore, the Committee made several general recommendations to the Spanish State, such as taking appropriate, effective measures to ensure that the histories of domestic violence are taken into account when stipulating custody and contact rights relating to children and so that the exercise of contact and custody rights does not put the safety of victims of violence, including children, at risk (section 11).

Unfortunately, this is not the only known case. There have been other cases of boys and girls murdered under similar circumstances in Spain. Such was the case of six-year-old Leonor, who in 2015 was murdered by her father, previously convicted of gender violence, on the day that he had to return the girl to her mother, from whom he was separating. Or the brother and sister Ruth and José Breton, aged six and two, murdered in 2013 by their father. These are tragic events to which many other cases of anonymous boys and girls would need to be added, murdered by their fathers when their mother decided to separate from him or during the regime of visits.

It is difficult to know how many boys and girls are really affected by violence against their mothers. According to data provided by the Government Office on Gender Violence, one child victim died in 2016, while between January and October 2017 a total of seven minors were murdered in cases of gender violence. Six mothers were affected since two of the victims were children of the same mother. However, these data have only been collected in very recent times and they are not reliable because of the general invisibility of the mistreatment of children in contexts of gender violence.

Neither do we have data on the consequences of judicial decisions on custody and contact for the children involved. We may also be concerned about the situation of the boys and girls who are left without mothers due to gender violence, and of those who have to live in an environment of permanent conflict and tension, where they act as a channel for the violence toward their mothers and are often used as instruments by the aggressor as a form of mistreatment of their mothers, to the point where some children lose their lives at the hands of their fathers who wish to harm their mothers 'where it hurts most'.

Faced with this situation, it is crucial to make visible the violence to which children have been and are exposed in contexts of gender violence experienced by their mothers (Reyes Cano, 2015, p. 184). This will make it possible to understand the highly negative impact these experiences of violence have on the children's well-being and development. Equally, it will make it easier to change social sensibilities and, in the long run, will make it possible to obtain answers from public policies, government and the judiciary. In this regard, Reyes Cano indicates that 'this is "extended violence" and those who always suffer in the end of that extension of violence are the sons and daughters who live in the same state of tension and alert as their mothers' (Reyes Cano, 2015, p. 182).

Legislative advances in the protection of women victims of gender violence and their children

Advances have been made in Spain in recent years both in respect of protection and improving information for victims in the procedural field and with regard to the protection of children.

One of these legislative responses has been the Law 4/2015, of 27 April, *regulating the standing of victims of crime* (which came into force on 28 October 2015).[8] Specifically, this Statute ensures procedural and extra-procedural rights for victims, including some specific provisions affecting victims of gender violence.

But above all, it has been the passing of the Organic Law 8/2015, of 22 July, and the Law 26/2015, of 28 July, *modifying the system for the protection of infancy and adolescence*, which has represented a substantial advance in relation to family law responses to gender violence.

The most significant modification made by the Organic Law 8/2015, of 22 July, is considering children and minors under the care and custody of abused women to be primary victims of gender violence and not mere witnesses of gender violence, as they were considered before. Therefore, the civil or criminal judge will be able to adopt protective measures that involve prohibiting the aggressor from approaching and communicating with the child.

Specifically, children who live in environments of gender violence are classified as primary victims due to the disturbance that exposure to violence means for their development. The Final Provision 3.1 of the Organic Law 8/2015 changed Article 1.2 of the Organic Law 1/2004, where it sets out its purpose:

> This law establishes integral protection measures the purpose of which is to prevent, penalise and eradicate [gender] violence and to assist women and their under-age children and minors under their guardianship or care and custody, victims of this violence.

This new provision puts an end to all the evasions found in existing doctrine and judicial practice. Children come to be considered *direct victims* of gender violence against them and not mere indirect victims or witnesses of the violence suffered by their mothers.

In spite of this undoubted improvement, it would have been more enlightened if the Law 4/2015 on the standing of victims of crime had established a conceptual distinction between, on the one hand, children as victims of domestic violence and, on the other, child victims of gender violence (Reyes Cano, 2015, p. 196). This is because, as is well known, they constitute very different realities, with different causes and consequences. The main difference is that child victims of domestic violence (or child abuse) come under the protection of the Social Services and may be dealt with by the Criminal Court. However, child victims of gender violence come under the protection of the Courts of Violence Against Women.

Articles 61.2 and 55 of the Organic Law 1/2004, also reformed by the Organic Law 8/2015, acknowledge the possibility of requesting precautionary measures to protect child victims of gender violence, including appeals to the Public Authorities who can harbour them. They also acknowledge the possibility of suspending parental authority or custody of children if a parent, custodian or guardian is accused in proceedings for domestic violence. The fact that the measure refers to the parent simply being accused means that suspension of parental authority or custody can be adopted as a precautionary measure before there is a conviction for an act of gender violence, without prejudice to the penalties that could finally apply or the decisions that are finally taken in the civil proceedings that regulate parental authority or care and custody of the child (Reyes Cano, 2015, p. 218).

Article 7 of the Law 26/2015 modifies Article 12 of the Organic Law 1/1996 and establishes that:

> ...when children are under the parental authority, guardianship, care or foster care of a victim of gender or domestic violence, the actions of the public authorities will be aimed at guaranteeing the necessary support to ensure that the children, regardless of age, remain with her, as well as their protection, specialised attention and recovery.

In this regard, the modification made by Final Provision 3 of the Organic Law 8/2015 to Articles 65 and 66 of the Organic Law 1/2004 is also important. As such, if the judge does not suspend parental authority, shared custody or contact with the children, he or she shall determine how these powers are to be exercised, adopting the measures necessary to ensure the safety, integrity and recovery of the children and women and requiring periodic monitoring of their progress. Although this modification does not constitute extra protection (Reyes Cano, 2015, p. 197), at least it obliges judges in all cases to analyse the situation of the child victim and to consider how the functions of parental authority are to be exercised given the accusation of gender violence, with the possibility of carrying out monitoring of their exercise. Finally, the status of children as direct victims of gender violence enables the Courts of Violence against Women to assume 'direct competence' with respect to gender violence that is perpetrated against children.

In summary, with these legal reforms of 2015, it has been understood that children who live in an environment where gender violence is present really are affected in many ways: in their well-being, development, health, etc., in addition to the intergenerational transmission of violent behaviour.

The child is considered to be a direct victim of gender violence from the moment that he or she is present in the place where aggression against the mother takes place, irrespective of whether he or she only witnesses the aggression or intervenes between the mother and the aggressor. Therefore, even though the aggressor acts directly against the mother and not the minor, in such cases minors deserve special protection by the law.

Impact of legislative change on judicial and institutional practice

These legal reforms have had a significant impact on judicial practice concerning shared custody and contact in contexts of gender violence. As stated previously, the possibility of suspending the aggressor's regime of visits, stays or relations and communication with children already existed in the Spanish legal system. However, since the legal reforms of 2015, a judge who adopts one of these measures must ensure periodic monitoring of their progress for the protection of the mother and the children in her charge.

Also relevant in the new legal regulations is the possibility of adopting additional precautionary measures with respect to the children in cases in which protection measures are put in place in respect of the woman, even if no aggressive episode towards the children has occurred up to that time, provided there is evidence that leads to the suspicion that the accused party could act against the children as some form of retaliation. That is, although the aggressor is only accused of acting against the mother, precautionary measures may be adopted if there is a well-founded concern that his harmful action against his ex-partner may continue through the children, when he no longer has access to her or simply when he wants to inflict greater pain.

Therefore, the judge can impose restraining orders not only with respect to the woman, but also with respect to the children, even though the violent acts alleged were not directed against them and only abuse of the woman is to be prosecuted. In addition, the laws of the Autonomous Regions ensure that a child affected by a change of residence as a consequence of a situation of gender or domestic violence is to be enrolled immediately in another educational institution, with the confidentiality of the reason for the change being respected. Similarly, situations of gender violence are also taken into account when providing educational support and access to the home where the mother and her children live.

Supreme court decisions

The legal reforms of 2015 have already been followed and reinforced by several Supreme Court decisions. The Supreme Court Sentence of 26 November 2015, referred to above, emphatically advanced a new jurisprudential approach in establishing that

> the judge or court may suspend the regime of visits with the child for the parent sentenced for the crime of abuse of their spouse or partner and/or for the crime of mistreatment of the minor or the other children, assessing the existing risk factors.

The arrangements to be adopted in the best interest of the child – whether shared custody or contact – may never further restrict or limit the rights of the protected children. In any event, the assessment of the risk factors must never be overlooked.

In turn, the important Supreme Court Sentence of 4 February 2016 (JUR 2016 30,008), establishes:

> Article 2 of Law 8/2015, of 22 July, modifying the system for the protection of infancy and adolescence, demands that the life and development of the child take place in an environment free from violence and that 'if all the concurrent legitimate interests cannot be respected, the interests of the child shall take precedence over any other legitimate interest that may arise'; criteria which, although expressed in a law subsequent to the action, incorporate those that this Chamber has taken into account repeatedly when determining the best interest of the child. A logical corollary is that set out in Article 92.7 of the Civil Code…

Therefore, as a result of the legal reforms of 2015 and backed by the jurisprudential shift established by the Supreme Court, a change is taking place in favour of the protection of the best interests of the child by judges and courts, with measures such as not granting shared custody, and limiting or suspending the regime of visits, stays and communication with children of the aggressor parent, after the divorce or separation of the parents.

This trend coincides with the demands of numerous institutions. Hence, for example, the Supreme Court Sentence of 26 November 2015 was received expressly 'with satisfaction' by the Ombudsman in a communiqué of 11 December 2015 which recalled that this institution had already 'recommended in November 2014 banning visits and communications with their children of those charged with mistreatment in order to avoid risks'. The arguments of the Sentence coincided with the view of the Ombudsman, who recommended guaranteeing by law 'an individualised examination of the regime of contact of each child affected by a family situation of gender violence' (Defensor del Pueblo, 2016).

The pact against gender violence

On 28 September 2017 the Spanish Parliament approved the so-called Pact against Gender Violence which represents a significant commitment given that it was approved by all the political parties. This State Pact considers children as victims of gender violence and amongst its 213 measures and proposals there are several of specific relevance to the issues discussed in this article.

Specifically, the Pact proposes that shared custody should not be granted in cases of gender violence or if a protection order is in place (proposal 144). In addition, visiting arrangements should be suspended in all cases where a minor has witnessed, suffered or had to live with acts of gender violence (proposal 145). It is also proposed that exclusive and specialist Family Meeting Points should be established for cases involving gender violence (proposal 151). The Pact also requires specific training in male violence for all personnel responsible for providing services to women and their children (proposal 150). This applies particularly to security forces and organisations, to the courts, to psychological services provided by the courts and to duty lawyers (proposal 159). Similarly, psycho-social teams specialising in gender violence will be trained to improve their intervention in this area and in family law in general (proposal 165).

However, the effectiveness of this State Pact is being questioned in Spain by many professionals involved in this area, including judges, gender violence magistrates, prosecutors, social workers and psychologists. While they recognise the considerable efforts made to achieve the Pact and that the proposals are appropriate, they remain sceptical about their implementation for reasons both political and financial. Furthermore, the feminist movement has warned that the Pact is not sufficiently detailed and comprehensive to be effective, and that it has been put into effect without the involvement of women's groups. They also point out that if no political agreement is reached on the country's budget in 2018, there will be no money to implement the Pact. In other words, without sufficient funding the Pact will simply be relegated to a catalogue of good intentions.

Judicial practice

As stated, an ever-increasing number of cases have been seen in Spain in recent years in which children have become objects of instrumentalised violence towards their mothers by aggressors. As such, some terrible acts of violence against the lives of children by their fathers have been front page news in the media, acts done with the clear purpose of harming the mother, especially in cases of separation and divorce and precisely by taking advantage of the father's regime of contact established by judicial ruling. All these facts have generated a great deal of social alarm and triggered the legal reforms highlighted above. In this regard, a new sensitivity is emerging in Spanish society which, as we have seen, has begun to be reflected in the practice of the judicial authorities and in the reaction of the institutions.

This new sensitivity is projecting itself little by little on judicial practice. From a jurisprudential point of view, the position of the Spanish Supreme Court in this regard is clear. But from the point of view of protection orders, progress is very slow.

If we expand the chronological perspective (Graph 1 and Table 1 above), the analysis of civil precautionary measures imposed by the Courts of Violence against Women shows

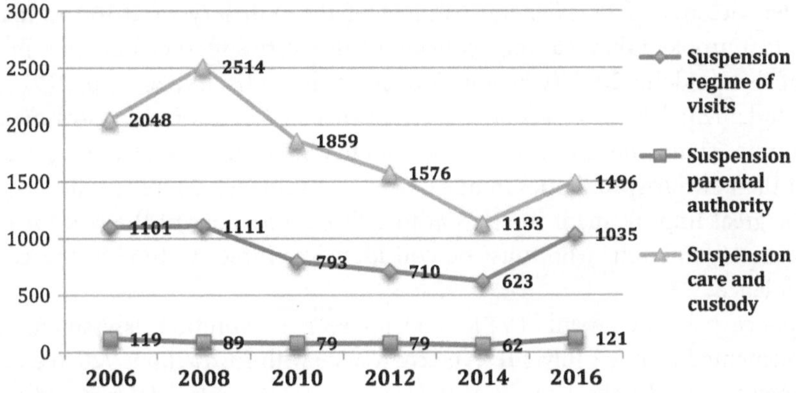

Graph 1. Suspensions of Parental Authority, Custody and Contacts in Decisions of the Courts of Violence Against Women (2006-2016)

Source: Preparing by the author based on statistics from the Observatory on Domestic and Gender Violence of the General Council for the Judiciary

that, with regard to the suspension of shared custody, there is a long way to go to reach the levels of 2008. A small recovery can be seen in relation to the suspension of parental authority and, more clearly, as regards children's contact with parents subject to criminal proceedings for aggression. Since the trend in recent years has been for a decreasing number of orders for the suspension of shared custody and contact to be made, the increase in these measures in 2016 compared to 2014 is significant. The number of orders suspending parental authority increased from 62 to 121; orders for the suspension of the regime of shared custody increased from 1,133 to 1,496; and orders for suspension of the regime of visits, where the most significant increase occurred, went from 623 to 1,035.

However, if we compare these data with those for all the precautionary measures adopted by these judicial bodies (see Table 1 above), it can be seen that the suspension of parental authority increased only from 0.4% of orders in 2014 to 0.7% in 2016; the suspension of shared custody only increased from 7.8% of orders in 2014 to 9.1% in 2016; and in the case of suspension of the regime of communication and visits, the increase was from 4.3% of orders in 2014 to 6.3% in 2016.

Risk assessment

An easy interpretation of these data would be to lay the blame for the slowness of change on the mentality of the judges, who according to some opinions are still stuck with traditional stereotypes. This may certainly be true to some extent, but it is also true that deciding on the risk of future violence and harm involves great complexity. Judges have to decide on the risk that the context of gender violence involves for the children and, in particular, on the risk that the children will be instrumentalised by the aggressor as a way of getting at their mothers. This complexity requires appropriate support mechanisms (see the Supreme Court Sentence of 26 November 2015, cited earlier).

In this respect, it should be emphasised that the new edition of the *Practical guide for Organic Law 1/2004 on Gender Violence*, approved by the group of experts on domestic and gender violence of the General Council of the Judiciary in 2016, begins to pay attention to a problem that was only considered in a very superficial manner in the first edition of this guide in 2005 (General Council of the Judiciary, 2016, p. 279).

It is fundamental to have support mechanisms in terms of risk assessment when taking any decision. This is another of the points on which the legislative reforms of 2015 and the new jurisprudential trends have had an impact. More specifically, there is a need for great improvement in relation to police assessment of the risk for mothers, but also for the children, who must be considered as direct victims in the context of gender violence.

New police risk assessments (VPR) and police risk evolution assessments (VPER) were implemented from 22 July 2016, in accordance with *Instruction* 7/2016 *establishing a new protocol for police assessment of the level of risk of gender violence and managing the security of victims*, issued by the Secretary of State for Security. This was a necessary revision that had been requested by numerous associations and by experts in the subject. But it remains to be specified how risk is to be assessed for children in the context of gender violence and whether the new indicators will be operative in this regard. Their application will need to be carefully evaluated. In this respect, in presenting the new protocol, the Secretary of State for Security stressed 'the complexity of tackling the security of children in the charge of victims'.[9] The security of children who are direct or indirect victims of gender violence must be protected, because this is what the Law determines. But in the risk assessment, the instrumental use of children to harm their mothers or, directly, to overcome the preventive barriers and commit aggression against them, needs to be taken into account.

Family meeting points

In addition, the new edition of the *Practical guide for the Organic Law 1/2004 on Gender Violence* from the Observatory on Domestic and Gender Violence of the General Council for the Judiciary highlights the need for the Family Meeting Points to protect victims. In this respect, it is indicated that:

> The creation of neutral and transitional points for visits to take place is the resource that has been progressively implemented to comply with the judicial resolutions affecting the communication of children with the non-custodial parent in cases of family relationships in crisis and, of course, in cases in which there is evidence of gender violence with the partner or former partner (General Council for the Judiciary, 2016, p. 279).

However, in view of the case described in the introduction to this article, it needs to be asked to what extent the Family Meeting Points are the solution or the problem. To begin with, these facilities were created for other purposes and not with the specific aim of protecting the victims of gender violence (Múrtulla Lafuente, 2016, p. 202). They were created in the 1990s by the social services in the Autonomous Regions to provide a neutral location staffed by a team of professionals (psychologists, social workers and mediators) to enable meetings of children with their parents and grand-parents in cases of a high degree of conflict between parents. Their aim, therefore, is to facilitate contact in cases of high conflict, not to regulate contact in cases of gender violence. They have also been greatly affected by economic cuts. For this reason, there are significant deficiencies in specific training on gender violence, which leads to added stress for the victims and may lead to new risks. As such, research conducted by the Aragon Institute for Women on the subject highlights that:

> It would be advisable for the professionals at the Family Meeting Points to have specific training on gender violence and its effects, both on the woman and on the children. This would, undoubtedly, result in better attention to both. (IAM-ADCARA, 2011, p. 92).

The Family Meeting Points represent a diverse reality in the various Autonomous Regions of the Spanish State and are now managed in many cases by associations or even service companies. The Family Meeting Points reporting to the Government of Aragon in Zaragoza, where the murder of Alexandra S discussed in the introduction took place, are managed by an association and a private company. The profile of service provision in other locations is similar and, obviously, the question to be raised is whether, apart from the fact that in their functioning they consider the specific circumstances of the cases of gender violence, their resources and training in gender violence are inadequate.

Given the situation described above, it is arguable that the decisions to grant or maintain shared custody and the regime of visits of aggressors with their children, with the problem of restraining orders and/or ensuring the safety of victims being 'resolved' by establishing that the contact between the aggressor and the children take place at the Family Meeting Point, are not appropriate for these cases. The supervision and prevention of risks to the children and the mother should involve specific measures for their protection. The best thing would be to avoid the risks always implicit in contexts of gender violence; but if the maintenance of the children's family ties with the aggressor continues to carry significant weight in judicial decisions, resorting to the Family Meeting Points will not be sufficient, at least until the operation of these centres changes significantly in relation to cases of gender violence.

Conclusions

One of the achievements of the Spanish Law is to address the problem of gender violence in all its aspects, with particular emphasis on prevention and the protection of victims. The creation of the Court for Violence Against Women with both civil and criminal competences represents a significant advance when compared to the previous lack of coordination existing between the Criminal Court and Family Courts before 2004.

Despite the progress made in recent years, there remain several issues which, as discussed in this paper, require considerable improvement. For example, while advances are being made in Spain in restricting the contact of fathers with their children in cases in which there is gender violence, visits and communication and even shared custody continue to be granted in cases of divorce or separation. This is despite the fact that shared custody in the context of gender violence has been expressly prohibited by law. However, until the latest legal reforms of 2015, Spanish judges allowed child contact with aggressor fathers and in many cases granted shared custody, giving priority to the father's rights over the protection of the physical and mental security of the children and their right to a life free of violence.

The social reality in Spain in recent years has shown an escalation in violence directed not only against women partners (or former partners) but also against their children, who have been used as an instrument to harm their mothers. Consequently, more effective measures are needed to protect the children.

Since the enactment of the Law 26/2015 and the Organic Law 8/2015, *for the protection of infancy and adolescence*, the protection of child victims of gender violence has become a direct principle of action for the public authorities, which may include measures such as the suspension of parental authority, custody and contact, and other measures that ensure the security, integrity and recovery of both the children and the mother, with the obligation on the part of the judges to ensure periodic monitoring of their progress. The most significant modification made by the Organic Law 8/2015 of 22 July, is that it considers children under the care and custody of abused women to be primary victims of gender violence. These children are no longer considered merely as witnesses of gender violence, as happened before. Therefore, the civil or criminal judge will be able to adopt judicial measures prohibiting the aggressor from approaching and communicating with the child.

According to the above, children fall within the concept of victim by the mere fact of living in environments of gender violence, due to all the disturbing effects that exposure to violence has on their development, thus affirming their right to a life free from violence. Consequently, Article 1 of the Organic Law 1/2004, *for integral protection against gender violence*, now extends its special protection to children under the guardianship, care or custody of victims. This makes it possible to adopt integral protection measures for any child, whether or not they are the aggressor's children. Therefore, the judge can agree to restraining measures and prohibition of communication not only with respect to the woman, but also with respect to the children.

In this regard, the Supreme Court Sentence of 26 November 2015 undoubtedly represented a great advance by establishing the 'need to assess the existing risk factors' to protect the best interests of the child, so that the grant of shared custody or the regime of communication and visits can in no case restrict or limit the rights of the child.

However, both the protective measures of suspension of shared custody and suspension of the regime of communication and visits have been shown to have been falling in Spain, at least until 2016. The increase in these measures in 2016 compared to 2014 was so small as to be practically insignificant.

The slowness of change cannot be attributed solely to the mentality of judges or their traditional resistance to change. Assessing the risks to children or their mothers is a task that requires adequate mechanisms and professional support. More specifically, there is a need for great improvement in relation to police assessment of the risk for mothers, but also for the children, who must be considered as direct victims in the context of gender violence. To begin with, many of the existing protocols and the professionals charged with their implementation lack the training and the necessary gender perspective.

On 28 September 2017 the Spanish Parliament approved the so-called Pact against Gender Violence that considers children to be victims of gender violence. Several of its proposals are of specific relevance to the issues discussed in this article. The Pact proposes that exclusive and specialist Family Meeting Points should be established for cases involving gender violence. It also requires specific training in male violence for all personnel responsible for providing services to women and their children. This is especially important if we consider that the Family Meeting Points are currently more of a problem than a solution. They were created for other purposes and not with the specific aim of solving the problem of compliance with restraining orders by establishing that contact between the aggressor and the children should take place at these Meeting Points. These institutions do not currently prevent the risks of violence being perpetrated on either the victim or the children.

In any case, if there is to be continued resort to the Family Meeting Points, they cannot remain as they operate at present. Appropriate infrastructure and human resources would be needed, with the priority of providing training in the protection of women and children and the prevention of male violence for the professionals who work in them. A further fundamental requirement is the coordination of all the support and protection services for the victim and the children in cases where contact with the children by the aggressor is maintained in cases of gender violence.

Notes

1. The Courts of Violence against Women are specialised courts created by the criminal courts whose competences are both criminal and civil in cases of gender violence.
2. 'Custody' in Spanish family law refers to general daily care and control of children.
3. *El Mundo* (2 August 2015) citing as a source the Spanish Federation of Associations of Divorced and Separated Women: see http://www.separadasydivorciadas.org/.
4. In general, restraining orders can be imposed either as a precautionary measure to protect the victim if there is a risk of violence or, as in the case of Alexandra, as an additional order following conviction for an offence of gender violence.
5. As such, the following can be mentioned, among others: SAP (Sentence of the Provincial Court) Badajoz no 2, of 17 April 2013; SAP Balearic Islands no 3, of 13 June 2008; SAP Barcelona no 12, of 9 March 2007; SAP Barcelona no 12, of 24 May 2007; SAP Las Palmas no 3, of 27 November 2007; SAP Murcia no 5, of 29 June 2006; SAP Toledo no 2, of 22 December 2006.
6. Spanish criminal courts are divided into two parts. The Court of Instruction investigates the facts and the evidence, and the Penal Court assesses the evidence and makes decisions on guilt or innocence. The Duty Criminal Courts are open 24 hours a day including weekends.
7. Parental authority is the historical legal concept derived from Roman Law and which continues to be used in the Spanish Civil Law.
8. Law adapted to the *Convention of Istanbul* of 15 May 2011 of the Council of Europe *on Preventing and Combating Violence against Women and Domestic Violence* and also transposing European Union directives on this matter. In particular, Directive 2012/29/EU, of 25 October (DOUE-L-2012–82,192).
9. Secretary of State for Security, *Instruction* 7/2016 *establishing a new protocol for police assessment of the level of risk of gender violence and managing the security of victims.*

Acknowledgments

This article was supported by the Project DER2014-55400-R: *The Treatment of Gender Violence in the Administration of Justice. Implementation and Effectiveness of L.O. 1/2004.*

Disclosure statement

No potential conflict of interest was reported by the author.

References

Águeda Rodríguez, R. M. (2016). *La guarda compartida y el interés superior del menor. Supuestos de exclusión*. Sevilla: Hispalex.

Calvo García, M. (2016). The role of social movements in the recognition of gender violence as a violation of human rights: From legal reform to the language of rights. *The Age of Human Rights Journal*, *6*, 60–82.

Defensor del Pueblo [Spanish Ombudsman]. (2016). *Los niños y los adolescentes en el informe anual del Defensor del Pueblo 2016*. Madrid: Defensor del Pueblo. Retrieved from https://www.defensordelpueblo.es/

General Council of the Judiciary. (2016). *Guía práctica de la Ley Orgánica 1/2004, de 28 de diciembre, de Medidas de Protección Integral contra la Violencia de Género [Practical guide for Organic Law 1/2004, of 28 December, on comprehensive preventive and protective measures against gender violence]*. Madrid: CGPJ. Retrieved from http://www.poderjudicial.es/

Gómez Pardos, L. (2011). *Menores víctimas y testigos de violencia familiar*. Zaragoza: PUZ. Retrieved from https://zaguan.unizar.es/

Gracia, J., & Jiménez, D. (2016). *Tristes tópicos. Representaciones Sociales desenfocadas*. Zaragoza: Laboratorio de Sociología Jurídica-Universidad de Zaragoza. Retrieved from http://sociologiajuridica.unizar.es/publicaciones

IAM-Fundación ADCARA. (2011). *Una mirada hacia los hijos e hijas expuestos a violencia de género. Orientaciones para la intervención desde los Servicios Sociales en Aragón*. Zaragoza: Instituto aragonés de la Mujer. Retrieved from http://www.aragon.es/estaticos/

Mujeres, F. (2017). *I Informe anual del fondo de becas "Fiscal Soledad Cazorla Prieto"*. Retrieved from http://www.fundacionmujeres.es/

Múrtulla Lafuente, V. (2016). *El interés superior del menor y las medidas civiles adoptadas en supuestos de violencia de género*. Madrid: Dykinson.

Pinto, C. (2015). La custodia compartida en la práctica judicial española: Los criterios y factores para su atribución. *Misión Jurídica: Revista de Derecho y Ciencias Sociales*, *9*, 143–175.

Reyes Cano, P. (2015). Menores y violencia de género. *Anales de la Cátedra Francisco Suárez*, *49*, 181–217.

Save the Children. (2011). *Informe sobre decisiones judiciales en materia de guarda y custodia y régimen de visitas*. Retrieved from http://www.violenciagenero.msssi.gob.es/

A voice or a choice? Children's views on participating in decisions about post-separation contact with domestically abusive fathers

Stephanie Holt

ABSTRACT
The United Nations Convention on the Rights of the Child explicitly calls for children to be granted the right to participate in legal proceedings that affect them. Despite this legal obligation and an evolving consensus that recognises children as social and competent actors, this rhetoric has struggled to achieve translation into meaningful practice reality, particularly when decisions are being made about contact arrangements for children where there has been a prior history of domestic violence. Drawing on the narratives of children who participated in three separate research projects in Ireland between 2009 and 2015, this paper will consider the manner in which they were involved in the decision-making process and the extent to which their views were ascertained and their voices heard. This paper concludes by raising the key question of how the child's best interests can be served if the child's views are not sought, heard or considered.

Introduction

Post-separation/divorce contact arrangements are considered an important opportunity for children and their absent parent to spend regular time together in order to maintain and sustain the parent-child relationship. A growing appreciation of the significant role that fathers play in their children's lives had led to many experts concluding that the absence of this role is damaging for children (Lamb, 2007). This perspective would suggest that supporting domestically abusive fathers to remain in contact with their children post-separation is important. Furthermore, this is often what both children and their parents want (Radford & Sayer, 1999). However, Thiara and Harrison (2016), amongst many other authors, also draw attention to the burgeoning empirical evidence which exposes the complex, challenging and potentially dangerous risks of post-separation contact with abusive fathers for both children and their mothers, arguing robustly that these risks far outweigh any potential benefits for children (Jaffe, Lemon, & Poisson, 2003; Women's Aid, 2016). Harne (2011, p. 65) asserts that the conviction that father involvement correlates unreservedly with children's welfare 'has overridden children and mothers' rights to protection' and has 'compromised their safety as a result', leading Coy, Perks, Scott and Tweedale (2012, p. 10) to argue that any debate about child contact should be grounded in empirical knowledge relating to children's exposure to domestic violence. In a similar vein, albeit some years earlier, Featherstone and Peckover (2007, p. 189) argued that father involvement needs to be 'located contextually' and that that context involves domestic abuse.

Considering this evidence base, it would seem imperative that some degree of caution is applied when decisions are being made about contact for children with domestically abusive men. This critical process of decision-making regarding contact is the focus of this paper, drawing on the narratives of children who participated in three separate research projects in Ireland between 2009 and 2015, to illuminate the manner in which they were involved in the decision-making process and the extent to which their views were ascertained and their voices heard. This paper is therefore positioned against the backdrop of an emergence of a more sharply focused lens of research and practice interest on childhood and children's experiences, reflecting the core ethos of the United Nations Convention on the Rights of the Child (UNCRC, 1989), which under Article 12.2[1] explicitly calls for children to be granted the right of participation in legal proceedings that affect them. The philosophical rhetoric underpinning the UNCRC reflects a construction of childhood that appreciates children as competent social actors (Emond, 2008), whose thoughts and opinions are worthy of consideration (Bosisio, 2012), and who are considered to not only have the ability to operate within 'adult-centred socially constructed meanings of citizenship', but also the capacity to influence them as well (Bacon, 2014, p. 22). In more recent years, the issue of engaging with children and involving them in private law proceedings in order to afford them a 'voice' in their parents' divorce, has developed considerable impetus (Sutherland, 2014). This reflects an empirically grounded awareness that this involvement is not only a right, but also that such participation can improve children's skills and self-esteem, inform decision-making and, as such, promote children's safety and welfare (Ewing, Hunter, Barlow, & Smithson, 2015; Powell & Smith, 2009).

However, despite legal obligations under the UNCRC and an evolving consensus that recognises children as competent actors, this rhetoric has struggled to achieve translation into meaningful practice reality (Skjorten, 2013), remaining controversial for a number of reasons (Neale, 2002). Not least among these is the tension between two of the three 'P's' at the very heart of the UNCRC, those of the right to participation and that of protection (Kjorholt, 2002). This tension is also encapsulated in the rights versus welfare debate centred on a particular concern that rights to participation risk over-burdening children with responsibility and thus potentially jeopardising their right to protection while simultaneously denying them their childhood (Morrow, 1999). Cossar, Brandon, and Jordan (2016) challenge the extent of that tension, arguing that participation can in fact be protective for children by reducing risk.

Drawing on Irish empirical research with 24 children and young people aged between four and 24 years, this paper will consider these issues in greater depth, focusing on the position of children within this debate and identifying the manner in which their discernible wishes are ascertained and indeed represented.

Literature review

Post-separation contact as a site for ongoing abuse of children and mothers

Concurring with Jaffe et al.'s (2003, p. 29) contention that 'separation is not a vaccination against domestic violence', many experts posit that post-separation contact is a potentially harmful experience for children who are 'caught in the crossfire' (Kernic, Monary-Ernsdorff, Koepsell, & Holt, 2005, p. 991) and exposed to the ongoing abuse of their mother (Thiara & Harrison, 2016). Furthermore, there is a strong correlation between child contact and child abuse, with Brown and Alexander (2007, p. 14) asserting that child abuse in the context of parental separation and divorce typically involves multiple forms of abuse, 'at the more severe end of the child abuse continuum'. Echoing Mullender et al.'s (2002) earlier research with children experiencing domestic abuse pre- and post-separation, Thiara and Harrison (2016, p. 2) conclude that child contact has 'serious implications for the health and development of children and their mothers', with research on child outcomes largely pessimistic (Holt, Buckley, & Whelan, 2008). Reflecting on this evidence base, McDonald (2014) cautions that the drive towards father involvement which overrides child and mother safety considerations has resulted in the ongoing presence or 'absent presence' (Thiara & Humphreys, 2017) of abusive men in the lives of women and children. This pro-contact culture is further grounded in a number of assumptions about what is generally believed to be good or bad for children (Herring, 2014), two of which warrant further discussion in the context of this paper.

Underlying assumptions

The most influential of the assumptions referred to above concerns the idea that children need two parents to co-operate with each other and maintain their parental relationships and responsibilities. Herring (2014) argues that this presumption endorses the non-resident parent's right to contact with their child without adequate consideration of the child's welfare, something Caffrey (2017) asserts leads to unsafe contact arrangements. Holt's (2016b) review of the literature on 'Quality Contact' argues strongly for the need to pay less attention to the logistics of contact arrangements and more to what actually happens during contact. A second powerful assumption concerns the belief that participation in decision-making in family law is harmful for children. Children's competence to participate is questioned, and participation is restricted on the grounds of age and maturity (Cossar et al., 2016; Kjorholt, 2002). So what are the implications of this for children's participation?

Assumptions can be considered problematic as they limit the practice of deciding what is best for each individual child in their unique circumstances, by applying expert knowledge about an abstract or universal child's needs and interests to each and every individual child, without attending to the needs and wishes of the child in question (Herring, 2014; Piper, 2000). Indeed, general indicators of age and stage capacity provided by developmental psychology (Buss, 1999), do not give the complete guidance that professionals require, only a general picture. Concurring with this concern about the authority of that 'general picture', James, James and McNamee's research (2004) examined a random sample of 481 contact court files in the United Kingdom and concluded that interviewing each child seemed unnecessary because the professional already 'knew' what was best for the child based on universal assumptions of children's best interests. Adhering steadfastly to a 'single voice of childhood' (Roche, 1999, p. 33) may preclude a child ever being heard, particularly if the child's views deviate from universally held assumptions. Herring (2014, p. 20) argues that the population of children who come before the court represent a 'highly unusual' sample, rendering the knowledge we have about 'usual' children of little significance.

James et al. (2004) concluded that children can be ordered to engage in contact not only because it is presumed to be in their best interests, but also because it is seen as their right to have a relationship with their father. This particular construction of the legal concept of the child's right to contact, James et al. (2004) suggest, denies their corresponding right not to have contact. According to Stanley (2006) gender constructs and gender relations can exacerbate this situation, leading to cases where children are listened to if they want contact, but overruled if they do not, on the grounds that they have been unduly influenced by their mothers. Cossar et al. (2016) warned that the child's disagreement with the professional's view may be used to contest the child's competence. Holt (2011) and Harrison (2008) conclude that children are listened to selectively – listened to if they want contact and overruled if they don't on the grounds of age and maturity, because it is assumed that there could be no other reason for them not to want what is considered unquestionably to be in their best interests. Smart and Neale (1997) and Rhoades (2002) raise concerns about the differential approach to enforcement of orders, where a child can be forced against their will to engage in contact, but the non-resident parent cannot be forced to comply with contact arrangements.

While there is a clear rhetorical commitment to the concept of children's rights, the orthodox practice in family law has been to protect rather than empower children, maintaining their views and rights firmly within a protectionist agenda (Mantle et al., 2007). Birnbaum and Saini (2012, p. 400) assert that this agenda dominates cases of conflicted parental relations and conclude that 'tensions remain with respect to allowing children to participate in separation and divorce matters'. This also to some degree mirrors the experience of researchers wishing to interview children about their experience of domestic abuse (Overlien & Holt, 2018). From this evidence base, it would appear that the practice and understanding of children's rights in the context of separation/divorce, custody and access fall either side of a dichotomous debate concerning welfare and rights. Known interchangeably as the welfare discourse, or the caretaking or protectionist agenda, this conservative view believes reverently in children's right to remain as children, protected from involvement in adult affairs. Neale (2002) condemns this orientation for critically limiting children's participation, for positioning them as subordinate to adults and rendering their right to speak at the discretion of the adults' judgement. Overlien's (2012) research with children about their experiences of domestic violence is testimony to their capacity to participate.

At the other end of the continuum is the children's rights position which accepts children's capacity to participate in decisions that concern them, arguing that far from compromising children's welfare, affording children rights also affords them protection (Pryor & Rodgers, 2001; Roche, 1999). The children's rights agenda emphasises that participation is about listening and respect – the right to a conversation – as opposed to self-determination (Roche, 1999). They also consider this integral to child welfare. Indeed Birnbaum, Bala and Cyr (2011, p. 415) argue that to 'build an ethic for children's participation', adults need to 'listen respectfully and engage in a dialogue' with children that respects their capacity rather than focusing on their perceived limitations. In agreement, Houghton (2018) calls for those in policy, research and practice to 'listen louder' to the views and experiences of children and young people and recognise them as experts in their own lives. Indeed there is a wealth of literature documenting a clear rationale for children's participation in the decision-making process, where their participation legitimises their experiences (Smart, 2002). The next section focuses on the positive rationale for children's participation.

Rationale for ascertaining the voice of the child

Sutherland (2014) suggests that involving children in the decision-making process leads to better outcomes and supports abuse prevention while Van Bijleveld, Dedding, and Bunders-Aelen (2015) assert that this participation is associated with feelings of mastery and control. Buss (1996, p. 1704) argues that giving children a voice in the legal process actually empowers children, those whom she describes as the 'disempowered victims of the circumstances leading to the court's involvement'. Many experts highlight the potentially enhanced vulnerability of children where distress and the trauma of separation may render their parents emotionally unavailable to them, with children simultaneously avoiding any discussion for fear of causing further upset (Butler, Scanlan, Douglas, & Murch, 2002) and anxious to show loyalty to both parents (Hunter, 2007). In fact, the research reviewed reveals that significant numbers of children remain uninformed about their parents' separation/divorce or about the plans for their future (Maudeni, 2002; Smith, Taylor, & Tapp, 2003). Furthermore, research has found that when children's views are valued and their independence is maintained, their capacity to cope with adversity is enhanced (Bagshaw, 2007), their self-esteem is bolstered (Van Bijleveld et al., 2015) and decisions are better informed so that they improve children's protection and the quality of their lives (Stanley, 2006).

Ascertaining the voice of the child

It would seem that the discourses regarding the voice of the child in decision-making processes, are, at the very least, confounding. While there does appear to be a commitment to a 'conceptual framework of children's rights' (Piper, 1999, p. 93), these rights appear stifled within a welfare agenda when the focus is on family law proceedings. Moving from rhetoric to reality, there are, however, a number of ways in which children's views can be ascertained and represented in custody and access cases, including being party to the proceedings; being separately represented; participating via a court ordered 'welfare' report; being interviewed by the judge; or giving direct evidence (Holt, 2016a; Hunter, 2007). However, the dominant construction of the risk of harm to the child of divorce, combined with questions over their maturity and competence to participate, has resulted in a professional reluctance to decide on their capacity and maturity. Van Bijleveld et al. (2015), for example, comment that while it is clear that the child's views should be ascertained in line with age and maturity, it is considerably less clear who should assess the maturity of the child and, indeed, what criteria should determine that assessment. Caffrey (2013), similarly found that the concept of the ascertainable wishes of the child is so ambiguous that it is potentially vulnerable to subjective understanding.

Vis, Holtan, and Thomas (2012) highlight the importance of the process being 'child friendly', with Vis and Fossum's (2013) later research warning that children may opt out of the process if it is overly official and bureaucratic. Interestingly, when children are actually asked in an appropriate and child-centred manner what they want, it is not surprising to find that they are articulate in their responses. Indeed, from a very young age they are capable of understanding and participating, with being listened to one of their primary needs (Bosisio, 2012). They want information and consultation; they want to know what is happening and why, through open and honest communication (Trinder, Beek, & Connolly, 2002). This is particularly important with research highlighting differential recall of events by parents and children. For example, Butler et al.'s (2002) research with 104 children between 7 and 15 years of age, as well as their 99 parents, within 15 months after the divorce, found that one third of children reported that they had not been told by anyone about their parents' separation. In contrast, the overwhelming majority of parents stated that they had, either separately or jointly, unambiguously told their children about the separation.

When asked about parent-child relationships, children see themselves as proactive in the formation and maintenance of their relationships with their parents, not as passive and dependent recipients. They also see inter-dependency in that relationship rather than a sole dependency on their part and perceive themselves as givers as well as receivers of emotional and practical support (James & James, 1999; Morrow, 1999).

The research shows that children and young people believe strongly in their right to be heard, but may not want the authority to decide post-separation/divorce arrangements (Barnett & Wilson, 2004; Bosisio, 2012), particularly when that involves making choices between their parents (Tisdall, Bray, & Marshall, 2004). When asked, children also differ significantly concerning their desire to participate in family matters, with research clearly demonstrating both their capacity to hold views and articulately express them as well as a wish not to participate or take responsibility for decision-making.

Methodology

As stated earlier, this paper draws on the narratives of children participating in three separate research projects in Ireland (2009–2015), all of which had domestic violence as a central focus. The first, a doctoral study completed in 2009 (referred to in the findings as PSC), involved (among other things) 20 qualitative semi-structured interviews with 16 children and young people aged between 7 and 24 years of age (four children participated in two interviews). The second study, an evaluation of a pilot child contact study completed in 2013 (referred to in the findings as CCC) involved the participation of five children aged between 5 and 13 years of age (Murphy & Holt, 2013). The third study (referred to in the findings as SH), completed in 2015 (Holt, Ward & Brady, 2015) also involved the evaluation of a pilot domestic violence service and engaged, as part of that evaluation, with three children of between 5 and 13 years of age. Across all three studies, ethical approval was sought from and given by the author's academic institution. While the first study employed both focus group and individual interviews, the subsequent two studies relied solely on individual semi-structured interviews. All interviews relied on age-appropriate activity-based techniques, including vignettes, letters to an agony aunt that they had to respond to and art-based exercises. All of the interviews were recorded with consent from the children and transcribed verbatim. NVivo was employed to help with the management of the data during the analysis phase. For the purpose of this paper, the data on the children's interviews across the three studies was revisited with three specific questions in mind, as follows:

(1) Can and do children hold coherent views that should be taken seriously?
(2) What are children's experiences of consultation and participation?
(3) To what extent do children want to participate?

Presentation of findings

Question 1: Can and do children hold coherent views that should be taken seriously?

Neale's (2002) research clearly demonstrated children's capacity to hold views and articulately express them, and similarly, participating children in the Irish studies reported on here also expressed clear responses to a number of questions put to them. For example, when children were asked about their understanding as to why their parents separated or divorced, they could articulate a variety of reasons for this. Four year old Victoria recalled her mother crying all the time, and when probed about the reason for this, graphically acted out a violent incident where her father punched her mother, stating:

> *Daddy hit Mom on the head – bang!* Victoria (4) SH

While Victoria recalls a specific event precipitating her parents' separation, other research participants recalled events in more general terms:

> *They separated 'cos of the fighting and shouting and nasty bad behaviour....but it's still the same, maybe even worse. He just lives somewhere else now.* Robbie (8) PSC

Robbie's narrative here confirms the concerns, discussed earlier in the literature review, that separation does not necessarily bring a resolution to problematic pre-separation family life (Jaffe et al., 2003). As Holt (2016b) says, simply organising the logistics of contact does not guarantee a good 'quality' contact experience. This point is elaborated on by Jonathan:

> *Before, it was mental but we (sister and brother) could go upstairs, we'd put on loud music or run outside to get away from it. But now we're made stay with him every week, he goes on and on and on and there is no escaping it... He does our head in.* Jonathan (13) PSC

In this next extract from Jane's interview, she also refers to difficult post-separation experiences. More significantly, however, she also has some important advice for professionals when deciding on contact, particularly the need for a 'trial run':

> *It seemed kinda exciting at first, like what you see on those American sitcoms...seeing your Dad every Saturday....that's till you realise it's the same crap crammed into one day a week! Looking back, they [social workers] should have given it a trial run, cos you don't know what you want or if it's gonna work till you try it. How could I have known what 'contact' I wanted or how could they have known what would 'work'?* Jane (17) PSC

Children and young people also recalled painful contact experiences, painting a largely negative picture and citing evidence to support their viewpoints. Echoing the existing literature (Kernic et al., 2005; Thiara & Harrison, 2016), these negative experiences ranged from exposure to the abuse of their mother in the context of contact to the direct abuse of the children themselves.

Verbal abuse of the child was reported in a small number of cases by both children and mothers, with this occurring both as an ongoing and as an integral feature of contact, and in the context of more isolated incidents or outbursts. Ciara provides some insight into how this is experienced by her:

> *My dad said 'are you dumb and stupid?' and it upset my brother really, really bad because it's not nice for your parent to be asking you are you dumb and stupid because your parents should know that you are not dumb and stupid.* Ciara (9) PSC

However, the findings also suggest that physical abuse of the children is very much an insidious and integral part of the contact experience, as seven year old Sean asserted:

> *He's just bold, he'll hit ya.* Sean (7) PSC

Like the children's in Mullender et al.'s (2002) research, children expressed sadness when their father was abusive during contact, while conversely the data also recorded children's upset and distress with contact they did *not* want, or wanted on their *own* terms, with bed-wetting and nightmares cited as common nocturnal manifestations of this emotional anguish.

Concurring with the findings of Pryor and Rodgers (2001), these studies found that the participating children and young people were articulate and reasonable in their rationale for not wanting contact with their father. Young participants like Leah and Eva explained that their wish to end contact was directly related to what they perceived as their father's lack of interest in them, abuse of their mother and his inability to take responsibility for his own behaviour:

> *We wrote him a letter to tell him why we didn't want to see him any more and since then we haven't seen him... he needs to see what he's done and he needs to feel guilt and needs to apologise to us properly, but we didn't get a word back.* Eva (16) PSC

For her sister Leah, it was simply because:

> *I'm still scared of him. [In the letter, I said] 'I'm fed up waiting for you to be our Dad. We just can't forgive and we see this as the only way we can move on'.* Leah (12) PSC

With little direct evidence of abuse in her narrative, thirteen year old Emily nonetheless articulates her concern about the quality of her contact experience, something she could predict from one week to the next:

> *He doesn't really make a lot of effort when we go over ...like quite often he has no plan whatsoever, no clue what he wants to do. He says he's working on his phone and he's just*

constantly texting, or he's looking at his phone, and his phone is glued to his face. The other two [younger brother and sister] get bored and kick off and then he gets angry. Same every time, you can predict what's going to happen. Emily (13) SH

Emily's reflection on the quality of her contact resonates with other research evidence (Holt, 2016b). Similar to Emily, while many of the participating children and young people had 'father presence' in their lives, their narratives were consistent with Pryor and Rodger's (2001) assertion that the mere presence of fathers is not enough. For example, Leah stated:

I'm fed up waiting for him to be a father. Leah (12) PSC

Other children similarly could articulate their views on their relationship with their Dad. For example, when Sara (11) was asked about this relationship, she described herself as *'a pebble at the bottom of a stream'* and that her dad was this river and that she was *'being knocked against other stones all the time'* (CCE).

While separation can physically lead to the loss of a permanent father-figure in a child's life, the presence of domestic abuse often means that fathering is compromised, a deficit that separation alone cannot rectify, as Leah wistfully reflects:

Anyone can have a father, but he is not my Dad. Leah (12) PSC

Rachel could see similarities between the behaviour of her sister and of her father, but stated she could understand her sister's behaviour:

It's like walking on eggshells with Cathy. She just doesn't know how to handle her anger. But I only think Cathy is the way she is because she has seen what my Daddy did to my Mum. I'm not sure what his excuse is, that's if he has one. Rachel (11) PSC

Older children also expressed frustration at the manner in which judicial orders were enforced and recommendations complied with. This primarily concerned non-compliance with contact orders, non-payment of maintenance orders and failure to comply with recommendations for counselling or mediation. As with Smart and Neale's (1997) findings, the difficulty with enforcement emerged with a potent gender bias in the present research, with mothers predominantly resisting compliance with contact orders and fathers failing to exercise the contact accorded to them. The penalty approach to resident mothers and 'laissez-faire' or 'ambivalent' approach to fathers that Rhoades's (2002, p. 77–78) earlier research identified, also emerged with clarity in the children's narratives. Rhoades argued that this led to enforcement being 'a remedy that is effectively only available to the contact parent, in that the court will not coerce a person into maintaining a relationship with their child' (2002, p. 77–78). Indeed, Bailey-Harris, Barron and Pearce's (1999) finding that judges were undivided in their conviction that a parent cannot be ordered to engage in contact, resonated in the present research, as this quote from 16 year old Eva shows:

We are made see him, that apparently can be enforced but him paying Mam money can't be...it doesn't seem fair really, does it? Eva (16) PSC

The presumption that contact is either in the child's best interests and/or something they actually want, was challenged by a silenced majority of children in this research; children who felt that no one cared what they thought or listened to them on the rare occasions they were asked for their opinion. The next section will address the second question asked of the research findings across the three studies, namely the views and experiences of the participants of the manner in which children are consulted and their voices heard and represented.

Question 2. What are children's experiences of consultation and participation?

Considering that consultation and participation can occur along a continuing time line that commences with the separation process, there are many points at which children can be consulted. Interestingly, when the children who were interviewed were asked to recall the period immediately prior to and during their parents' separation, the majority could either not recall any consultation about post-separation contact, or simply said:

> *That conversation never happened.* Eva (16) PSC

This finding echoes assertions by Piper (1997) and Sawyer (2000) that professionals assume that parents will consult their children, and rely on that assumption. However, in reality, this is dependent on the emotional availability of those parents to their children at a stressful and traumatic time in the parents' lives.

The predominant criticism expressed in this research concerned the small number of cases where assessments were completed and children's views were sought, and where the participants perceived that the judge ignored or rejected the recommendations of those reports:

> *We didn't want to spend time with him [father] at all. The guy [psychological assessor] did (listen) but the Judge didn't (listen).* Todd (7) PSC

> *I think the social workers got a statement off me and Leah once or twice to say we didn't want to see him but it didn't do much (good). The second last time we went to court, a female judge said 'I can't physically make you go, you know but you kind of do have to see him'.* Eva (16) PSC

From a child-centred perspective, it is important to highlight that, while many children may wish to continue to see their fathers, some do not and others may be more ambivalent, but it may be difficult for the child to say that (Mullender et al., 2002). Where children and young people did experience being taken seriously and listened to, the experience had positive outcomes, as Eoin explains:

> *They [contact centre staff] were great. They really listened to me. [Staff] asked me if I wanted to see my Dad and when I said that I didn't, they said that that was ok. I thought they would try to make me, but they didn't.* Eoin (13) CCE

Alongside having her voice heard, was the critical importance for another participant, Sara, of feeling understood; that someone

> *had my back, not just listened to me but also understood why I felt the way I did. They were there for me and supported me through it. They understood my situation better than other people would.* Sara (11) CCE

Children and young people's direct participation in the decision-making process was not simply dependent on the opportunities that were afforded them, but also down to their interest in and willingness to participate. As Bosisio (2012) found, all the children and young people participating in these three research projects demonstrated the capacity to clearly articulate their views, but not all wanted decision making-capacity. The third question is now addressed.

Question 3. To what extent do children want to participate?

A small number of participating children clearly rejected the notion of child participation, expressing concern about being asked to participate in the decision-making process. Robert explains:

> *My mum does ask questions like does my Dad tell me that he wants me to live with him and then I was saying to my Dad then that if I lived with one of my parents, I wouldn't be able to see the other parent and that's what's happening (now), (and) I can't cope with it.* Robert (8) PSC

On the other hand, some children stated they would welcome being given the opportunity to choose and were very clear that this was an option they would take if offered:

> *(I'd tell the Judge) that I want to stay with my mum and that my dad should give us money and he should have to see us like every Saturday and show up; we can go if we want to or (not go) if we don't want to. I just want a choice...I think I should be let (have) a choice.* Rachel (11) PSC

Rachel's views echo those of the young participants in Morrow's (1999) research, where it is clear that, like them, she is asking for respect, not control. However, for a minority of other children, involvement at the level of talking to the Judge was over and above what they were comfortable with:

> *I don't think I want to do that (talk to the Judge)...what would they want me to say? I want to live with her, with him? I don't really care, cos it's a win lose situation whichever way it works out and it's between them. It's nothing to do with me.* Tim (15) PSC

Where children had either been given a choice, or been allowed to exercise their will not to have contact, and this wish was respected by the court, their sense of empowerment and self-esteem was palpably evident. Eva explains:

> *When we wrote that letter to him saying we didn't want to see him any more because he just kept hurting Mam and that hurt us too and we just couldn't take any more...it's hard to explain, but it's always been his move, like in chess, we were always waiting for his move...it feels now that we have check-mated him and he doesn't know what to do 'cos that never happened before.* Eva (16) PSC

Equally so, and in agreement with Butler et al. (2002), where children experience being listened to and where decisions are taken on their behalf that reflect their viewpoints, children also experience empowerment without the burden of decision-making power, as Sara (11) explains:

> *Them [Contact Centre] making the decision that it wasn't safe for me to see my Dad made it easier for me...I knew that they weren't just 'listening' to me, that they had actually heard me and that made me feel very safe. I'm not sure I could have made that decision myself...I don't think I should have to.* Sara (11) CCE

It is clear from the narratives that the participating children and young people could clearly articulate a rationale for separation/divorce and were further able rationally and reasonably to articulate their position regarding contact, giving concrete examples to support their viewpoints. The rhetoric of 'listening to the voice of the child' however, was not often found to have been translated into reality in this research. When it was, contact arrangements were made safer and children were empowered. Participation does not necessarily mean having a choice, but it does demand we consider children's voices. In relation to the need to consider the voices of children and young people and, in particular, to pay attention to their capacity and insight, the final word rests with Eva:

> *I don't really believe in fathers, like I think they're a bit useless, but that's just because of our experience, but maybe some of them could be, you know, ok, and they should be investigated properly, and have proper detailed statements from children whether or not they want to see them, instead of assuming it was good for ya and you'd miss out otherwise. They thought we were missing out, but how can you miss something (relationship with father) if you never rightly had it? I've never had it so I can't miss it. It's not rocket science...if anyone had really bothered to listen, they could have figured it out pretty quickly, but their starting point was all wrong.* Eva (16) PSC

Discussion: positioning children in the post-separation domestic abuse contact debate: seen but not heard?

Three issues emerge as central to the debate. Firstly, there is the question of whether or not children should be participants in the deliberations about post-separation contact; secondly, there is the issue of the manner in which that participation takes place and thirdly, is the appropriate weight given to their views, or simply put, what happens to their views?

Regarding the first issue, the debate around children's participation in the decision-making forum of post-separation contact has revolved around welfare versus rights, as explored in detail earlier. The process of reflection on that debate, which has involved the inclusion of children and young people in this research, leads this paper to conclude that promoting children's welfare by protecting them from involvement in the process, is somewhat akin to closing the stable door after the horse has bolted and adds further insult to the injury of their invisibility within the domestic abuse domain. Concurring with other observers (Butler et al., 2002; Thomas & O'Kane, 1998), it is palpably apparent that children *are* already involved in the process of their parents' separation or divorce and that, furthermore, the reality of their exposure to domestic abuse has been emphatically established and remains unquestioned. This experience, therefore, needs to be acknowledged and respected. Roche (1999) asserts that this respect is reflected in their right to participate, while Emond (2008, p. 192) suggests that the manner in which participation is achieved represents a 'finely balanced position between recognising and respecting the abilities of children whilst at the same time viewing them as inherently vulnerable'.

The second issue concerns the manner and means by which children's views are ascertained. The starting point of this paper is to concur with Mantle et al. (2007, p. 792) who argue against a 'naïve positivism underlying any assumption' that the views of the child are simply 'out there waiting to be collected'. It is also pertinent to note that, while on the one hand the oppressive context of domestic abuse may not have facilitated free expression, resulting in the child's need for considerable support and preparation in order to be able to participate, the evidence from this and other research nonetheless attests to children's participatory competence (Neale, 2002; Overlien, 2012; Smith et al., 2003). This current paper, therefore, supports Smith et al.'s (2003) criticism of the 'escape clause' against children's participation that is provided for by the imposition of standards of age and maturity, and supports the view that the argument should not be one of proving the child's ability to participate, but more one of responsibility on adults to be competent enough to elicit those views in the context of a trusting relationship with the child. Similarly, both Overlien and Holt (2018) and Thomas and O'Kane (2000) argue that when children are judged incompetent to participate, we should, perhaps, firstly question whether the methods used to elicit their views were appropriate and secondly, whether those methods were 'competently' administered. Indeed, the issue of competency emerges with clarity concerning the skills and proficiencies of professionals to elicit those views, by engaging in a wide range of methods including interview, observational and play methodologies (Mantle et al., 2007). This also involves, as Smart (2002) has argued, the practice of allowing the child to speak, the skill in eliciting their views, as well as the ability to hear what they are saying, a process Schofield (1998) asserts is more complicated than simply obtaining a view from the child. Taking Houghton's (2018) call for professionals to 'listen louder' to what children and young people are saying, this complex task involves not only attention to what they are saying, but also consideration of what they are not saying, via their non-verbal messages. It requires an adept understanding of the psychological complexity of children and an ability to understand their 'internal world', particularly where abusive experiences have rendered them confused and vulnerable (Schofield, 1998, p. 430).

Those involved in the business of 'ascertaining children's views' also need to question the fall-back position of relying on assumptions about the best interest of the child in general, rather than attending to the needs of the child in question (Piper, 2000). This presumption of contact also potentially serves to promote unsafe contact (Caffrey, 2017; Herring, 2014). Faced with the decision of transposing the child's testimony into the report for the court, James, Jenks, and Prout (1998) suggest that, while some practitioners use direct quotes from children in order to represent their views as accurately as possible, others 'interpret' the child's views for the court, which raises obvious questions about the accuracy of that representation. Arguing against this, Trinder (1997, p. 302) recommends instead that professionals adopt 'a stance of uncertainty, treating each child as unique and avoiding expert or adult constructions of what that child is like'. Attempting to resolve the problem of balancing the child's own view of their best interests against the professional's adult judgement of those same interests, James et al. (1998) advocate for the direct involvement of children in the writing of their own testimonies to the court, perhaps via a letter to the judge.

Having ascertained their views then, the next question concerns what happens to those views. The children and young people in this current research concluded, as other research has done, that their voices were 'seldom heard and, if heard, usually discounted' (Morrow, 1999, p. 154). Roche (1999, p. 71) suggests that this occurs when the child's narrative is filtered through a professional adult lens, a lens that views this narrative as 'inherently suspect', particularly when it does not conform to the dominant discourse and in a climate that views children as unreliable (Neale, 2002). Neale (2002) asserts that the court process is focused on what is considered to be in the child's future interest, even where that contradicts the child's unique construction of their own welfare. Roche's (1999, p. 33) suggestion that 'there is no single voice of childhood' is a theme taken up by other observers who argue against 'blanket rules' governing a 'theoretical' child's needs (Neale, 2002, p. 468), as these rules or presumptions render the need to consult with children somewhat superfluous. The present research also argues against those blanket rules, advocating instead for an approach which views each child as unique and prioritises his or her subjective views and experiences.

The research drawn on in this paper confirms children's competence to participate in the discussion about their experiences: their past as well as their future. The majority of children and young people in this research did not expect nor did they want their views to be determinative, but believed that they should be given appropriate weight. Their intimate knowledge of, and unique position within their own families warranted the respect that listening to them would accord, as they felt that this would demonstrate to them a clear sense that what they thought was important. Echoing Schofield's (1998) assertion, this was not viewed as a pointless exercise, even where their wishes were not reflected in the final decision.

This research also concurs with Masson's (2003, p. 80) observation that the construction of childhood in family law represents merely a 'need to comply with international standards' rather than a belief in a child's right to participate, because in reality, no fundamental restructuring of adult attitudes towards children has taken place, despite a clear rhetorical paradigm shift. James et al. (1998, p. 155) conclude that, until a point is reached where the child is conceptualised as having 'active agency', professionals will continue to struggle to recognise and assert the importance of children's thoughts, wishes and feelings in the decision-making process, because it is specifically these individual expressions that represent each child's unique individuality and agency. This, Roche (1999, p. 71) asserts, would require a 'major cultural shift in family law practice' to one that reflected a more appropriate balance between protection and participation in order to 'enable children to be heard without exploiting them, protect children without silencing and excluding them and pursue rigorous inquiry without distressing them' (Alderson & Morrow, 2004, p. 12).

Conclusion

Although it is claimed that children and their needs are the central consideration in the child contact debate, the decision-making processes reflects an implicit assumption that it is necessary to increase their protection by limiting their involvement in that process. Indeed, a belief in the need to consult was negated by an assumption that this would further harm and distress those children. Inherent in this is the assumption of knowing, in the absence of any consultation with children, what is in their best interests. This assumption can be challenged by the weight of evidence from the narratives and testimonies of the children and young people who participated in this research. Their accounts highlight that, by according them agency in the contact process, they can feel recognised as the experts of their own lives and lived experiences. Indeed, if empowered to use their own voices, the unique stories of children and young people can provide the foundation for unique solutions to the challenges that they face in negotiating safe and meaningful contact with their fathers. For this to happen professionals involved with children and families need to avoid being constrained by expert or adult constructions or assumptions about *a* child and to adopt a position of uncertainty about what will be best for *each* individual child. Most importantly, they need to start from a position that accepts the uniqueness of *each* child and their lived experiences and to commit to practice that values and prioritises the right of children to use their voices to participate in decisions being made about them.

Note

1. Article 12.2 states: 'parties shall assure to the child who is capable of forming his or her own views the right to express those views freely in all matters affecting the child, the views of the child being given due weight in accordance with the age and maturity of the child. For this purpose, the child shall in particular be provided the opportunity to be heard in any judicial and administrative proceedings affecting the child, either directly or through a representative or an appropriate body, in a manner consistent with the procedural rules of national law'.

Disclosure statement

No potential conflict of interest was reported by the author.

References

Alderson, P., & Morrow, V. (2004). *Ethics, social research and consulting with children and young people*. Barkingside: Barnardos.

Bacon, K. (2014). Rethinking children's citzenship: Negotiating structure, shaping meanings. *International Journal of Children's Rights, 1*, 21–42.

Bagshaw, D. (2007). Reshaping responses to children when parents are separating: Hearing children's voices in transition. *Australian Social Work, 60*, 450–465.

Bailey-Harris, R., Barron, J., & Pearce, J. (1999). From utility to rights? The presumption of contact in practice. *International Journal of Law, Policy and the Family, 13*, 111–131.

Barnett, C., & Wilson, C. J. (2004). Children's wishes in the Australian family court: Are they wishful thinking? *Psychiatry, Psychology and Law, 11*, 73–78.

Birnbaum, R., Bala, N., & Cyr, F. (2011). Children's experiences with family justice professionals in Ontario and Ohio. *International Journal of Law, Policy and the Family, 25*, 398–422.

Birnbaum, R., & Saini, M. (2012). A qualitative synthesis of children's participation in custody disputes. *Research on Social Work Practice, 22*, 400–409.

Bosisio, R. (2012). Children's right to be heard: What children think. *International Journal of Children's Rights, 20*, 141–154.

Brown, T., & Alexander, R. (2007). *Child abuse and family law: Understanding the issues facing human service and legal professionals*. Sydney: Allen & Unwin.

Buss, E. (1996). 'You're my what?' The problem of children's misperceptions of their lawyers' roles. *Fordham Law Review, 64*, 1699–1762.

Buss, E. (1999). Confronting developmental barriers to the empowerment of child clients. *Cornell Law Review, 84*, 895–966.

Butler, I., Scanlan, L., Douglas, G., & Murch, M. (2002). Children's involvement in the parents' divorce: Implications for practice. *Children & Society, 16*, 89–102.

Caffrey, L. (2013). Hearing the 'voice of the child'? The role of child contact centres in the family justice system. *Child and Family Law Quarterly, 25*, 357–3179.

Caffrey, L. (2017). The importance of perceived organisational goals: A systems thinking approach to understanding child safeguarding in the context of domestic abuse. *Child Abuse Review, 26*, 339–350.

Cossar, J., Brandon, M., & Jordan, P. (2016). ''You've got to trust her and she's got to trust you': Children's views on participation in the child protection system. *Child & Family Social Work, 21*, 103–112.

Coy, M., Perks, K., Scott, E., & Tweedale, R. (2012). *Picking up the pieces: Domestic violence and child contact*. London: Rights of Women/Child and Woman Abuse Studies Unit, London Metropolitan University.

Emond, R. (2008). Children's voices, children's rights. In A. Kendrick (Ed.), *Residential child care: Prospects and challenges* (pp. 183–195). London: Jessica Kingsley.

Ewing, J., Hunter, R., Barlow, A., & Smithson, J. (2015). Children's voices: Centre-stage or side-lined in out-of-court dispute resolution in England and Wales? *Child and Family Law Quarterly, 27*, 43–62.

Featherstone, B, & Peckover, S. (2007). Letting them get away with it: fathers, domestic violence and child welfare. *Critical Social Policy, 27*(2), 181-202. doi:10.1177/0261018306075708

Harne, L. (2011). *Violent fathering and the risks to children: The need for change*. Bristol: The Policy Press.

Harrison, C. (2008). Implacably hostile or appropriately protective? Women managing child contact in the context of domestic violence. *Violence Against Women, 14*, 381–405.

Herring, J. (2014). The welfare principle and the children act: Presumably it's about welfare? *Journal of Social Welfare and Family Law, 36*, 14–25.

Holt, S. (2011). Domestic abuse and child contact: Positioning children in the decision-making process. *Child Care in Practice, 17*, 327–346.

Holt, S. (2016a). The voice of the child in family law: A discussion paper. *Children and Youth Services Review, 68*, 139–145.

Holt, S. (2016b). 'Quality contact' post separation/divorce: A review of the literature. *Children and Youth Services Review, 68*, 92–99.

Holt, S., Buckley, H., & Whelan, S. (2008). The impact of exposure to domestic violence on children and young people: A review of the literature. *Child Abuse & Neglect, 32*, 797–810.

Holt, S., & Ward, M. (2015). *Evaluation of the Sonas Safe Home Project*. Dublin: Sonas Domestic Violence Charity.

Houghton, C. (2018). Voice, agency, power: A framework for young survivors: Participation in national domestic abuse policy-making. In S. Holt., C. Overlien, & J. Devaney (Eds.), *Responding to domestic violence: Emerging challenges for policy, practice and research in Europe* (pp. 77–96). London: Jessica Kingsley Publishers.

Hunter, R. (2007). Close encounters of a judicial kind: 'Hearing' children's 'voices' in family law proceedings. *Child and Family Law Quarterly, 19*, 283–303.

Jaffe, P. G., Lemon, N. K. D., & Poisson, S. E. (2003). *Child custody and domestic violence: A call for safety and accountability*. Thousand Oaks: Sage Publications.

James, A., Jenks, C., & Prout, A. (1998). *Theorizing childhood*. Cambridge: Polity Press.

James, A. L., & James, A. (1999). Pump up the volume: Listening to children in separation and divorce. *Childhood, 6*, 189–206.

James, A. L., James, A., & McNamee, S. (2004). Turn down the volume? Not hearing children in family proceedings. *Child and Family Law Quarterly, 16*, 189–202.

Kernic, M. A., Monary-Ernsdorff, D. J., Koepsell, J. K., & Holt, V. L. (2005). Children in the crossfire: Child custody determinations among couples with a history of intimate partner violence. *Violence Against Women, 11*, 991–1021.

Kjorholt, A. T. (2002). Small is powerful: Discourses on 'children and participation' in Norway. *Childhood, 9*, 63–82.

Lamb, M. E. (2007). Improving the quality of parent-child contact in separating families. In M. Maclean (Ed.), *Parenting after partnering: Containing conflict after separation* (pp. 11–28). Oxford: Hart Publishing.

Mantle, G., Moules, T., Johnson, K., Leslie, J., Parsons, S., & Shaffer, R. (2007). Whose wishes and feelings? Children's autonomy and parental influence in family court enquiries. *British Journal of Social Work, 37*, 785–805.

Masson, J. (2003). Paternalism, participation and placation: Young people's experiences of representation in child protection proceedings in England and Wales. In J. Dewar & S. Parker (Eds.), *Family law: Processes, practices, pressures* (pp. 79–98). Oxford: Hart Publishing.

Maudeni, T. (2002). Seen but not heard? Focusing on the needs of children of divorced parents in Gaborone and surrounding areas, Botswana. *Childhood, 9*, 227–302.

McDonald, G. (2014). *Domestic violence and private family law proceedings: Promoting child welfare or promoting contact.* Bath: University of Bath.

Morrow, V. (1999). 'We are people too': Children's and young people's perspectives on children's rights and decision-making in England. *International Journal of Children's Rights, 7*, 149–170.

Mullender, A., Hague, G., Iman, U., Kelly, L., Malos, E., & Regan, L. (2002). *Children's perspectives on domestic violence.* London: Sage.

Murphy, C., & Holt, S. (2013). *Evaluation of the Barnardos and One Family Pilot Child Contact Centre Project.* Dublin: Barnardos/One Family.

Neale, B. (2002). Dialogues with children: Children, divorce and citizenship. *Childhood, 9*, 455–475.

Overlien, C. (2012). *Domestic violence: Children's strategies.* Oslo: University of Oslo.

Overlien, C., & Holt, S. (2018). Including children and adolescents in domestic violence research: When myths and misconceptions compromise participation. In S. Holt, C. Overlien, & J. Devaney (Eds.), *Responding to domestic violence: Emerging challenges for policy, practice and research in Europe* (pp. 97–112). London: Jessica Kingsley Publishers.

Piper, C. (1997). Ascertaining the wishes and feelings of the child. *Family Law, 27*, 796–800.

Piper, C. (1999). The wishes and feelings of the child. In S. Day-Sclater & C. Piper (Eds.), *Undercurrents of divorce* (pp. 77–98). Aldershot: Dartmouth.

Piper, C. (2000). Assumptions about children's best interests. *Journal of Social Welfare and Family Law, 22*, 261–276.

Powell, M. A., & Smith, A. B. (2009). Children's participation rights in research. *Childhood, 16*, 124–142.

Pryor, J., & Rodgers, B. (2001). *Children in changing families: Life after parental separation.* Oxford: Blackwell Press.

AMICA; Radford, L., & Sayer, S. (1999). *Unreasonable fears? Child contact in the context of domestic violence: A survey of mothers' perceptions of harm.* Bristol: Women's Aid Federation of England.

Rhoades, H. (2002). The 'no contact mother': Reconstructions of motherhood in the era of the 'new father'. *International Journal of Law, Policy and the Family, 16*, 71–94.

Roche, J. (1999). Children and divorce: A private affair? In S. Day-Sclater & C. Piper (Eds.), *Undercurrents of divorce* (pp. 35–75). Aldershot: Dartmouth.

Sawyer, C. (2000). Effective support services for children and young people when parental relationships break-down: A child centred approach. *Child and Family Law Quarterly, 11*, 447–452.

Schofield, G. (1998). Making sense of the ascertainable wishes and feelings of insecurely attached children. *Child and Family Law Quarterly, 10*, 429–443.

Skjorten, K. (2013). Children's voices in Norwegian custody cases. *International Journal of Law, Policy and the Family, 27*, 289–309.

Smart, C. (2002). From children's shoes to children's voices. *Family Court Review, 40*, 307–319.

Smart, C., & Neale, B. (1997). Arguments against virtue: Must contact be enforced? *Family Law, 27*, 332–336.

Smith, A. B., Taylor, N. J., & Tapp, P. (2003). Rethinking children's involvement in decision-making after parental separation. *Childhood, 10*, 201–216.

Stanley, N. (2006). *Domestic violence and child protection: Directions for good practice.* London: Jessica Kingsley.

Sutherland, E. (2014). Listening to the child's voice in the family setting: From aspiration to reality. *Child and Family Law Quarterly, 26*, 152–172.

Thiara, R., & Harrison, C. (2016). *Safe not sorry: Supporting the campaign for safer child contact.* Bristol: Women's Aid.

Thiara, R., & Humphreys, C. (2017). Absent presence: The ongoing impact of men's violence on the mother–Child relationship. *Child & Family Social Work, 22*, 137–145.

Thomas, N., & O'Kane, C. (1998). When children's wishes and feelings clash with their 'best interests'. *The International Journal of Children's Rights, 6*, 137–154.

Thomas, N., & O'Kane, C. (2000). Discovering what children think: Connections between research and practice. *British Journal of Social Work, 30*, 819–835.

Tisdall, K. M., Bray, R., & Marshall, K. (2004). Children's participation in family law proceedings: A step too far or a step too small? *Journal of Social Welfare and Family Law, 26*, 17–33.

Trinder, L. (1997). Competing constructions of childhood: Children's rights and children's wishes in divorce. *Journal of Social Welfare and Family Law, 19*, 291–305.

Trinder, L., Beek, M., & Connolly, J. (2002). *Making contact: How parents and children negotiate and experience contact after divorce.* York: Joseph Rowntree Foundation.

United Nations. (1989). *Convention on the rights of the child.* HMSO: London

Van Bijleveld, G. G., Dedding, C. W. M., & Bunders-Aelen, J. F. G. (2015). Children's and young people's participation within child welfare and child protection services: A state-of-the-art review. *Child & Family Social Work, 20*, 129–138.

Vis, S. A., & Fossum, S. (2013). Representation of children's views in court hearings about custody and parental visitations: A comparison between what children wanted and what the court rules. *Children and Youth Services Review, 35*, 2101–2109.

Vis, S. A., Holtan, A., & Thomas, N. (2012). Obstacles for child participation in care and protection cases: Why Norwegian social workers find it difficult. *Child Abuse Review, 21*, 7–23.

Women's Aid. (2016). *Nineteen Child Homicides.* Bristol: Author.

The approach in Scotland to child contact disputes involving allegations of domestic abuse

Kirsteen M Mackay

ABSTRACT

This article considers the approach taken in Scotland to the processing of child contact cases in which there are allegations of domestic abuse. Four key features of the processing of cases which may facilitate outcomes that prioritise safety are considered. These are: the availability of legal aid; the cautious process of successive child welfare hearings; the use of child welfare reports; and the taking of the child's views. All these features occur within a policy context that recognises domestic abuse as gender-based violence and where courts have a statutory duty to protect a child from abuse. Drawing on the author's court based analysis of papers from 208 child contact disputes and from interviews with sheriffs, this article discusses the strengths and limitations of all four process features in terms of protecting women and children, and the risks to these features posed by perpetually reducing government budgets.

Introduction

Scots family law, criminal law, and child protection systems have always been separate from those of the other nations that make up the United Kingdom. Even during the 290 years that the U.K. parliament at Westminster passed legislation for Scotland, this legislation had to be consistent with the distinctive nature of Scots law. Scotland also has a separate court structure, with family actions most usually being heard by a sheriff within the local Sheriff Court.

Since 1999, Scotland has once again had her own Parliament and this has enabled a more rapid pace of change to legislation (and to the underlying policy) both in respect of family law, but also in respect of policy and practice responses to domestic abuse. Partly because Scotland is a relatively small jurisdiction (having a population of just around 5.5 million), and also because of the consultative approach of Scotland's Parliament to the passage of legislation, it has been possible for organisations that support abused women and their children to directly influence both policy and the wording of legislation relevant to domestic abuse. That is, the Scottish Government regularly undertakes consultations to inform proposed legislative changes and includes key practitioner and third sector organisations, as well as academics, who may make written and oral representations on existing policy and practice and on the proposed changes.

Key ongoing reviews of policy and of legal process in family actions in Scotland include the Scottish Government's 'Family Justice Modernisation Strategy' launched in 2016. Two key pieces of work following on from this include changes introduced to the methods of hearing children in family actions (principally through modification of the form sent to children to obtain their views and the related rules of court); as well as changes introduced to court procedural rules in respect of the processing of child contact cases (in an attempt to speed up resolution by reducing the number of hearings in a case). These changes have been led by the Family Law Committee of the Scottish Civil Justice Council who advise and prepare draft procedure for the civil courts of Scotland.[1]

The Scottish Government has also recently announced that it is to review the substantive law underpinning Scots private family law as a part of the 'Family Justice Modernisation Strategy' (Scottish Government [SG], 2017a). Public law child protection systems in Scotland are also the subject of an on-going review by the Child Protection System Review Group, who consulted with key players in the field in the second half of 2017. In addition, the Scottish Law Commission, which makes recommendations to the Scottish Government with a view to simplifying and modernising Scots law, is also to include a review of family law in Scotland in its 10th Programme of legislative review in 2018.

This article is specifically concerned with private law child contact disputes raised within the civil court system in Scotland. These private law actions are raised by a party to the action even when domestic abuse may be the cause of the separation of the couple and the reason for the dispute over contact. As such, the parties are likely to have to pay for the legal advice and representation they receive, as well as for the cost of court hearings. However, Scotland differs markedly from England in that financial assistance in the form of legal aid administered by the Scottish Legal Aid Board remains available for family actions to those on low incomes. There is currently no statutory requirement for parties (whatever income bracket they fall into) to demonstrate they have considered mediation prior to the raising of a court action, nor is there any need to evidence recent abusive behaviour in order to qualify for legal aid to raise a court action. However, where Scotland is similar to England is that Government *spending* on family court process (including legal aid costs) has been the subject of intense scrutiny, with an independent review group set to once again consider the legal aid system of Scotland despite relatively recent reviews (SG, 2017b).

This article provides a 'snap shot' of the present substantive law and legal processes applied in Scotland to child contact disputes, within an ever shifting practice context. It draws heavily on findings from court based research completed by the author in 2011 and includes commentary on the likely impact of recent and proposed changes.

It will be seen that the substantive law of Scotland places an emphasis on the need to protect children from domestic abuse and that there are also a number of potentially protective features of Scots legal *process*. These include (i) The availability of legal aid for family actions; (ii) the 'process' nature of child welfare hearings (as opposed to rapid decision making based on pleadings); (iii) the use of court appointed child welfare reporters to investigate all the circumstances of the child; and, (iv) the statutory requirement that the child should be given an opportunity to express their views. It will be seen that, while each of these features may facilitate the protection of women and children leaving abuse, they are not without their problems.

The article will first review the Scottish Government's policy approach to domestic abuse and the core criminal and civil remedies available. This will highlight the 'gender based abuse' approach adopted in Scotland. It will then briefly outline the substantive law in respect of determining child contact disputes in Scotland, including a review of the extent to which domestic abuse actually features in the background of the disputes before the court. Thereafter, consideration will be given to each of the aforementioned potentially protective features of Scots legal process, including a discussion of the leading case of *NJDB v JEG* [2012] UKSC 21 which informs ongoing changes in the processing of child contact cases.

Domestic abuse as gender-based abuse

Within Scotland the term 'domestic abuse' rather than 'domestic violence' is generally used within policy documents and in legislation. This term 'abuse' may be more easily applied to non-physical actions such as mental or emotional abuse and coercively controlling behaviours (such as preventing access to money or to other people).

As previously observed, Scotland regained her Parliament in 1999. By the year 2000, the first 'National Strategy to Address Domestic Abuse' in Scotland was published by the (then) Scottish Executive (known as the Scottish Government since 2007). From the outset, Scotland's policy documents around domestic abuse recognised this as gender-based abuse. Although not denying that men can also be victims, and that domestic abuse may occur in same sex relationships, the policy document states that 'domestic abuse requires a response which takes account of the gender specific elements and the broader gender inequalities which women face' (Scottish Executive, 2000, p. 6). More recently, in 2014, the Scottish Government published 'Equally Safe', Scotland's strategy to tackle all forms of violence against women and girls. This strategy states that violence against women 'stems from systemic, deep rooted women's inequality'. This 'gender based' approach in Scotland is based on the 1993 United Nations Declaration on the Elimination of Violence Against Women (SG, 2016, p. 13), which holds that gender based violence is a function of gender inequality, and an abuse of male power and privilege and of women's and girls' subordinate status in society.

The most recent statistics on the incidence of domestic abuse as reported to the police in Scotland demonstrate that of the 58,810 reported incidents in 2016–17, 79% had a male perpetrator and a female victim (SG, 2017c, p. 2). Where the relationship between the two individuals was known, 55% were partners and 44% involved ex-partners – a pertinent illustration that separation from an abusive individual need not bring an end to violence but is rather, a known risk factor for violence (Saunders, 2004; Women's Aid, 2016).

Criminal law responses to domestic abuse

There has been a robust policy response to the policing of domestic abuse in order to shift any tendency to treat reports of incidents as 'just another domestic'. In Scotland there is a Joint Protocol between the Crown Office and Procurator Fiscal Service

(COPFS) and the Police Service. This commits the police to treating all incidents of domestic abuse as a high priority as well as establishing an assumption of prosecution (Police Scotland and COPFS, 2017). A specialist Domestic Abuse Court was established in Glasgow in 2004 to hear cases of domestic abuse and this is now also the case in Edinburgh.

Of those incidents of domestic abuse which were reported to the police in 2016–2017, 47% resulted in the recording of at least one offence or crime. Most usually these are 'common assault' (37%) or Breach of the Peace (33%) (Scottish Government, 2017c, p. 2).

At the time of writing (March 2018) the Domestic Abuse (Scotland) Act 2018 has just been passed. This introduces a specific criminal offence of 'domestic abuse' which expressly includes coercively controlling behaviour, such as a person isolating the other, or controlling and monitoring their day-to-day activities, or frightening, humiliating or punishing them. This is a significant shift as it will enable psychological and emotional abuse to be tried in a criminal court.

Civil remedies for domestic abuse

Victims of domestic abuse may not wish for criminal charges to be brought against their partner or former partner, or the abuse to which they are subjected may not ever come to the attention of the police or to the wider criminal justice system. Yet victims may wish to be protected from ongoing abuse. Civil protection orders such as common law non-molestation interdicts [injunctions], as well as non-harassment orders (under the Protection from Harassment Act 1997) can be sought. So, also, can exclusion orders (excluding the offending partner from the family home) as well as matrimonial interdicts (prohibiting certain behaviours such as presence in a specified area) under the Matrimonial Homes (Family Protection) (Scotland) Act 1981. An advantage of civil protection orders is that there is a lower standard of proof (balance of probabilities) rather than the need to establish the behaviour occurred beyond reasonable doubt.

Women may only become aware of such protection orders when they flee to a support agency seeking refuge or when they approach their local Citizens Advice Bureau[2] or consult with a solicitor when considering leaving a spouse or partner. Requests for such orders may then become part of a subsequent family court action in which the woman seeks both residence of her children and protection from on-going abuse.

The next section outlines the substantive law applicable to disputes over child contact, prior to exploring key findings from the author's research into child contact disputes in Scotland. This includes the finding that there are relatively few requests for civil protection orders, given the prevalence of allegations of abuse.

Child contact disputes in scotland

Substantive family law in Scotland is constituted with a view to protecting family life and based on the assumption that children have a right to know and be cared for by their families. This is consistent with United Nations Convention on the Rights of the Child 1989 (UNCRC) to which the UK is a signatory,[3] as well as with Article 8 of the

European Convention on Human Rights and Fundamental Freedoms 1950 (ECHR). The ECHR became part of the domestic law of the UK (including that of Scotland) via the UK Human Rights Act 1998.

In Scots case-law it has been said that it may usually be assumed that a child will benefit from ongoing contact with each parent without there being the need for that parent to lead evidence of this (*White v White* 2001 SLT 485). That is, by default there may be an assumption that contact will best promote the welfare of a child. The extent to which a parent's abusive behaviour towards the other parent diminishes the strength of this assumption is within the discretion of individual sheriffs – with sheriffs being directed by statute to consider the need to protect a child from abuse as part of their decision-making process.

Parents seeking to secure the residence of their children or, at least, ongoing contact with those children, may raise a court action under s. 11 of the Children (Scotland) Act 1995, in the event that they are unable to secure the agreement of the other parent to their proposed arrangements. Both parents of a child are vested with 'parental rights' and 'parental responsibilities' (PRR) under the Children (Scotland) Act 1995, and this expressly includes the right to maintain personal relations and direct contact with the child on a regular basis where the child is not living with the parent (s. 2(c)).

The court applies three principles when deciding whether or not to make an order for contact. The first of these is that the welfare of the child is to be the court's paramount consideration (the welfare principle); the second that the court is not to make an order unless it is satisfied that the making of an order is better for the child than not doing so (the 'no-order' or 'status quo' principle). The third principle is that the court is required to give the child an opportunity to say if he or she wishes to express a view and if the child does, then to give that child the opportunity to do so *and* to give due weight to those expressed views. This is consistent with Article 12 of the UNCRC (requiring State Parties to enable children to be heard in judicial proceedings in matters affecting them).

A lengthy amendment was made to the 1995 Act by the Family Law (Scotland) Act 2006 specifying that when a court is determining whether to make an order in repect of parental rights it must consider the need to protect the child from abuse and from the risk of abuse. Section 11 (7C)(a) of the amended Children (Scotland) Act 1995, defines 'abuse' to include violence, harassment, threatening conduct and any other conduct likely to give rise to physical or mental injury, fear, alarm or distress. The conduct to be deemed within scope includes 'speech' and 'presence in a specified area'. The Act also requires the court to consider the need for cooperation between two or more individuals – given that contact handovers may be used as an opportunity to harass, interrogate, criticise, or assault the other parent of a child.

Domestic abuse as a factor in child contact disputes

In 2011, the author completed doctoral research, funded by the Economic and Social Research Council (ESRC), in which court papers pertaining to all child contact disputes between parents, raised over the course of one calendar year within two sheriff courts in Scotland, were systematically reviewed. All 208 cases (affecting 299 children) had been raised after the 2006 amendments had come into force (requiring courts to consider the need to protect a child from abuse). In addition to this court data, surveys were undertaken with legal practitioners and with former litigants. Interviews were also undertaken with sheriffs, solicitors, family support workers, and with parents and children who had experience of a court based child contact dispute. A significant amount of data on the background of the cases was collated, as well as on the ways in which children were heard. The most pertinent findings in respect of allegations of domestic abuse within child contact disputes are given in this section. Subsequent sections will also use illustrative findings from the court data set and from interviews where these are helpful to illustrate the point being made.

Allegations of domestic abuse of a physical or sexual kind were made in cases affecting half of the 299 children.[4] In those cases where these allegations were made, 92% of the allegations were made by the mother of the child who was the subject of the dispute. The mothers of a quarter of the children were in refuges for women at the time the court action was raised. Women who had fled abuse stated they had left to protect themselves from physical abuse as well as to escape verbal intimidation and threats.

Allegations of domestic abuse within either the initial writ (submitted by a female pursuer [applicant] in the case), or within the defences (where the mother was defending the case) were statistically more likely to result in the court taking a proactive approach to the determination of the case. That is, while the legal system of Scotland is adversarial (and the judge's role is to determine the case on the basis of what is put before him or her), within family actions, where the welfare of the child is the paramount consideration, the court has options available which enable it to take a more inquisitorial approach. Principally, the rules of court afford the court discretion to appoint a solicitor to act as a child welfare reporter (formerly known as 'bar reporters') to investigate all the circumstances of the case and in particular, the arrangements for the care and upbringing of any children.[5] The court may also appoint a lawyer to act as a *curator ad litem* to protect the interests of the child.[6] In the cases reviewed, child welfare reporters were appointed in 57% of cases in which allegations of domestic abuse were made, compared to just 35% of cases where allegations of domestic abuse were not made, whilst *curators ad litem* were appointed to 7% of the children across the court data set.

Crucially, at the time the study was conducted, child welfare reporters had broad discretion in respect of the issues they investigated and they habitually approached the police for records of criminal convictions as well as records of calls to the family home which were related to incidents of abuse or other offences. Where present in the court papers, these reports were a mine of potentially corroborating information in respect of domestic abuse. Due to the presence of these child welfare reports, the review of the court papers revealed evidence of police involvement with two-thirds of the families where domestic abuse was alleged, while statutory social workers were also involved with a third of these families. The court papers also revealed that, in those cases in which domestic abuse was alleged, just under a fifth of children had a father who was the subject of criminal proceedings at the time the child contact dispute was raised. Seventeen percent of these children had a father who had previous convictions for domestic or child abuse at the time the action was raised. Ten children's fathers were in prison at the time of the child contact dispute.

Ten children's fathers were also subject to a civil interdict at the time the action was raised. While interdicts against removal of the child were requested in respect of 54 children, only 24 women requested a non-molestation order as part of the court action. There were also only two cases in which a non-harassment order was requested, and only four cases in which an exclusion order was requested. These various orders were only *granted* in cases in which there had been extreme violence. For example, one father, who had a history of assault upon the mother and the child of the action, had also assaulted the pursuer's elderly mother who had subsequently died. He had then also breached his conditions of bail to stay away from his former partner. That is, despite broad statutory definitions of the behaviours that individuals needed to be protected from, in application, courts appeared reluctant to grant the protective orders unless significant risk to life and limb existed.

The findings in respect of the prevalence and nature of domestic abuse in the background of cases that go before the courts vividly illustrate why the introduction of a statutory assumption of ongoing contact could place children at risk of harm. To date, Scotland has resisted repeated public petitions (usually raised by a litigant or former litigant) calling for either the introduction of a statutory assumption of ongoing parental contact post-separation, or for shared parenting (where children spend equal, or near equal time with each parent).[7] However, despite the lack of a statutory assumption of contact, 54% of children from cases in which domestic abuse was alleged, were found to be exercising contact with the alleged perpetrator by the final hearing in the case. This was most likely to be the case when child welfare reports had not been ordered and when there was no known prior involvement of statutory agencies (such as the police and social work). It was also more likely when the children were deemed to be of 'tender years' and therefore were not approached for their views (see also Mackay, 2013).

One sheriff in interview observed the need for training of the judiciary following the introduction of the statutory requirement to consider the need to protect a child from abuse.

> They were rushed through at the end [of the legislative process] and we now have a duty to consider domestic abuse but there were no resources put into their implementation. We are not told how to make the assessment. Training, information and resources are needed. (Sheriff no. 3)

While some optional training is available to sheriffs within the Judicial Institute for Scotland, it remains the case that specific training on the impact of domestic abuse upon victims and their children is not currently mandatory for family law practitioners. It is however currently being considered for solicitors who undertake child welfare reports for the court (SG, 2017d, p. 7).[8]

This article moves now to consider in more detail four key features of the current legal process for managing child contact disputes in Scotland. While these potentially enable women and children to be protected from ongoing abuse, in practice they may not always do so.

Legal process features of child contact disputes in scotland

The four key features of Scots family law process to be considered in greater detail here are: (i) the availability of legal aid; (ii) the cautious process of child welfare hearings (as opposed to rapid decision making); (iii) the use of child welfare reports; and, (iv) the statutory requirement that the child should be given an opportunity to express their views. These are each discussed in turn – with the inclusion of a review of the leading case of *NJDB v JEG* [2012] UKSC 21 in the section on the process nature of a child contact dispute. It is notable that these process features have all been the subject of either a recent or current review, or both.

Legal aid

In Scotland legal aid – access to state funds to cover legal actions – enables individuals to access advice on their rights and options from a legally trained and qualified professional lawyer. That person may then also represent them in a court of law. In principle, there is a strong moral resistance to limiting access to the courts in family actions in Scotland, whether by limiting funding or otherwise. When charged with undertaking a review of the funding of civil litigation in Scotland in 2011, Sheriff Principal Taylor observed that 'Access to justice is a right and it has been said with some force that its absence is "an enemy of the rule of law"' (Taylor, Sheriff Principal n.d., p. 1). Consistent with this assertion is the fact that the thresholds for legal aid are set a level that enables those who are out of work or on low incomes to qualify, while there is a sliding scale of contributions for those above this level. Legal aid in Scotland is administered by the Scottish Legal Aid Board (SLAB). At present civil legal aid is available to individuals with an annual disposable income of £26,239 or less and disposable capital of £13,017 or less (Law Society of Scotland [LawSoc] 2017a, p. 57).

Within the court data set over two thirds of male pursuers were in receipt of legal aid and three-quarters of female pursuers were in receipt of legal aid. This appears broadly consistent with the finding in more recent research that on average solicitors estimated that 79% of family clients would not have had access to legal advice, assistance or representation if they had not received legal aid (LawSoc, 2017b, p. 34).

In 2016–2017 legal aid spending on family actions was £19,581,000 (Law Society of Scotland, 2017b, p. 11). The cost per funded individual is estimated to equate to a relatively modest sum of £1,416 – taking account of the fact that the costs of legal aid are repaid to the SLAB by the party if the action results in any monetary gain (or retention of property) (Law Society of Scotland, 2017b, p. 11). However, since 2010, the legal aid budget of Scotland has been cut from £161.4 million to £126.1 million in 2016–2017. Family actions have been subject to particular attention as they account for approximately 60% of all grants of civil legal aid (SLAB, 2017, p. 71).

The SLAB has had to respond to the reduced budget by tightening the purse strings and requiring solicitors to comprehensively demonstrate the need for a family action to go to court rather than using an alternative process such as mediation (Scottish Legal Aid Board, 2017, p. 61). This is in the context that neither the existing statutory provisions, nor the rules of court, require individuals to consider or attend mediation, although a court may choose to refer parties to mediation.[9] Block fees paid to solicitors in family actions have also not increased for seventeen years (LawSoc, 2017a, p. 18). When new procedural rules are introduced that require additional steps to be taken by solicitors when representing a client, no similar changes are made to the fees paid (Law Society of Scotland, 2017a, p. 62). Consequently, an estimated third of civil legal aid work is 'pro bono' (unpaid) (Law Society of Scotland, 2017a, pp. 9–10). Not surprisingly many firms have abandoned legal aid work and only represent private (self-funding) clients, with a 12% fall in the number of outlets providing civil legal aid between 2004 and 2009 alone (SWA, 2009, Para 3.3.4). So, while the principle underpinning legal aid in Scotland is laudable, the practice reality in the context of ever shrinking budgets tells a different story.

When a parent cannot access funds to cover legal costs this may have serious welfare implications for children. In one case in the author's court data set a mother – who was working and not in receipt of legal aid – could not afford to pay for the child welfare report.[10] The Local Authority Social Work department eventually stepped in and completed a report which provided a record of the father's criminal convictions for assault and harassment and previous abduction of an older child during contact. They also reported on the child's disturbed behaviour – at only 8 years of age she threatened to kill herself and would stand with a knife pressed to her chest. The availability of legal aid for those who are unable to cover legal costs in family actions is clearly an essential requirement for the protection of women and children and for the promotion of the welfare of the children.

The 'process' nature of child welfare hearings

The length of time it can take for a child contact dispute to resolve is regularly raised as a cause for concern (Scottish Government, 2017d, Annex A). However, the need for several hearings can reflect the court's concern to make a decision consistent with the promotion of the welfare of the child. That is, in order to do this the court is likely to need additional information (over and above that provided by the parties) as well as feedback on any interim contact ordered. To do otherwise would risk the application of a formulaic or blanket approach to determining a child contact dispute – which would by default be likely to equate with the ordering of contact, given that across families in general it may usually be assumed this would benefit the child.

The court hearings regulating Parental Rights and Responsibilities (such as child contact) were constituted as 'Child Welfare Hearings' (CWH) in 1996. The focus of these hearings is the welfare of the child concerned. They are closed to the public and intended to be less formal hearings, with the sheriff removing his or her wig, and the legal representatives their gowns. The sheriff may also speak directly with the parties to the action in order to facilitate agreement or at least compliance. It is usual for there to be a number of CWH in a single case in order to facilitate resolution of the case without the need for an expensive proof hearing (in which witnesses are called and cross examination takes place). In the author's court data set, by the last CWH in the case, contact had either resumed or continued in respect of 70% of all children, while for some children the status quo of 'no contact' was maintained at the final hearing in the case (27% of all children for whom the outcomes were discernible). The number of CWH in the cases varied from just a single hearing (in 5% of cases) to, at the extreme end, 25 CWH. However, 60% of cases actually became inactive in five or fewer CWH and 91% of cases became inactive within 10 hearings or less.

The sheriffs interviewed as part of this research listed several advantages of the CWH. One particularly approved of the fact that 'I am able to speak directly with the parents' whilst also noting that, 'The sheriff principal has noted that there have been fewer family appeals to him since the introduction of the child welfare hearings'. Additionally, this sheriff observed: 'they [CWH] are, of course, labour intensive as one has to have a series of hearings to monitor contact – however by this means it is usually possible to avoid a proof' (Sheriff no. 4). A further sheriff observed that, 'some are of the view that one should only have one child welfare hearing and then go to proof. I don't agree with this, they enable a monitoring of the situation' (Sheriff no. 5).

It was indeed noticeable within the court data set that the courts were generally supportive of requests that contact be (re)introduced gradually, or that contact should be monitored, where contact had broken down due to welfare concerns or there had been no contact between the child and the non-resident parent for a significant time.

In those cases where the court ordered a child welfare report, it was often the case that no contact would take place until the report was received. At one of the two courts from which data was collected in particular, after receiving the report, the court would then often require the reporter to directly observe the contact that took place – most usually within a child contact centre. One sheriff in interview observed:

> Where domestic violence is alleged I would put contact on hold until this is investigated by a reporter [...] If, after making an inquiry, I am satisfied that it is better for the child that there be contact than no contact, I would begin by ordering contact in a child contact centre. (Sheriff no. 4)

Child contact centres are run by charitable organisations and provide a space in which a child can have contact with their non-resident parent in a public space (as opposed to a private home), 'supported' by volunteers.[11] Thirty-eight percent of children from cases in which domestic abuse was alleged were ordered to have contact in a child contact centre at some stage of the court process.

Using this cautious approach to resolving child contact disputes meant that almost all actions resolved without the need for an expensive proof hearing. While proof hearings were set at some stage in 14% of cases across the data set, these were only held in 1% (3 cases) in the court data set.

While there are advantages to this cautious approach in terms of protecting women and their children, an obvious disadvantage is that it usually takes the reinstatement of contact as the starting point. This normative starting point may carry significant risks for the child and their mother in the context that any 'interim' contact ordered is with a domestically abusive father – even if only temporarily reinstated. A relatively recent reported child contact dispute, *NJDB v JEG* [2012] UKSC 21, illustrates the potential for a coercively controlling individual to use sustained legal process to pursue a former partner for increasing amounts of care and control of the child,[12] although, rather than doing this via a series of CWH alone, unusually, the pursuit of contact in this case included appeals as far as the UK Supreme Court (the highest appeal court for Scottish civil cases). Despite being an exceptional case, *NJDB v JEG* has led to changes in the processing of family actions and is worthy of closer attention.

In *NJDB v JEG*, the initial court action and subsequent appeals were all raised by an unmarried father who had enjoyed around three years of informally arranged contact with his son (born in 2000) as well as with the older daughter of his former cohabiting partner. The father sought PRR and the residence of both children at the time that his former partner was marrying another man. In January 2004 (the month of her wedding) the court of first instance awarded the father PRR in respect of both the children and also made a contact order in respect of his biological child. Shortly after this the father raised proceedings to find the mother in contempt of court as contact did not take place when the child was unwell, an action which, if successful, could have resulted in the imprisonment of the mother. While this action for contempt was later abandoned by the father, he again requested residence of his son in December of that same year (2004). The mother sought the cessation of all contact at that time. This was then followed by the father accusing the mother's husband of sexual abuse of the children (and involving the police). It was found that the allegations were unfounded. The son was allegedly expressing ever more urgent wishes not to be ordered to go to contact with his father, and contact ceased in August 2007 when the child:

> lay kicking and screaming on the couch. He accused the defender and her husband of forcing him to do things that he did not want to do. He said that he hated his father and repeatedly asked why no one was listening to him. (*NJDB v JEG* [2010] CSIH 83, para. 11)

A proof hearing on the issue of contact was eventually held in the court of first instance in 2009 which included an extraordinary 52 days of evidence and took over a year to complete. The father was denied any further contact on the basis that it would not promote the welfare of the child to order him to have contact to which he was so vocally opposed. The father then appealed to the Inner House of the Court of Session and it is in the report of this case, *NJDB v JEG* [2010] CSIH 83, that we learn that the mother had at some point been a victim of a violent episode at the hands of the father, to her serious injury (at para. 13). The Court of Session did not uphold the father's appeal and it was then that he appealed to the UK Supreme Court, who also concluded that contact would not be in the best interest of the boy. The Supreme Court judgment included scathing commentary on the cost of the case (over £1 million) and on its duration ([2012] UKSC 21, paras. 21–37).

Despite being an exceptional case, the comments of the UK Supreme Court, and the fact that the case was heard at a time when government budgets were being drastically cut, has meant the case has influenced changes in the processing of child contact disputes. The key change, in place since 2013, is intended to prevent long proof hearings. The rules of court now require the representatives of both parties to agree and put in written form (via a joint minute) the scope of what is in dispute, as well as the scope for agreement and for the instruction of a joint 'expert witness'. They also have to include an estimate of the time needed for examination and cross examination. This is put before the sheriff and informs a case management hearing in advance of the proof. One possible negative impact of these changes on women seeking to protect their children from the other domestically abusive parent, may be that they are prevented from presenting expert evidence from a specialist (such as a child psychologist) who has assessed the impact upon the child of being ordered into contact against their will (which was the case in *NJDB v JEG*). Given that it may normally be assumed that a child will benefit from contact with both parents this could have serious implications.

Child welfare reports

In *NJDB v JEG* [2012] UKSC 21 there is no mention of a child welfare report being undertaken prior to the initial order in the sheriff court which awarded the father PRR and contact. As previously discussed, such reports enable the court to obtain key background information prior to the ordering of any contact such as evidence of domestic abuse and the prior involvement of the statutory agencies, such as the police. It would be hard to overstate the significant import of such reports and, as such, they are worthy of further consideration as a key feature of child contact legal process in Scotland; particularly as a person was appointed to undertake a child welfare report in respect of 47% of all the children in the court data set (one quarter of whom were social workers and the rest, solicitors). Almost all these reports were ordered at the first hearing in the case.

In the wake of the discussion of *NJDB v JEG*, it is pertinent to restate that a child welfare report may also prevent cases needing to go as far as an expensive proof hearing. As one sheriff interviewed observed:

> A report is really a dress-rehearsal for a proof and unless it is very wrong in emphasis this can be a catalyst for a party saying ok, I realise I am not going to get contact of the type I want. (Sheriff no.1)

It is also relevant to note that reports were sometimes ordered in the court data set even though the case was undefended (12 cases). In these cases, the views and experiences of the mother were not available to the court, with the only information before the court often being that the father had produced a birth certificate naming him as father of the child and that he wanted an order for contact. In one undefended case, the court clerk prepared the document (interlocutor) for the sheriff to sign in order to make the orders as sought. The sheriff however returned this to the clerk with the following note attached:

> The child is not just one year old! He (the pursuer) 'believes' he is the father as a result of a 'brief' sexual relationship [...] A reporter should be appointed to investigate the circumstances...

In another of these cases, the appointed reporter gleaned that the father, who was seeking overnight contact with a baby, had convictions for murder (amongst other crimes/offences), and that the baby had been born prematurely, with the mother having previously reported domestic violence by the father to the police.[13] Contact was not granted in either case.

Child welfare reports were undoubtedly instrumental in facilitating the protection of these children and it is imperative that they are not lost from the processing of child contact disputes. However, these reports regularly cost around £3,000 each and over £4 million a year to the Scottish Legal Aid Board (SG, 2011). As part of the need to reduce legal aid expenditure, their scope has been restricted by new rules of court which came into effect in March 2016.[14] These require that the appointing court specify the enquiries to be undertaken via the use of a checklist. This checklist includes the option of obtaining a criminal conviction certificate under section 112 of the Police Act 1997 and the option to 'interview domestic abuse case worker' along with 'interview social worker.' If these are not 'checked' then the reporter cannot undertake these tasks. It is not clear however if reporters may continue to obtain records of police call outs in response to domestic abuse. Most incidents of domestic abuse do not result in a charge being brought, let alone conviction, yet 'records of police attendance at the home address' is not included on the checklist. Only future research will be able to provide data on the impact of these rules on women leaving abuse.

What is also worrying is that the Scottish Government has recently recommended to the Scottish Civil Justice Council (who draft rules of court) that consideration be given to a rule requiring that a child welfare report is not ordered except as preparatory to a proof hearing (Scottish Government, 2017d, p. 4). This would represent a significant shift from current practice - given that only 1% of cases in the author's dataset proceeded to a proof, and similarly low percentages have been found in previous research (Laing & Wilson, 2010; SE, 2004). Surely it is better the court is made aware of the issues that are usually behind the resistance to contact (abuse, neglect, mental illness, substance misuse, distressed children) at the *start* of the action, rather than to leave it to the final hurdle when the parties are even more highly distressed, often considerably poorer, and may be losing confidence in the judicial process.

Hearing the views of children

The court data set revealed that older children were more likely to have their views taken, with children aged seven years and over being more likely to have their views taken than not (56%). This increased to 77% for children aged 11–12 years of age, 92% for children aged 13–14 years of age, and 100% for children aged 15 years.

Most usually children's views were taken as part of the child welfare report. However, the passage of the UNCRC led to an amendment to the rules of court so that they require the parents' solicitors to include a request either that the child be made aware of the court action (known as 'intimation') or that this should be dispensed with. Intimation was granted by the court in respect of 52 of the data set children - meaning that these children were then sent a form (Form F9) giving them the specific opportunity to tell the court their views on the issue of contact. All but two of the children intimated in this way were aged between 7–17 years of age. Twenty-five of the children returned their completed form to the court.

In addition, being 'intimated' via a Form F9 significantly increased the likelihood of a child (and his or her siblings) expressing their view to the court by other means as well. There were nine children who wrote letters directly to the court and three children who instructed their own solicitor and all of these children had either been intimated via a Form F9, or had an older sibling who had. The sheriff also chose to speak directly with the child in three cases.

Analysis of the court data revealed that just under two-thirds of the children who expressed a view had a contact outcome that was broadly consistent with the views they had expressed (such as for more or less contact or in relation to whether there were overnight stays). Overwhelmingly these were children who were not expressly opposed to contact or who appeared to be ambivalent.

Worryingly, in respect of child protection, a third of the children whose express views were known, were ordered into contact against these express wishes. Ninety-six percent of these children were from cases where domestic abuse was either alleged or uncovered by a child welfare reporter. That is, children's wish not to be forced to have contact with a parent whose behaviour upset them, was insufficient to dislodge the assumption that their welfare is best promoted by ongoing contact with both parents. Examples of the views expressed by children exposed to domestic abuse included:

> I don't want to go to dad because he shouts and swears. He grabs my collar and he hurts me….He makes us clean his house. When he drinks he falls asleep on the couch. (Boy, aged 10)

> My dad […] made me do all the chores and if I didn't he hit me. He treats the other children [step siblings] like they are number one and I am invisible. They wouldn't let me phone home and would not let me go home. This makes me really sad. (Girl, aged 10)

> As you all well know my dad is not a pleasant human being to live with. He is violent and dangerous. I would not want to be miserable or permanently in hospital. I want nothing whatsoever to do with him in the future or now. (Girl, aged 13)

What did help to shore up the views of children who were opposed to contact, and often resulted in the court not making an order for contact, was when the specific individual appointed to undertake the child welfare report took the impact of exposure to domestic abuse and the children's fears seriously. Similar cases could have a different outcome depending on the understandings of the child welfare reporter. Two cases from the court data set illustrate this clearly. In one case the older of two children (aged 6) had witnessed her father attempt to strangle her mother when she told him she was leaving. Police records confirmed they had been involved with the family and the family health visitor reported that the child psychologist, who had worked with the child since the event, was of the view contact was not in the best interests of the child. The reporter put it to the father that the child might feel fear given the circumstances, but the father responded that 'if [the child] is expressing fear, that must have been created in her by her mum'. This reporter concluded that the father 'appeared to have no insight into the effect of his behaviour on the children' and concluded that 'in all the circumstances, I cannot recommend that an order for contact be made as there is a risk that to do so would be injurious to the well-being of the children.' No contact was ordered.

However, in another similar case, the reporter did recommend contact. In this case the children had witnessed their father assaulting their mother by punching her in the head. Their screams alerted their neighbour who called the police. The court reporter gleaned that the father had three previous criminal convictions for drunk driving and for breach of peace. The children told the reporter: 'they do not want to see their father and say they will run away if they are made to see him' (child welfare report). The children also told the reporter that their father left them outside the pub during contact and that they had to sit on the step in the dark and were frightened. Their mother told the reporter that the younger child had started to wet the bed at night and was soiling herself due to being fearful of being made to see her father. Nonetheless the reporter concluded:

> There appear to be no child welfare based reasons why contact should not operate [....] I do not feel that either of the girls are sufficiently mature to be able to evaluate their feelings objectively. [....]The girls are obviously fearful of their father, but I do suspect this is a result of the perception of their mother's reaction rather than a genuine fear of spending time with the pursuer.

An obvious conclusion is that training should be provided for solicitors undertaking child welfare reporting, as well as for those sitting on the bench in family actions. This should be both regularly delivered and mandatory. While training for the Judiciary is an operational matter for the Judiciary and the Scottish Courts and Tribunals Service (Scottish Government, 2017d, p. 31), it is encouraging that the Scottish Government has suggested that the forthcoming review of the 1995 Act provides an opportunity to consider the introduction of powers to regulate child welfare reporters - including assuring appropriate training (Scottish Government, 2017d, p. 7).

Concluding discussion

This article has discussed the substantive law underpinning the processing of child contact disputes in Scotland where there are allegations of domestic abuse. It has been seen that these cases are considered within a wider policy context in which domestic abuse is recognised as a form of gender-based violence and where abuse is defined widely and includes coercively controlling behaviours and not just physical and sexual violence, while within the legislation governing court decision making, there is an express statutory requirement to consider the need to protect a child from abuse, and from the risk of abuse.

However, while the legislation and wider policy are in place to provide protection to those leaving abuse, there are indicators of concern within the findings from the court based research. One of these is the low numbers of women leaving abuse who are supported to seek civil protection orders by their legal representatives and the fact that these were only granted in cases of extreme (life limiting) violence. Similarly, we also saw that more than half the children in cases in which domestic abuse was alleged were exercising contact with their fathers at the final hearing in the case. Thus, while allegations of domestic abuse did impact statistically on final contact outcomes (with children from cases in which domestic abuse was alleged being less likely to be exercising contact in the final hearing in the case), the extent to which women and children seeking protection from a domestically abusive parent were protected, varied between similar cases.

Through the discussion of four key features of legal process in Scots child contact disputes, it has been seen that each of these offers the potential for protection but inconsistently delivers on this potential. While legal aid in Scotland theoretically remains available without the need to demonstrate prior domestic abuse or to attend mediation, in practice the SLAB is putting increasing pressure on legal practitioners to urge their clients to find alternate methods of resolving their dispute that stops short of a court action. Yet, access to court is essential given that only a court can lawfully remove a person's parental right of contact with a child.

At the time that the court data set was collated, either a solicitor or a social worker was appointed to undertake a child welfare report in almost half of all cases. We have seen the extent to which these enabled the protection of children through providing the court with vital background information. However, we have also seen how non-receipt of legal aid can prevent a party from being able to afford the report that might protect her child. We have also seen how the knowledge and understanding of the person undertaking the report, in respect of the impact on children of exposure to the abuse of their parent, significantly impacts on the recommendations made by that reporter. It is to be hoped that the proposed review around the training of solicitors who are to act as child welfare reporters will be robust and require demonstration of understanding (and not just attendance on a course).

We have also seen that the laudable approach in Scotland to enabling children to say whether they wish to express a view or not, as part of the legal process, can ensure more robust decision making. However, at present very young children are far more likely to be ordered into contact than older children, as their views are either not taken or not accepted as their own. Clearly there is a need for specialist children's workers to engage with children and report to the court so that courts do not 'default' to the assumption of contact just because the child is not old enough to abscond from contact.

Yet, the current economic climate is such that it is highly unlikely that specialist workers will be utilised in the process of obtaining either the views of children, or to undertake child welfare reports generally. As this article has made clear, child contact disputes and their funding have been the focus of repeated consultations seeking to reduce the time and cost to the State of their resolution. We have seen how the exceptional case of *NJDB v JEG* [2012] UKSC 21 has been used to inform a review of the processing of all child contact disputes and that it is now being suggested that child welfare reports may only be ordered in advance of a proof hearing. This would reduce the use of child welfare reports from almost half of all child contact cases, to well under 5%. The wish to avoid extreme cases such as *NJDB v JEG* is understandable, however we must not lose sight of the fact that a cautious approach to contact can be the best approach to the resolution of a child contact dispute. It was not the appointment of a child welfare reporter, or the succession of child welfare hearings that cost so much in *NJDB v JEG*, but the proof hearing and subsequent appeals.

What can be concluded from this discussion of the Scottish approach to the resolution of child contact disputes where there are allegations of abuse, is that it is essential that any changes in law and policy continue to be informed by those working with individuals who have experienced domestic abuse. It is also essential that those charged with putting into practice the substantive law, and the rules of court, do so with a clear understanding of what it means to promote the welfare of children who have experienced domestic abuse. Gender sensitive and progressive policy is only as good as its application.

Notes

1. The Scottish Civil Justice Council was established in 2013 by the Scottish Civil Justice Council and Criminal Legal Assistance Act 2013, following the Report of Scottish Civil Courts Review (Gill, 2009).
2. These are local registered charities who provide free information and advice on issues such as housing, debt, consumer rights and family breakdown. https://www.cas.org.uk/about-us/consumer-advice
3. Article 7 UNCRC includes the right of the child to know and to be cared for by his or her parents. Article 8 includes the right of the child to preserve family relations and Article 9 includes the right of the child not to be separated from his or her parents against his or her will.
4. Previous court based research undertaken in Scotland found allegations of domestic abuse in 36% of cases (Scottish Executive, 2004).
5. In Scotland, child welfare reporters are usually family law solicitors. Currently there is no requirement that they undertake additional specialised training for the role of child welfare reporter. Where social workers are already involved with the family, they may be asked to undertake the child welfare report. At the time of this research, the appointment of a court welfare reporter was entirely within the discretion of the individual Sheriff. Since March 2016, court rules require that a court welfare reporter is only appointed if the court is satisfied that the appointment is in the best interests of the child, and will promote the effective determination of the issues.
6. Courts in Scotland have the power at common law to appoint a *curator ad litem* in respect of anyone lacking legal capacity. They are most usually a solicitor. They present to the court what they consider to be in the best interests of the individual who lacks legal capacity.
7. Since 2014, these petitions include PE01570; PE01513; PE01528 and PE01589.
8. A recent small-scale study with legal practitioners similarly concluded there remains a need for training of family practitioners (Whitecross, 2017).
9. In my dataset only 2% of cases were sisted [suspended] to enable the parties to attend mediation.
10. Under the rules of court it is the parties to these private law civil actions who have to pay for child welfare reports.
11. For a critique of research on child contact centres see Morrison and Wasoff (2012).
12. The father was described in the court of first instance as 'sanctimoniously insensitive and dogmatic': *NJDB v JEG* [2010] CSIH 83, para. 13.
13. There was insufficient information in the court papers to indicate whether the child's premature birth was related to domestic violence.
14. Act of Sederunt (Rules of the Court of Session 1994 and Ordinary Cause Rules 1993 Amendment) (Child Welfare Reporters) 2015, SSI 312/215.

Disclosure statement

No potential conflict of interest was reported by the author.

Funding

This work was supported by the Economic and Social Research Council [PTA-031-2006-00040]

References

Gill, Rt. Hon. Lord. (2009). *Report of Scottish civil courts review.* Vol 1, Chapters 1–9. Edinburgh: Scottish Government. Retrieved from: https://www.scotcourts.gov.uk/docs/default-source/civil-courts-reform/report-of-the-scottish-civil-courts-review-vol-1-chapt-1—9.pdf?sfvrsn=4

Laing, K., & Wilson, G. (2010). *Understanding child contact cases in Scottish sheriff courts.* Edinburgh: Scottish Government Social Research. Scottish Government. Retrieved from http://www.gov.scot/resource/doc/334161/0109246.pdf

Law Society of Scotland. (2017a). Independent strategic legal aid review: Response to the independent strategic legal aid review call for evidence. *Law Society of Scotland* Retrieved from https://www.lawscot.org.uk/media/10441/final-law-society-of-scotland-response-to-independent-strategic-legal-aid-review-call-for-evidence-aug-2017-corrected.pdf

Law Society of Scotland (2017b). Social return on investment in legal aid: Technical report. Law Society of Scotland Retrieved from https://www.lawscot.org.uk/media/359230/social-return-on-investment-in-legal-aid-technical-report.pdf

Mackay, K. M. (2013). *The treatment of the views of children in private law child contact disputes where there is a history of domestic abuse: A report to Scotland's commissioner for children and young people.* Edinburgh: SCCYP.

Morrison, F., & Wasoff, F. (2012). Child contact centers and domestic abuse: Victim safety and the challenge to neutrality. *Violence Against Women, 18*, 711–720.

Police Scotland and the Crown Office and Procurator Fiscal Service. (2017). Joint protocol: In service challenging domestic abuse. *Police Scotland.* Retrieved from http://www.scotland.police.uk/assets/pdf/keep_safe/175573?view=Standard

Saunders, H. (2004). *Twenty-nine child homicides: Lessons for domestic violence and child protection.* Bristol: Women's Aid. Retrieved from http://familieslink.co.uk/download/jan07/twenty_nine_child_homicides.pdf

Scottish Executive. (2000). National strategy to address domestic abuse. Scottish Government. Retrieved from http://www.gov.scot/Resource/Doc/158940/0043185.pdf

Scottish Executive. (2004). Contact disputes involving allegations of domestic abuse: Feasibility study. *Scottish Government.* Retrieved from www.gov.scot/Publications/2004/10/20004/43946

Scottish Government. (2011). A sustainable future for legal aid. *Scottish Government.* Retrieved from http://www.gov.scot/Publications/2011/10/04161029/0

Scottish Government. (2016). Equally safe: Scotland's strategy for preventing and eradicating violence against women and girls. *Scottish Government.* Retrieved from http://www.gov.scot/Resource/0049/00498256.pdf

Scottish Government. (2017a). Review of the Children (Scotland) Act 1995. *Scottish Government.* Retrieved from http://www.gov.scot/Topics/Justice/law/17867/review-of-children-scotland-act-1995

Scottish Government. (2017b). Review of legal aid. *Scottish Government.* Retrieved from https://news.gov.scot/speeches-and-briefings/review-of-legal-aid

Scottish Government. (2017c). Domestic abuse reported to the police in Scotland, 2016 - 2017. *Scottish Government* Retrieved from http://www.gov.scot/Resource/0052/00526358.pdf

Scottish Government. (2017d). Scottish civil justice council: Family Law Committee, policy paper by the Scottish Government: Family justice modernisation strategy (Paper 5.1A). Retrieved from http://www.scottishciviljusticecouncil.gov.uk/docs/librariesprovider4/flc-meeting-files/flc-meeting-papers-08-may-2017/paper-5-1a-case-management-in-family-actions—policy-paper-by-the-scottish-government.pdf?sfvrsn=2

Scottish Legal Aid Board. (2017). *Annual report and accounts for the year ending 31st March, 2017*. Scottish Legal Aid Board Retrieved from https://www.slab.org.uk/export/sites/default/common/documents/Annual_report_2016_17/2016-17_Annual_Report_and_Accounts.pdf

Scottish Women's Aid. (2009). *Research Report: The use and effectiveness of exclusion orders under the Matrimonial Homes (Family Protection)(Scotland) Act 1981 in preventing homelessness*. Retrieved from: https://womensaid.scot/wp-content/uploads/2017/07/ExclusionOrderReport.pdf

Taylor, Sheriff Principal. (n.d.). Review of expenses and funding of civil litigation in Scotland: Press statement. *Scottish Government* Retrieved from http://www.gov.scot/Topics/archive/reviews/taylor-review/ConsultationPaper/press-statement

Whitecross, R. W. (2017). Section 11 orders and the abuse provisions: Family lawyers' experience and understanding of section 11(7A)-(7E). *Edinburgh Law, 21*, 269–275.

Women's Aid Federation. (2016). *Nineteen child homicides*. Bristol: Women's Aid. Retrieved from. https://1q7dqy2unor827bqjls0c4rn-wpengine.netdna-ssl.com/wp-content/uploads/2016/01/Child-First-Nineteen-Child-Homicides-Report.pdf

Enhancing judicial skills in domestic violence cases: the development, implementation, and preliminary evaluation of a model US programme

Peter G Jaffe, Claire V Crooks, Maureen Reid, Jennifer White, Danielle Pugh-Markie and Linda Baker

ABSTRACT

The overwhelming number and complexity of domestic violence cases in criminal and family courts has resulted in the development of education programmes to assist judges. There is limited research on judicial education in this area. This paper reviews one such initiative entitled 'Enhancing Judicial Skills in Domestic Violence Cases' (EJS) that has been developed and implemented over the last 20 years by the National Judicial Institute on Domestic Violence, a partnership of the US Department of Justice Office on Violence Against Women, National Council of Juvenile and Family Court Judges and Futures Without Violence. We present findings of a preliminary evaluation of the programme based on the self-reports of 480 judges who had taken the four-day workshop between 2006 and 2010. Overall, judges reported the programme to be engaging and effective. At a six-month follow-up, most of the judges identified specific benefits and behavior changes in the areas of access to justice, judicial leadership, victim safety, and abuser accountability as a result of participating in the programme. Critical issues in judicial education are highlighted based on the authors' experiences in the development and implementation of this programme.

Introduction

Domestic violence is a serious social issue that impacts millions of people across the globe (WHO, 2014). The impact of domestic violence on the health and wellbeing of its victims has been repeatedly documented over the past quarter century (Black, 2011; WHO, 2014). As an indication of the potential volume of cases that might come before the courts, one in four women in the United States reports experiencing violence by a current or former spouse or boyfriend at some point in her life (Smith et al., 2017). In the US, since the mid-1980s, multiple factors like public awareness and the development of police mandatory charging policies have led to increasing numbers of cases that

---

The opinions, findings, conclusions and recommendations expressed are those of the authors and do not necessarily reflect the views of the Department of Justice, Office on Violence Against Women or the host organisations.

now come before the criminal court as well as different civil proceedings (Department of Justice Office of Justice Programs, National Institute of Justice, 2009).

Increasing domestic violence cases before the courts

Domestic violence cases now represent a substantial and increasing proportion of all cases processed by criminal and civil state courts. There is historical data that outlines these trends such as data from the Court Statistics Project of the National Center for State Courts (NCSC), which indicate that from 1989 to 1998 domestic violence filings in State courts increased by 178% (Keilitz, 2004). Over three decades ago, similar findings were reported by Gover, Brank, and MacDonald (2007), noting that between 1984 and 1997 domestic relations cases that included domestic violence increased by 177% in the United States. Ostrom and Kauder's (1997) work found that domestic violence is a serious problem in all states, and most jurisdictions experienced an increase in their domestic violence caseload between 1993 and 1995, with 18 states reporting a 20% increase during this period. This study also found that domestic violence cases were the fastest growing segment of domestic relations cases, and domestic relations cases were the fastest increasing segment of state civil court caseloads. The Bureau of Justice Statistics (BJS) studied felony assaults charged in state courts of 15 urban counties in May of 2002 and found that one third were related to domestic violence (Smith, Durose, & Langan, 2008). In addition to constituting a growing segment of judicial work, domestic violence cases are extremely taxing on judicial officers. Symptoms of burn-out and vicarious trauma are common among judges who hear these and other abuse cases (Jaffe, Crooks, Dunford-Jackson, & Town, 2003).

A host of factors account for the increased rates of domestic violence cases being processed by the civil and criminal justice system. The passage of the Violence Against Women Act (VAWA) in 1994 created awareness nationally, sparked legislative improvements, and put real dollars behind the justice and advocacy response to domestic violence; funding helped hire and train police, support civil advocacy and legal representation for victims, raise awareness and education among prosecutors and judges, and bring system players together with community groups and experts to coordinate responses. Between 2014 and 2016, five VAWA funded grant programmes used funds for court activities. In this two-year period, one of these five programmes reported that courts receiving funding disposed of 6,424 criminal cases, of which 66% resulted in convictions and that courts engaged in judicial monitoring of an average of 1,824 offenders for compliance with court-ordered conditions at 13,345 individual review hearings (Department of Justice, Office on Violence Against Women, 2016). During the two-year reporting period, VAWA funded professionals provided assistance to victims in securing 69,035 final civil protection orders (Department of Justice, Office on Violence Against Women, 2016).

The importance of judicial education on domestic violence

Cases involving domestic violence require specialised knowledge. Due to the unique dynamics of domestic violence, it is crucial for judges to understand and develop skills related to a wide range of legal and social issues including victim recantation, lethality assessment, admissibility of evidence of past violence, and children exposed to violence. Recent research has highlighted the complexity in judges' decision-making around protective orders, for example (Agnew-Brune, Moracco, Person, & Bowling, 2017). Judges need to gain the experience and have access to appropriate education programmes to effectively handle domestic violence cases. An understanding of the diverse presentations of domestic violence victims and perpetrators and an awareness of the community resources available promote a more informed and thoughtful judicial response to the problem (Helling, 2005).

The importance of specialised domestic violence educational programmes for judges is well founded in the literature. Several authors have documented the most appropriate environments and methods to enhance judicial education. Judges as a profession have distinct qualities that influence their learning styles and preferences (Armytage, 2015). These styles and practices as learners which are distinctive to judges have important implications for educators (Armytage, 2015). Scholars and judicial educators argue that education focusing on substantive legal and social issues is insufficient. Judicial education must also develop judges' internal character and integrity, along with their decision-making, critical thinking, and interpersonal skills (Benton & Sheldon-Sherman, 2015). Senior judges have also highlighted the need for judicial education programmes that reflect on judges' fundamental leadership role in promoting access to justice and fairness in all proceedings (Martinson & Jackson, 2017). Some of the distinct characteristics of judges as learners are a result of the following: the nature and criteria of judicial appointment, tenure, the preferred learning styles and practice of judges, doctrinal constraints of judicial independence, the nature of a judge's role, the environment surrounding the judicial office and a judge's reasons or requirements for attending ongoing professional education (Armytage, 2015). As a result of these factors, judges tend to be rigorously autonomous and are extremely motivated to further their competence for its own sake as opposed to being motivated for a material or promotional enhancement. Furthermore, judges experience significant distress related to feeling chronically short of time (Jaffe et al., 2003), and accordingly can be critical of professional development activities that seem to be a waste of their valuable time.

Various continuous learning vehicles have been explored to meet the educational needs and learning style preferences of judges. Frequently used methods of judicial education include conferences and continuing education courses. Most judicial officers highly regard formal conferences and courses since they offer information, knowledge, skills, and collegial contact at a number of levels for people engaged in a solitary career (Goldring, 2003). Beyond the formal presentation at conferences and courses, the informal exchange of ideas between and among judges is seen as a highly valuable experience (Goldring, 2003). Judicial education is described as most effective when it is voluntary, respects the independence of the judiciary, creates an opportunity to be critically reflective and allows for individualised learning (Armytage, 2015; Goldring, 2003). Increasingly, scholars advocate, and judicial educators utilise programming with active or experiential learning techniques. One commonly promoted technique uses concrete experiences, discussion and reflection, abstract conceptualisation, and application (Labriola, Bradley, Sullivan, Rempel & Moore, 2012). Faculty for these educational programmes must be well informed and able to involve the audience through meaningful, inclusive, and appropriate means of presentation.

Judges largely require presenters who are interesting, understand the independence of the bench and are acknowledged experts within their fields (Goldring, 2003).

One of the challenges of developing judicial education on domestic violence is making the curriculum relevant for all judges regardless of the cases they are currently presiding over (e.g. dissolution cases, dependency cases, criminal cases) and their level of court. Education must benefit judges with different levels of experience and opportunities to hear cases where domestic violence is a factor. For instance, some participants in judicial education will be in general courts while others are in specialised domestic violence courts. In 2010, the Center for Court Innovation identified at least 208 courts that have specialised dockets or dedicated judges for domestic violence cases, an increase of more than 150 courts since the last national study a decade before (Labriola et al., 2012). These innovative measures create a distinct collaborative and multidisciplinary approach to case management that allows for a unique opportunity to hold perpetrators accountable and provide resources as well as enhanced safety measures for victims.

Domestic violence courts offer insights into potential policies and practices that may be most helpful in these complex cases as well as themes for judicial education programmes. The key issues identified appear to be effective management of domestic violence cases; specialised intake and court staffing; improved assistance for victims by court staff; court processes to ensure victims' safety; increased court monitoring and enforcement of batterer compliance with court orders; and increased recognition of the impact of domestic violence on children.

The range of experiences of participating judges creates opportunities for valuable informal and structured exchanges in education programmes. For instance, judges in specialised domestic violence courts or with dedicated domestic violence dockets frequently receive focused training (Labriola et al., 2012), and bring to education programmes their specialisation in an area of law that requires precision, a vast knowledge and understanding of the law, and the ability to process challenging cases in a more efficient manner (Helling, 2005). Justice system practitioners, victim advocates and researchers identify one of the major benefits of specialised domestic violence courts as judges' greater understanding of how domestic violence affects victims and their children (Keilitz, 2004). Exchanges between judges from different courts, jurisdictions, and variable years of experience create rich opportunities for national education programmes. In its study of domestic violence courts, the Center for Court Innovation found that more than 91% of the courts surveyed reported that their dedicated judges had received specialised training but noted the need for continued training and retraining of judges and other team members (police, attorneys, and court personnel) on domestic violence dynamics and related legal issues (Labriola et al., 2012).

The development and implementation of the 'Enhancing Judicial Skills in Domestic Violence Cases' programme 1999–2018

The 'Enhancing Judicial Skills in Domestic Violence Cases' programme (EJS) described in this paper emerged in response to the increasing volume of domestic violence cases before the criminal and civil courts as well as an analysis of the critical skills required by judges to address these complex matters. The National Council of Juvenile and Family Court Judges together with Futures Without Violence held several consultations in 1998 and 1999 with judges and judicial educators together with lawyers and social scientists to develop the curriculum based on the perceived needs of judges and the courts (for more background on these organizations see http://www.ncjfcj.org/and https://www.futureswithoutviolence.org/). The EJS was developed by many judges on behalf of other judges in a manner that considers judges' learning styles and their special role in the community. The host organisations had received significant feedback from judges that specialised education on domestic violence was necessary to enable the court to deal more effectively and efficiently with domestic violence cases on criminal and civil court dockets. This judicial education programme was developed to have an impact on domestic violence by reducing recidivism, improving access to resources for victims, creating more effective case management, and increasing the monitoring and enforcement of compliance with court orders. There is no evaluation on these overarching goals, so research has had to focus on changes in judges' knowledge and attitudes. EJS was created to provide an opportunity for judges to learn from each other and leading experts in the field about the challenging dynamics in domestic violence cases and how to deal effectively with victims, perpetrators, and children in the context of legal proceedings.

The EJS is founded on the principles of adult education and an understanding of the needs and learning styles of judges (Kolb, 2014). The founding organisations retained consultants in this area as well as a panel of experienced judges to develop the initial curriculum. The EJS workshop contains six major curriculum segments that are covered over a four-day period. The six segments include: Practical Courtroom Exercises, Victim and Perpetrator Behaviour, Fact-Finding, Access to Justice, Fairness and Cultural Issues, and Decision-Making. Each of the segments is described below in terms of some of the overall learning objectives. More detail about the curriculum is available from the funder and host agencies.

The EJS programme budget is approximately $US65,000 for approximately 50 judges including a full day faculty planning meeting the day before. EJS is funded through the VAWA technical assistance grants programme (TA Programme). The Department of Justice Office on Violence Against Women (OVW) TA Programme provides funding to enhance the success of local projects being implemented with OVW grant funds. OVW goals include building the capacity of criminal justice and victim services organisations to respond effectively to sexual assault, domestic violence, dating violence, and stalking. The funds are also geared to foster partnerships among organisations to address violence against women. (For more information, see Violence Against Women Act Measuring Effectiveness Initiative at the Muskie School of Public Service, University of Maine, available at http://muskie.usm.maine.edu/vawamei/taprovidermain.htm). There is no mandate in VAWA for judges to attend EJS. Some states have judicial organisations or chief judges that suggest or require training. Judge participants attend using discretionary VAWA grant money, state/local funding and scholarships from the National Council of Juvenile and Family Court Judges, or sometimes their own personal funding. In some states or counties, there may be a new domestic violence court that is beginning, and judges assigned to the court will choose EJS as a training ground. State judicial organisations have a wide variety of training opportunities for their judges. EJS is unique as a national opportunity to network and learn from other judges.

The EJS faculty is led by senior judges who have shown leadership in the area of domestic violence at a national and/or state-wide level. The judges are complemented by other faculty with expertise in legal and social science research and practice as it relates to emerging knowledge in dealing with domestic violence cases. The faculty takes part in its own development sessions to ensure the curriculum design and delivery is grounded in the principles of adult education. The EJS stands in contrast to many other legal continuing professional education programmes that are based on traditional methods of instruction that use lecture to focus primarily on the transfer of information to participants. For example, rather than relying on several hours of traditional lecturing, the programme intersperses mini-lectures with video examples, case studies, experiential exercises, and small group learning opportunities. The EJS programme promotes and models alternate, more interactive learning methods that focus on the needs of learners rather than presenters, builds on the judges' existing experiences, and helps to engage judges through a multidisciplinary, multicultural faculty.

The EJS programme was initially developed in 1999 and has been delivered three or four times a year ever since in different locations across the US. The basic structure of the programme has stayed the same but the content has been updated with emerging legal decisions and social science research on domestic violence. The programme fosters interactive learning through small group discussions that centre on case dilemmas throughout the four days. The cases are presented through video or role play dramatisation and through written materials related to pleadings or case summaries. The participants are seated at tables for six to eight together with a table facilitator who has graduated from the programme, demonstrated knowledge, and received training in effective facilitation skills. The small group discussions are not geared to solve the many case dilemmas but rather foster an open dialogue in which judges identify critical considerations and engage in diverse analyses. Judges are encouraged not to make decisions during the first three days (other than in the 'Practical Courtroom Exercises' as described below) but rather consider the relevance of different evidence and fact finding related to the dynamics of domestic violence. Each segment has detailed learning objectives that are reviewed with participants. The programme segments are briefly outlined below.

Programme segments

The 'Practical Courtroom Exercises' segment gives judges an opportunity to discuss complex civil and criminal cases involving domestic violence. There are five case scenarios that are presented through role plays by faculty and participants acting the parts of litigants and their counsel together with supporting documentation. The cases illustrate difficult dilemmas with no straightforward decisions and were chosen to flag some of the issues that are presented in the subsequent segments of the programme. Judges are asked to consider how they might handle the case and their analysis is then discussed in groups of eight to ten judges. The session provides a chance for the participants to practice ruling on realistic, hypothetical domestic violence cases. The cases give rise to discussion about the dynamics of domestic violence and the challenges of handling domestic violence cases. The participants can assess how domestic violence negatively affects the victim, perpetrator, and children as well as identify factual, legal, procedural, and resource issues that arise frequently in domestic violence cases. This first segment sets the stage for EJS in terms of identifying issues and establishing the interactive, learner-driven educational style of the programme.

The 'Victim and Perpetrator Behaviour' segment gives judges an opportunity to evaluate the impact of domestic violence on adult victims and children who are exposed to violence as well as to identify the safety and restoration requirements of domestic violence victims. This segment addresses the context of violent behavior and patterns of abusive behavior. These patterns are discussed in terms of potentially effective intervention for perpetrators of domestic violence and accountability mechanisms. Consideration is given to the decision-making and courtroom presentation of victims and perpetrators and the complexity of these relationships. Judges participate in an immersive exercise where they assume the role of a victim and are forced to make a series of complicated choices with limited resources while balancing the possibilities of life-generated and perpetrator-generated risks. The role of abuse victims and perpetrators as parents is addressed as well as access to appropriate resources and the court's role to make sure they have access to these resources.

The 'Fact-Finding' segment gives judges an opportunity to evaluate the facts of the case before they are asked to make a specific ruling, including the assessment of factors associated with the potential dangerousness of a perpetrator of domestic violence. Judges discuss how best to apply an understanding of domestic violence to judicial fact-finding and identify and resolve evidentiary issues of primary concern to judges. Learning objectives also involve the challenges of determining credibility, the assessment of bias, motive, and perspective of witnesses and parties. The unique challenges associated with pro se litigants, highly common in civil and family law domestic violence cases, are highlighted in the context of ensuring procedural fairness within the bounds of judicial ethics. Judges discuss appropriate leadership roles they could take in developing practices and policies that ensure they routinely have the information they need.

Participants spend part of their time on case illustrations and the impact of higher court decisions such as the US Supreme Court judgment on whether a hearsay statement is testimonial or non-testimonial (Crawford v. Washington, 124S. Ct. 1354 (2004); see e.g. Mendez, 2004). *Crawford* was not a domestic violence case; it was an attempted murder and assault case that has nevertheless had a long-term impact on domestic violence cases because of its treatment of the admission of hearsay evidence in criminal matters. The *Crawford* decision focused on the right of a criminal defendant to confront witnesses against him, the intent of which, as enshrined in the 6th Amendment to the US Constitution, is fairness for criminal defendants. In that case, the Court determined that when a party seeks to introduce statements that are hearsay, or out of court statements that are submitted to a court to prove the truth of a matter asserted in the statement, and the declarant does not testify, prosecutors must overcome two hurdles in order to successfully admit the evidence. The prosecutor must show that the declarant is unavailable to testify, for which the legal definition of unavailability applies and includes circumstances such as the speaker's death. Domestic violence, however, is a unique crime in which the perpetrators and victims are often intractably entangled in enduring relationships because of children, shared property, family ties, economic necessity, fear, or a host of other factors. It is common for prosecutors to struggle to provide victim witness testimony in these cases. As a result, the decision in *Crawford* and its progeny had a sharp and sustained impact on victims, law enforcement, defence lawyers, and the courts since many victims are reluctant to appear in court. Judges need to be prepared to consider the *Crawford* decision in domestic violence proceedings.

The 'Access to Justice' segment provides a time for judges to reflect on the impact of their role as a judge on court system players by exploring, defining, and refining their role as a judge, with the goal of advancing access to justice in their court and community. A central focus in this segment is the application of judicial ethics rules that govern judges' participation in activities such as court and community councils, legislative proposals, and education programmes by and for non-judge providers. An important theme discussed is the fact that judges are only as effective as the resources available and the extent to which these resources are coordinated. In addition, there is an emphasis on the critical role for the court in violence prevention through public education and helping to change attitudes about domestic violence. Participant judges have an opportunity to share innovative projects and activities in their jurisdictions that promote access to justice.

Embedded in the learning objectives in the 'Access to Justice' section is the potential leadership role of judges. There is an ongoing debate on the role of judges and their personal level of comfort in relation to leadership activities. In the US, judicial leadership is a concept that involves some parameters rather than any prohibitions, while the rules of judicial ethics are interpreted through ethics decisions and advisory opinions which are sometimes unpublished. So in effect, a jurisdiction's rules may say that judges 'are encouraged to engage' (an expression often cited in state ethics rules and taken from the comment to Rule 3.1 in the ABA Model Code of Judicial Conduct) subject to 'the other rules in the code' such as to avoid the 'appearance of impropriety' or activities that would 'undermine a judge's independence'. However, a jurisdiction's ethics opinions and advisory opinions may reflect a lenient or a rigid view of a judge's role. The support for or antagonism towards judicial leadership is hard to ascertain from a simple reading of the rules of conduct and published opinions. In large part, judicial leadership is a product of the individual judge's perspective and the culture of his or her court and bench. In the authors' observation, however, judges who specialise in domestic violence courts often play a leadership role in their communities to promote enhanced coordination of services and improved counselling and legal resources for litigants.

The 'Fairness and Cultural Issues' segment helps judges identify ways in which culture is relevant in the courtroom and recognise individual and structural explicit and implicit biases that may impact on the administration of justice. Participants have an opportunity to assess implicit biases that are brought to the bench that might influence courtroom demeanour or the interpretation of facts and making of decisions in domestic violence cases. Judges have the opportunity to apply knowledge about culture in cases involving domestic violence as well as to consider the need for specialised resources such as interpretation services. The theme of this segment is that culture cannot and should not be used as an excuse for domestic violence, but cultural awareness may help shape meaningful remedies for victims, perpetrators, and their children. Participants are encouraged to reflect on how their own understanding of cultural context can help shape appropriate access and responses that bring about justice in civil and criminal cases involving domestic violence.

The 'Decision-Making' segment gives judges an opportunity to integrate the information shared in all the prior segments to inform safe and effective decisions in civil and criminal cases. The overall theme is how an understanding of domestic violence might affect how judges make decisions in a number of areas such as drafting and issuing effective protective orders, requiring appropriate batterers' treatment, and facilitating enforcement in criminal and civil domestic violence cases. Some of the critical issues addressed include the impact of domestic violence on cases involving custody and visitation of children, the evaluation of batterers' intervention programmes, appropriate treatment/intervention options, and the potential benefits of conducting review hearings (in conjunction with probation services) to monitor perpetrators' conduct in domestic violence cases. Decision-making is discussed in the context of current federal legislation (and states' emerging legislative reform) in regard to multiple issues such as stalking and firearms. This segment ends with judges reflecting on the challenges and opportunities to make a difference in dealing with domestic violence cases and their thoughts about a judicial philosophy in approaching this complex endeavour from the bench.

Aside from the formal programme outlined above, there is a special session to discuss vicarious trauma (or compassion fatigue) in judges as well as stress and burnout from the challenges of dealing with domestic violence. Psychologists present emerging research about the impact of exposure to trauma that many professionals may experience especially when dealing with a range of material from child sexual abuse, sexual assault, and homicides. This session was developed in response to judges' requests about having an opportunity to have a safe and respectful environment to address the emotional toll of their work. Over the years, judges have completed surveys to describe the impact of their work and effective strategies to cope. Some of these results have been published and shared with new participants (Jaffe et al., 2003).

Programme evaluation 1999–2010

Ongoing evaluation has been an integral part of the EJS programme since its inception in 1999. Prior to 2006, the workshop evaluations were based on a five-point rating scale (1 = Poor, 2 = Fair, 3 = Good, 4 = Very Good, 5 = Excellent) on the value of each segment and the skills of the various faculty members. The evaluation form also provided additional space for comments by judges. Each educational segment was appraised separately. Judges were asked to rate the segments in terms of whether their expectations were met and to give an overall impression of the segment. The average ratings were between 4.1 and 4.3 out of 5 (excellent) for the various times the EJS programme was delivered between 1999 and 2002 based on evaluations from 350 judges. Overall the judges identified the interactive nature of the programme and the opportunity to learn from other participants as effective. Their most common criticisms were about the volume of the materials and length of the full days (8am–5pm). The preliminary evaluation of the EJS programme in the early years demonstrated an appreciation for the quality of the faculty and all segments of the curriculum. However, the evaluation did not provide insight into the benefit of the programme in terms of achievement of learning objectives and the assessment of knowledge and skills that judges brought back to their courtrooms. Thus, the preliminary evaluation provided an important foundation for developing a more informative evaluation.

Based on the gaps identified with the preliminary evaluation approach, the EJS programme organisers developed a more comprehensive evaluation strategy. The organisers undertook an objective third-party evaluation of the curriculum development and delivery process. Questionnaires were developed to assess the impact and relevance of the programme. Part of a more rigorous assessment of the programme's ability to effectuate actual change in behavior was to ask participants to complete a pre-programme questionnaire, reflect on their learning during each segment of the programme and then to complete a questionnaire a short time after the programme. The highlights of this evaluation and results are discussed below.

The EJS evaluation included data collection with judges at different points in time. Three measures were used to evaluate the EJS programme. Judges were asked to complete a pre-workshop survey prior to attending the four-day workshop. Judges were also asked to complete a brief questionnaire on their reflections after every half-day segment of the programme. Approximately six months after the programme, judges were asked to complete an on-line survey (post-workshop survey) assessing their views on the impact of the workshop. The three measures were to be completed anonymously and all information gathered remained confidential. Only group information is reported. All research protocols were approved by the North Carolina State University's Research Board.

The pre-workshop survey provided demographic and background information on the judges as well as their current knowledge and views about domestic violence. This information provides an overview of the participants and their learning needs. In the pre-workshop survey, judges were asked to respond to 15 questions concerning attitudes toward domestic violence in the court system. A five-point scale was used ranging from Strongly Agree to Strongly Disagree in response to each question. The 15 questions were divided into four themes related to judges' views on the impact of the court on domestic violence, judges' satisfaction in dealing with domestic violence cases, satisfaction with attorneys and community resources and limitations on the role of judges. This survey was sent with an information letter to ensure that judges understood the voluntary and confidential nature of the data collection.

To assess the value of knowledge and skills covered in each segment of the programme, the judges were asked at the end of every half-day to reflect on the key learning points and how they could use them upon their return to the bench. The three questions assessed what they learned, how they would use the information, and how they would improve the segment.

Approximately six months after completion of the EJS programme, the judges were asked to complete an on- line survey as a follow-up. Judges were asked to consider how they utilised the programme information and skill development in their daily work. The independent research contractor maintained a code for each participant to link the pre- and post-survey for comparison purposes. Different numbers of participants completed each of the measures. In summary, 480 judges attended the EJS programme over a four-year period (2006–10). Out of those judges, 341 (71%) completed a pre-test survey, 425 (93%) completed a reflection form during each half-day of the programme and 134 (28%) completed a follow-up survey (only 87 or 25.4% of judges who did the pre-survey could be matched).

Overall there were 199 male and 142 female judges who completed the pre-workshop survey, of whom 80% indicated they were Caucasian and 9.5% identified as African-American. The remaining judges identified themselves as Asian Americans (6 judges), Native Americans (8 judges) and Hispanics (8 judges). In terms of communities served, 51% of judges worked in an urban center and 34% in a rural community. The remaining 12% indicated that their jurisdiction included both urban and rural communities. The judges came from all over the US states and territories with 43 different states represented. Wisconsin, Michigan, North Carolina, New Hampshire, New York, Washington, and Texas had amongst the highest number of judges who attended. In addition, judges attended from Puerto Rico (6 judges), and Guam (1 judge).

Judges were asked about their length of experience on the bench. At the time of participation in the EJS programme, the average number of years served as a judge was 7.9 years with a range of less than one year to 29 years. There was a wide range of court assignments, with approximately half of the participants coming from general jurisdiction courts. One third of participants worked in civil courts, and smaller numbers in criminal, juvenile dependency, and specialised domestic violence courts. There were also questions about why and how judges came to attend the EJS training. The majority of judges indicted that their reason for attending the EJS programme was to gain skills or better understand the issues surrounding domestic violence (76%) or prepare for court (9%). In terms of funding for the session, 40% of judges indicated that their local OVW grantee programme supported their attendance. Other sources of funding included courts (16%), scholarship (9%), personal (2%) or some combination of sources (30%).

Judges were asked to indicate the percentage of their time devoted to cases that involve domestic violence. There was a full range of answers in that 21% of Judges said less than 10%, 60% of Judges said between 10-40%, and 10% said between 40-80%. There were 30 Judges (9%) who indicated that over 80% of their time was spent on domestic violence cases. In the pre-workshop survey concerning attitudes toward domestic violence in the court system, a number of observations were apparent: there was variability in judges' attitudes on all four domains; there were a number of areas where judges felt pessimistic about the effectiveness of the court response (i.e. changing batterer behavior, and to a lesser extent, ensuring victim safety); the perceived needs of the judges matched the EJS learning objectives well (e.g. less than 30% of judges felt that judges appreciated the cultural diversity represented in court); and there were some clear opportunities for enhancing the judicial role. For example, fewer than 60% of judges thought it was permissible to become involved in community education activities despite the fact that most judicial codes of ethics permit this type of engagement.

Judges were also asked to list three requests (wishes) that would enhance their knowledge, skills, and effectiveness in dealing with domestic violence. The results were coded for content and several common themes emerged. Some of the most common responses included the wish to better understand domestic violence (19.7%), to have better resources (16.4%) as well as more training (9.9%) and knowing what works (9.1%).

Judges were also asked to summarise their vision in their role as a judge in their community for the next 10 years. The major themes reported centred on improving access to justice and enhancing collaboration with community partners. Many judges expressed ideas about the ideals of judicial integrity and neutrality – summarised by one participant as 'I hope to be a judge who does and is perceived to do honest, effective work that improves the lives of all interested persons of the cases I handle'. Judges' visions ranged from optimistic to more modest and many included an impact far beyond their courtrooms.

The final section of the pre-test was a self-assessment of individual expertise judges identified with in terms of their awareness and skills for domestic violence cases. Judges read descriptions of three career stages in dealing with domestic violence cases from just learning about handling these matters to working collaboratively with court-related services and community partners. Stage 3 was the highest stage and indicated the most in-depth knowledge and experience of domestic violence. Using a seven-point scale judges indicated where they perceived themselves on the continuum. The average rating was 4.32 and the range was from 1 to 7. These scores were then coded into the 3 separate stages. Stagel (1-2 on the seven-point scale) represents judges who have been recently appointed or assigned to hear cases involving domestic violence. Stage 2 (3-5) corresponds to judges who have been working for a longer period of time and Stage 3 (6-7) is the highest level, where judges have a deeper understanding of domestic violence and have been involved as mentors to new judges in this area. The majority of judges (65%) indicated that they were in the middle stage (Stage 2) at pre-test. Of the remaining judges, 14% indicated that they were at the early stages of their career in dealing with domestic violence and 21% reported that they were at the more advanced stage of their career.

Follow-up survey with the judges

A follow-up (post-workshop) survey was completed on-line by 134 judges approximately six months after the training. The post-survey asked many of the same questions as the pre-survey as well as several questions that asked specifically about the impact of the training experiences.

Approximately one-third of the judges who attended the programme completed the post-survey. Given that only a sub-sample of judges completed the post-survey, statistical analyses were completed to examine possible differences between the sub-sample of 134 and the full sample (pre-survey) of 341 judges. There were no significant differences between these two groups for years of experience, time spent on domestic violence cases, reported stage in career, or gender and race. As a result, we can conclude that this sub-sample is representative and thus results are applicable to the entire population of judges who attended the EJS programme and completed the pre-survey.

In the post-training survey judges read the same descriptions as in the pre-survey regarding three career stages and using the same seven-point scale indicated where they perceived themselves on the continuum before the training and after the training. The average rating before the training was 3.56 (range 1-7) and the average rating after the training was 4.87 (range 2-7). No judges believed they were still at Level 1 in Stage 1 after the training. These responses were collapsed into the 3 separate stages (1- 2, 3-5, 6-7). Before the training only 10% of judges indicated they were in the third stage whereas after the training 42% said they were in Stage 3. See Figure 1 for a comparison of pre- and post-programme ratings assessed at post-test.

There are two interesting findings with respect to the career stage identified by judges. First, there is a clear shift in the confidence, skills, and awareness of judge-participants as

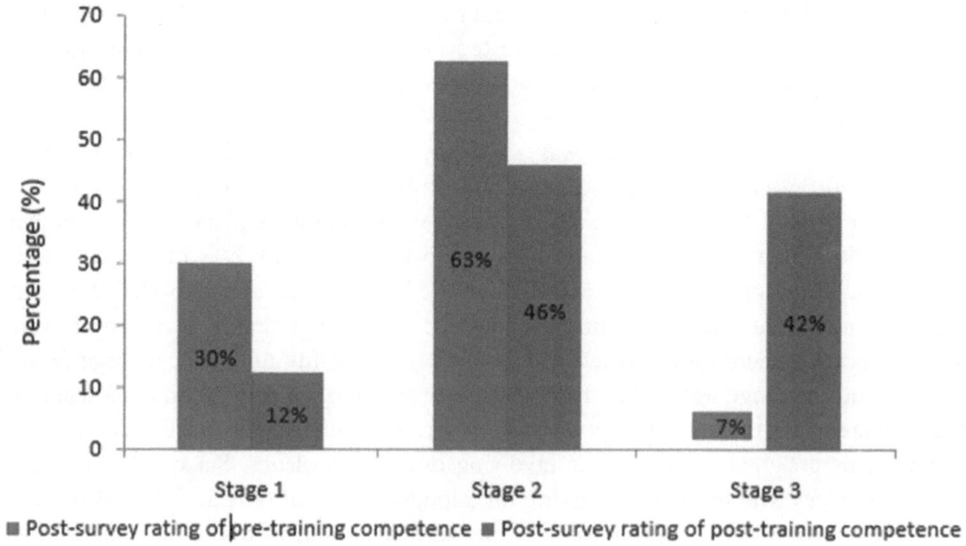

Figure 1. DV career stages before and after training assessed post-test.

evidenced by the higher scores (on the scale of 1 to 7) and the greater number of judges rating themselves in Stage 3. The shift to Stage 3 is particularly noteworthy as it is a Stage that goes beyond individual competence to assuming a leadership and mentoring role. Essentially, judges are experiencing a qualitative shift in their ability to deal with the complexity of DV cases after engaging in EJS training.

The second important finding regarding self-identified competence is the gap between how judges rated themselves prior to EJS training, and how they subsequently saw their pre-training stage *after* the EJS training. A comparison of assessed career stage pre-test and post-test rating of pre-training career stage, indicates that after training, judges rated their pre-training skills and awareness lower. This phenomenon is confirmed by examining the pre-training scores on the seven-point scale (X = 4.35, SD = 1.68) and post-training ratings of pre-training competence (X = 3.61, SD = 1.57) for the sample of judges who completed pre- and post-tests that could be matched (87 judges or 25.4% of the sample). Once judges have the experience of identifying and approaching the complexities of these cases, they realise that they were not as advanced as they originally thought. The training made judges more aware of the complexity of DV cases and diverse skill set required to handle these cases effectively. It also increased their skills, awareness, and confidence in being able to meet the demands of these cases.

In the follow-up survey, questions were asked regarding the effectiveness of the training programme in four specific areas: access to justice, providing judicial leadership, enhancing victim safety, and improving batterer accountability. Judges could respond by saying 'occasionally', 'frequently' or 'always', and were provided an opportunity to endorse examples of these outcomes. The vast majority of judges reported improvements in these areas and many were able to identify specific ways in which these improvements were realised. A summary of these results appears in Table 1.

Table 1. Judges' self-report on improved practice.

Area of Improvement	Never	Occasionally	Frequently	Always	Examples Provided
Access to Justice	4%	31%	48%	17%	*address cultural barriers that impact access to justice *improve access to justice through court administration
Exercise Judicial Leadership	6%	48%	37%	9%	*helping to determine whether to participate in extra-judicial activities like public education *motivation to undertake greater judicial leadership
Enhancing Victim Safety	1%	24%	55%	20%	*identifying cultural considerations *making and enforcing decisions that help victims to evaluate and reduce danger from an abuser
Holding Batterers Accountable	4%	32%	47%	17%	*differentiating how persons might use violence in different contexts *ordering batterers to participate in appropriate intervention programmes

The first impact question asked judges whether they felt EJS had improved their ability to provide access to justice. Approximately two thirds of judges answered that EJS provided them with the tools to improve access to justice always or frequently (see Table 1). Judges were asked *how* the EJS programme helped them improve access to justice and endorsed the following items most frequently:

EJS helps me to...

- identify and address cultural barriers that impact access to justice, including due process protections
- identify and control battering behaviours that can impede access
- improve access through administration of the court
- contribute to the community response to domestic violence to promote better access

The next question asked if the training helped the exercise of judicial leadership in the community. Nearly half of the respondents indicated that it improved their judicial leadership either always or frequently. For the judges who indicated that the EJS programme helped them exercise judicial leadership in their community, they endorsed the following statements most frequently:

EJS helps me exercise judicial leadership in my community by...

- providing ideas for and examples of engaging appropriately and ethically, in judicial leadership activities
- motivating me to undertake greater judicial leadership
- answering key, specific questions pertaining to judicial leadership
- helping me determine whether to participate in extrajudicial activities like education, legislation, discussions with the media, etc., and how to do so ethically
- helping me to connect with my colleagues to discuss and consider alternatives in resolving judicial leadership questions

EJS helps me exercise greater leadership on the bench with respect to...

- examining and accepting pleas
- warning of collateral consequences
- evaluating adequacy of legal representation

The third follow-up question asked if the training helped enhance the safety of victims. Three-quarters of the judges indicated improvement in this area. Judges who indicated that EJS helped them enhance the safety of victims of DV endorsed a variety of mechanisms through which these benefits were incurred. The most frequently endorsed items are included below:

EJS helps me enhance victim safety by...

- obtaining greater and better factual information for consideration by the fact finder at different stages of criminal and civil proceedings
- identifying and referring victims to appropriate resources, including culturally appropriate services
- identifying cultural considerations and helping victims to improve their access to justice by overcoming potential cultural barriers
- examining my personal 'blinding preferences' [implicit biases] and avoiding to the extent possible inappropriate actions or inactions based on these preferences
- enforcing relevant federal and state gun laws
- making and enforcing decisions that help victims to evaluate and minimise danger from an abuser and to secure resources to promote the safety and stability of non-abusive family members.

The fourth question asked the participants if the training had helped hold batterers more accountable and encourage changes in batterer behaviour. Two-thirds of judges indicated improvements in this area. Respondents indicated that EJS helped them with batterer accountability and change in a number of ways, as follows:

EJS helps me hold batterers more accountable for their behaviour by...

- differentiating how persons might use violence in different contexts, including for example classic battering (based on power and control) vs. fighting back as a defensive measure
- identifying cultural considerations and taking culture into account when structuring appropriate sentences or civil remedies
- making and enforcing decisions that impose appropriate sanctions on batterers and overseeing their compliance with the court's orders
- ordering batterers to participate in appropriate intervention programmes and overseeing their compliance with the court's orders through review hearings or other enforcement mechanisms

Summary

This article provides an overview of the 20-year development, implementation and evaluation of a national judicial education programme entitled 'Enhancing Judicial Skills in Domestic Violence Cases' (EJS) that was developed by the National Council of Juvenile and Family Court Judges together with Futures Without Violence. Initial evaluations demonstrated consistently positive ratings of the faculty and programme. There was little information about how judges utilised the educational opportunity upon their return to their work, so an additional evaluation was undertaken. Judges from diverse courts and jurisdictions across the US completed the pre-workshop questionnaire. A follow-up questionnaire six month after programme completion was submitted by a representative sample of 134 judges.

Judges' ratings of their competence with domestic violence cases indicated that they learned a great deal from the programme and saw themselves in a leadership role in their home jurisdiction as a result of their participation. Post-programme, some judges revised their estimate of their pre-programme knowledge - that is, with hindsight, they realised they did not know as much as they thought prior to the programme. The majority of judges surveyed indicated that the programme helped them in their work and suggested specific areas in which they felt changes had taken place - on the bench, in their interactions with peers and with their work in the community.

Limitations

There are several limitations in the evaluation of this judicial education programme. The programme needs to be understood in the context of US courts and the growing expectations to deal effectively with a high volume of domestic violence cases. There was no comparison group of judges who did not attend or attended an alternative programme. The evaluation is based on judges' self-reported views and changes reflected on after the programme and not based on third party objective measures of change. Approximately one-quarter of the judges responded to the requests for follow-up information about the impact of the programme. The evaluation did not differentiate judges based on prior training, length of experience on the bench or the nature of their court assignment. Judicial education is best understood as part of a career long commitment to professional development which may vary according to judges' interests, jurisdictional requirements, and specialisations, so it is difficult to evaluate a one-time programme such as this four-day intensive and specialised programme on domestic violence. Finally, it is important to keep the findings of this evaluation in context. We evaluated self-reported gains in knowledge, attitudes, self-efficacy, and some behaviour, but ultimately the extent to which this programme is having an impact on the experiences of victims, perpetrators, and children who come before the court is unknown.

Future directions

This article highlights the importance of judicial education on domestic violence across different criminal and civil court proceedings. Future research could evaluate different kinds of training methods and differentiate the impact across diverse judges based on experience on the bench, court assignment and urban versus rural court jurisdictions. Ideally, it would be good to track the impact of training over time and the benefits of more in-depth programmes. For example, the EJS host organisations also provide advanced training for judges, 'Continuing Judicial Skills in Domestic Violence Cases', that provide continued education for judges on civil, family, or criminal court assignments and on specialised topics, such as supervised visitation and exchange and batterer accountability. Examples of these expanded trainings are available at http://www.njidv.org/. There is very limited research on evaluating judicial education beyond satisfaction by the consumers, so this study provides a more in-depth method of assessing the value of programmes. There are many gaps in terms of understanding what works for whom in terms of these programmes.

There could also be improvements in our research methodology to produce a larger sample at follow-up to identify patterns of progress better. For example, in this research, judges who did not find the EJS experience positive might have been less likely to participate in follow-up surveys. It might be useful to shorten the survey and explore incentives for participation. Brief checklists could be developed based on current open-ended answers (e.g. wishes for additional content such as cyber-stalking, mental health). Nonetheless, the data collected in the evaluation of EJS provided a rich opportunity to research judges' attitudes and learning styles in general. Future evaluation efforts should consider obtaining consent to use these data for a variety of purposes beyond programme evaluation (e.g. basic research purposes on judicial attitudes about domestic violence and required court or community interventions).

Conclusion

This article highlights the implementation and evaluation of the EJS. Since 1999, 3556 judges from across the US have benefited from the programme and provided positive feedback. The key components of the four-day programme focus on common dilemmas in domestic violence cases, dynamics with victims, perpetrators and their children, fact-finding, access to justice, fairness and cultural issues and decision-making as well as judicial vicarious trauma and compassion fatigue. A more in-depth evaluation on a diverse group of judges in terms of tenure, demographics, and court assignments who attended the programme between 2006 and 2010 indicated positive changes on a six-month follow-up. The majority of judges identified specific benefits and behaviour changes in the areas of access to justice, judicial leadership, victim safety and batterer accountability as a result of participating in the programme. The programme supports the need for ongoing judicial professional development and more research about the needs of different judges at various stages of their careers who deal with domestic violence cases.

Acknowledgments

The authors wish to express their appreciation to the initial leaders of EJS for the curriculum development and implementation in 1999 – Michael Runner and Billie-Lee Dunford Jackson. Dr. Julia Storberg-Walker (formerly of North Carolina State University and now Associate Professor and a Co-Director of the Executive Leadership Programme at George Washington University) played an important role in helping to design the evaluation and measures and to facilitate the initial data collection. The measures used in this study are available to other researchers from the senior author. More information about the curriculum and other judicial programming is available from Danielle Pugh-Markie, Program Director, Program Development and Judicial Engagement, National Council of Juvenile and Family Court Judges, P.O. Box 8970, Reno, NV 89507

Disclosure statement

The first three and last authors are all trainers with the judicial education programme described in this paper. The fourth author is an employee of Futures without Violence and the fifth author is an employee of the National Council of Juvenile and Family Court Judges. These two organisations jointly developed the programme and are the recipients of the grant to deliver it. This work was supported by the Office on Violence Against Women, U.S. Department of Justice (Grant No. 2008- TA- AX- KO38).

Funding

The EJS programme and evaluation was supported by Grant No. 2015-TA-AX-K026 awarded by the Office on Violence Against Women, US Department of Justice.

References

Agnew-Brune, C., Moracco, K. E., Person, C. J., & Bowling, J. M. (2017). Domestic violence protective orders: A qualitative examination of judges' decision-making processes. *Journal of Interpersonal Violence, 32*, 1921–1942.

Armytage, L. (2015). Educating judges: Where to from here? *Journal of Dispute Resolution, 2015* (1), 167–174.

Benton, D., & Sheldon-Sherman, J. A. (2015). What judges want and need: User-friendly foundations for effective judicial education. *Journal of Dispute Resolution, 2015*(1), 23–39.

Black, M. C. (2011). *Intimate partner violence and adverse health consequences: Implications for clinicians*. Atlanta, GA: Centers for Disease Control and Prevention.

Department of Justice Office of Justice Programs, National Institute of Justice. (2009). *Practical implications of current domestic violence research: For law enforcement, prosecutors and judges*. Retrieved from http://www.ojp.usdoj.gov/nij/topics/crime/intimate-partner-violence/practical-implications-research/ch7/dv-court-traits.htm

Department of Justice, Office on Violence Against Women. (2016). *The 2016 biennial report to Congress on the effectiveness of grant programs under the Violence Against Women Act*. Retrieved from http://muskie.usm.maine.edu/vawamei/attachments/congressreports/2016RTC_MASTER_12.19.16.pdf

Goldring, J. (2003). The reflective judge: Aims and content of judicial education. *Journal of Judicial Administration, 12*, 216–222.

Gover, A. R., Brank, E. M., & MacDonald, J. M. (2007). A specialized domestic violence court in South Carolina: An example of procedural justice. *Violence Against Women, 13*, 603–626.

Helling, J. A. (2005). *Specialized criminal domestic violence courts*. Minnesota Center Against Violence and Abuse. Retrieved from http://www.bwjp.org/assets/documents/pdfs/specialized_criminal_domestic_violence_courts.pdf

Jaffe, P. G., Crooks, C. V., Dunford-Jackson, B. L., & Town, M. (2003). Vicarious trauma in judges: The personal challenge of dispensing justice. *Juvenile and Family Court Journal, 54*, 1–9.

Keilitz, S. (2004). *Specialization of domestic violence case management in the courts: A national survey*. Williamsburg, VA: National Center for State Courts.

Kolb, D. A. (2014). *Experiential learning: Experience as the source of learning and development*. Indianapolis: FT press.

Labriola, M., Bradley, S., O'Sullivan, C. S., Rempel, M., & Moore, S. (2012). *National portrait of domestic violence courts*. New York: Centre for Court Innovation.

Martinson, D., & Jackson, M. (2017). Family violence and evolving judicial roles: Judges as equality guardians in family law cases. *Canadian Journal of Family Law, 30*, 11–70.

Mendez, M. A. (2004). 'Crawford v. Washington': A critique. *Stanford Law Review, 57*, 569–610.

Ostrom, B., & Kauder, N. (1997). *Examining the work of state courts, 1997: A national perspective from the Court Statistics Project*. Williamsburg, VA: National Center for State Courts.

Bureau of Justice Statistics, & United States; Smith, E. L., Durose, M. R., & Langan, P. A. (2008). *State court processing of domestic violence cases*. Washington, DC: US Departmet of Justice, Office of Justice Programs.

Smith, S. G., Chen, J., Basile, K. C., Gilbert, L. K., Merrick, M. T., Patel, N., ... Jain, A. (2017). *The National intimate partner and sexual violence survey (NISVS): 2010–2012 state report*. Atlanta, GA: National Center for Injury Prevention and Control, Centers for Disease Control and Prevention.

World Health Organization. (2014). Violence against women. Retrieved from http://www.who.int/mediacentre/factsheets/fs239/en/

Specialised domestic violence courts in Canada and the United States: Key factors in prioritising safety for women and children

Jennifer Koshan

ABSTRACT

This paper reviews the response of specialised domestic violence courts in Canada and the United States to contact disputes where there are allegations of domestic violence. It begins with a discussion of legal reforms responding to domestic violence in Canada and the United States, including the different types of DV courts and their rationales, key features, merits and drawbacks. Evaluations of Integrated DV courts in the United States and Canada are then reviewed. The research shows that although IDV courts hold more promise to deal with contact disputes given their inclusion of family law matters, there are few studies analysing the impact of IDV courts on these disputes, and some suggest these courts may actually increase contact and hence the potential for safety issues to arise. The final section discusses the strengths and weaknesses of IDV courts in relation to contact disputes, identifying the factors that make these specialised courts more or less successful in prioritising safety and minimising harm for women and children.

Introduction

Extensive legislative, administrative and judicial reforms have occurred in Canada and the United States since the 1970s and 1980s to respond to the legal treatment of domestic violence cases.[1] Many of these reforms were spurred by women's groups and anti-violence activists, who called on government actors to treat domestic violence as a public rather than private issue and to take it more seriously (Coker, 2001; Currie, 1990; Epstein, 1999; Moore, 2009; Sack, 2004; Schneider, 2000). Justice system personnel also undertook their own initiatives to develop strategies for responding to the particular challenges of domestic violence cases in their courtrooms (Mazur & Aldrich, 2003; Tutty, Ursel, and Lemaitre, 2008).

Most recently, these reforms have included the establishment of specialised domestic violence courts ('DV courts') in Canada and the United States (Labriola, Bradley, O'Sullivan, Rempel, and Moore, 2009; Ursel, Tutty, & Lemaistre, 2008). The latest development – which has been utilised primarily in the United States – is integrated domestic violence courts ('IDV courts'), where criminal matters are heard alongside family and civil matters in a one judge-one family model that is intended to provide a more holistic approach to cases involving domestic violence issues (Hyman & Aldrich, 2011; Koshan, 2014).

In spite of these reforms, however, there continue to be multiple instances each year where women and children are injured and killed by abusive men in North America, just as in other jurisdictions. In many of the cases there was justice system involvement and no contact orders were either in place or had been considered by the courts (see, e.g., *Lenahan (Gonzales), Jessica et al. v United States*, Inter-American Commission on Human Rights, No 80/11; Turpel-Lafond, 2009, 2012). To take a recent Canadian example, two young girls, Chloe and Aubrey Berry, were allegedly killed by their father, Andrew Berry, on Christmas Day in 2017 in British Columbia. In 2013, amendments to British Columbia family laws took effect, providing for explicit consideration of family violence – including coercive control – in disputes about allocating parenting time (*Family Law Act*, Statutes of British Columbia 2011, ch. 25). Yet questions have been raised about whether the judge who heard the case between Andrew Berry and his ex-partner Sarah Cotton adequately accounted for the context of family violence in permitting Berry to have contact with his daughters (*Cotton v Berry* [2017] BCSC 907). Commentators argue that the case is part of a broader pattern of judges failing to give full force to the new law by continuing to minimise family violence and to over-value shared parenting (Boyd & Lindy, 2016; Calder & Boyd, 2018). Given that the law was substantively strong on family violence as a factor in parenting disputes, these deaths squarely raise the issue of what legal procedures for resolving contact disputes have the best potential to protect women and children, and whether specialised courts can make a difference in this regard.

This paper reviews the response of specialised domestic violence courts in Canada and the United States to contact disputes where there are allegations of domestic violence. The next part discusses the different types of DV courts in Canada and the United States, along with their rationales, their key features, and the merits and drawbacks of these courts. Because most DV courts focus on criminal matters, contact disputes have not been their specific focus; IDV courts hold more promise for dealing with these disputes given their inclusion of family law matters and their focus on victim safety and offender accountability. Evaluations of IDV courts in Canada and the United States are reviewed in the following part, focusing on the extent to which these courts deal with contact disputes and how they are handled. The research shows that there are few studies analysing the impact of IDV courts on these disputes, and those studies that do so suggest that IDV courts may actually increase contact between the parties, and hence the potential for safety issues to arise. The final part discusses the strengths and weaknesses of IDV courts in relation to contact disputes, identifying the factors that have made these courts more or less successful in prioritising safety and minimising harm for women and children who are victims of domestic abuse. I also identify the need for future research that is more attentive to the ways in which specialised domestic violence courts deal with contact disputes and whether they may have unintended consequences in this area, for example, for members of marginalised groups.

Overview of specialised DV courts in Canada and the United States[2]

As noted by Keilitz, Guerrero, Jones and Rubio (2000, p. 2), 'Courts are the newcomers in most jurisdictions' when it comes to institutional reforms to improve the justice system's response to domestic violence. Justice system reforms in Canada and the United States beginning in the 1970s and 1980s focused on the criminal realm and included the adoption of mandatory arrest, charging and prosecution laws and policies, as well as the development of specialised police, prosecution and probation units (Brown, 2000; Sack, 2004; Tsai, 2000; Tutty, Ursel, & Douglas, 2008). In Canada, there have also been reforms to the *Criminal Code* to include the domestic violence context as an aggravating factor for sentencing (*Criminal Code* 1985, s. 718.2(a)(ii)), although domestic violence itself is still not the subject of a specific criminal offence. In the United States, criminal laws are enacted at the state level and so they vary considerably in the context of domestic violence. The federal *Violence Against Women Act*, first passed in 1994 and most recently reauthorised in 2013, created new penalties for inter-state domestic violence crimes and a new civil rights remedy for domestic violence.

Starting in the 1970s, many jurisdictions in the United States and later, Canada, also enacted legislation providing for civil protection orders in domestic violence cases (Busby, Koshan, & Wiegers, 2008; Sack, 2004). In Canada, civil protection order legislation may also require death reviews where individuals are killed in circumstances of family violence (see, e.g. Alberta's *Children First Act* 2013), and in other jurisdictions such reviews are implemented independently of civil protection order legislation (see, e.g. Ontario, 2015; Turpel-Lafond, 2009, 2012). In the United States, the *Violence Against Women Act* 1994 provides for inter-state enforcement of civil protection orders, which is only available in some Canadian jurisdictions (Neilson, 2015).

Family law reforms in both jurisdictions have included amendment of laws to require consideration of domestic violence as a factor relevant to the best interests of children for the purposes of resolving parenting disputes and child protection matters (Goodmark, 2004; Jaffe, Crooks, & Bala, 2008; MacDowell, 2011; Nixon, Tutty, Weaver-Dunlop, & Walsh, 2007). Definitions of domestic violence differ in family law statutes, but as noted above, jurisdictions such as British Columbia have defined domestic violence broadly to include psychological, emotional and financial abuse, coercive control, threats to other persons, pets or property, and children's 'direct or indirect exposure to family violence' (*Family Law Act* 2011, s. 1).

Specialised DV courts first developed in North America in the 1990s, in part because the earlier wave of domestic violence reforms had created a significant increase in the volume of cases (Center for Court Innovation, 2009; Tutty et al., 2008). This suggests that one of the rationales for specialised DV courts was efficiency (Keilitz et al., 2000; Moore, 2009; Shaffer, 2004). It is significant that particular judges and other justice system personnel led the development of DV courts, sometimes in collaboration with community actors (Mazur & Aldrich, 2003; Tutty et al., 2008; Wolf, Aldrich, & Moore, 2004). DV courts were also created to respond to the perceived problems in how the courts and other justice personnel had traditionally dealt with domestic violence cases, and to better respond to the complex and unique challenges these cases presented, including low reporting rates, high rates of withdrawal of charges and prosecutions, and high rates of recidivism (Bennett, 2012; Tsai, 2000; Ursel et al., 2008). Specialised courts are intended to provide a more coordinated, collaborative response to domestic violence, characterised by better informed and more consistent decision-making and the provision of victim support and offender treatment services (Keilitz et al., 2000; Labriola, et al., 2009; Moore, 2009; Tutty et al., 2008).

There is much diversity in the jurisdiction of specialised DV courts. There are numerous civil protection order courts or dockets in the United States (Center for Court Innovation, 2011a; Sack, 2002; Shelton, 2007), but this form of specialisation does not exist in Canada, where applications for protection orders are made in front of non-specialised magistrates, justices of the peace or family or superior court judges (Busby et al., 2008). In both jurisdictions, civil protection orders typically include provisions restraining the respondent's contact with the victim and potentially with the children of their relationship, although provision may also be made for access to the children, sometimes to be arranged through or supervised by a third party. Civil protection orders may also provide exclusive occupation of the family home to the victim and children, and require the respondent not to attend at specified places such as the victim's workplace or the children's school. Breaches of civil protection orders may result in the arrest and conviction of the respondent, but many studies indicate that breaches tend to be under-enforced, especially where civil protection order legislation is not dealt with by specialised courts (see, e.g. Busby et al., 2008; Koshan & Wiegers, 2007; Neilson, 2015; Sack, 2002).

The most common type of specialised DV court in both Canada and the United States is the criminal DV court, with over 50 such courts in Canada and over 200 in the United States (Cissner, Labriola, & Rempel, 2013; Quann, 2006; Tutty et al., 2008). Criminal DV courts normally have screening processes that allow appropriate cases to be identified, after which they are dealt with in dedicated courtrooms on a separate docket from other criminal cases by specially trained judges, prosecutors, probation officers and other staff (Keilitz et al., 2000; Labriola et al., 2009; Moore, 2009; Sack, 2002; Ursel et al., 2008; Weber, 2000). In the United States, DV court judges are usually specialised and dedicated to DV courtrooms, whereas in Canada DV courts are more likely to have different judges rotating through the court to avoid concerns about impartiality. Many of these courts have the mandate to intervene in domestic violence matters as early as possible, and encourage victim participation by providing information, support, and referrals to other services (Labriola et al., 2009; Tutty et al., 2008, 2008).

Criminal DV courts may impose no contact orders as a condition of bail or sentencing, and in Canada, as a condition of a peace bond, which is a diversion option used by some DV courts that allows the defendant to avoid criminal conviction where they promise to 'keep the peace and be of good behaviour' (*Criminal Code* 1985, s. 810; Tutty & Koshan, 2013). In addition to the usual enforcement mechanisms for breaches of criminal no contact orders, many DV courts monitor defendants' compliance with such orders, as well as with conditions to attend batterer treatment programmes. In the United States, this monitoring is typically conducted by judges, whereas in Canada, it is normally conducted by probation officers (Center for Court Innovation, 2011b; Labriola et al., 2009; Tutty, Ursel, and Dougas, 2008).

Another form of specialised court is the unified family court (UFC), which responds to the federal nature of jurisdiction in Canada and the United States and the resultant fragmenting of family law matters into different levels of court. UFCs consolidate jurisdiction in one court to deal with a range of family law matters, but do not typically include powers to hear criminal matters, nor do they specialise in domestic violence issues (Dunford-Jackson, Frederick, Hart, & Hofford, 1998-1999; Evaluation Division,

2009). IDV courts in the United States grew out of the movement towards UFCs and also built on the American experience with criminal DV courts (Aldrich & Kluger, 2010; Katz & Rempel, 2011; Picard-Fritsche, 2011).

IDV courts have jurisdiction to hear criminal, family and civil protection matters in one setting, in recognition of the problems associated with having multiple proceedings in different forums dealing with the range of legal issues that arise in domestic violence cases. These problems include the lack of information sharing between civil, family and criminal courts, which can lead to inconsistent and conflicting decisions and orders that can cause confusion and may affect the safety of victims and children (Bennett, 2012; Dalley, 2013; Epstein, 1999; Jackson & Martinson, 2015; Katz & Rempel, 2011; Neilson, 2012). Conflicting orders may also flow from the different and often contradictory objectives of various courts, from family courts' focus on the best interests of children (which may favour maximising contact between parents and children), to criminal courts' focus on protection of victims and children (which may favour more limited contact) (Birnbaum, Bala, & Jaffe, 2014; Cleveland, 2010; Hester, 2009; Martinson, 2012). Perpetrators may take advantage of the existence of multiple forums to bring applications in different courts, perpetuating harassment and abuse of their partners. Fragmented proceedings also result in access to justice concerns, including multiple court appearances, the requirement to re-tell one's story several times, increased costs to the parties and the justice system, and delay in the resolution of disputes, particularly family matters when criminal cases are prioritised (Bala, Birnbaum, and Martinson, 2010; Breger, Elkins, & Fosbinder, 2010-2011; Hyman and Aldrich, 2011; Levy, Ross, & Guthrie, 2008; Martinson, 2012; Mosher, 2015; Neilson, 2012; Vollens, 2010).

As is the case for DV courts more generally, IDV courts are said to focus on the goals of victim safety and offender accountability, with the provision of victim support services and mandated offender treatment as key features. Children are often provided with independent counsel as well (Cissner, Picard-Fritsche, & Puffett, 2011; Ontario Court of Justice, n.d.). According to a recent study, IDV courts have four main objectives:

(a) a more holistic and multi-disciplinary approach to family problems;
(b) more effective judicial monitoring to increase accountability for the offenders and compliance with court orders;
(c) improved judicial decision-making as a result of the judge having more information about the family; and
(d) better access to and coordination of support services (i.e., legal and social services) for the victims and children. (Birnbaum, Saini, & Bala, 2017).

The one judge-one family model may also assist with the management of litigation-related conflict (Bala et al., 2010).

There are now dozens of IDV courts in the United States, mostly concentrated in New York state, and one in Toronto, Canada (Center for Court Innovation, 2009; Ontario Court of Justice, n.d.). It must be emphasised that despite the principle of 'one courtroom for all related cases' (Center for Court Innovation, 2011c), not all IDV courts have jurisdiction over all legal issues that arise in domestic violence cases. For example, few IDV courts hear child protection matters, and some may only hear minor criminal matters (Koshan, 2014; Ontario Court of Justice, n.d.). In terms of process, some IDV courts have separate intake units, while others hear matters that are transferred from criminal, civil and/or family courts based on eligibility criteria. Once in the IDV court, criminal and family matters are heard in sequence, ideally on the same day with criminal matters heard first (Hyman & Aldrich, 2011; Koshan, 2014).

Most assessments of DV and IDV courts have been undertaken with a focus on evaluations of specific courts, with little comparative analysis of different court models and their outcomes (for exceptions, see Cissner et al., 2013; Tutty et al., 2008). Before turning to these evaluations in the next section, it is useful to review some of the overarching concerns that have been raised with respect to DV and IDV courts.

While victim safety and offender accountability are widely stated as the goals of DV and IDV courts, it is often unclear how these goals are defined or measured (Koshan, 2014). To the extent that offender accountability is related to compliance with court orders such as those mandating batterer treatment programmes (Center for Court Innovation, 2005), it must be recognised that there is debate about whether such programs are effective (Tutty et al., 2008). It has also been argued that the focus of DV and IDV courts on batterer treatment programmes may displace resources that would otherwise be available to victims, posing a possible challenge to the goal of victim safety (Bennett, 2012). Another concern is that there has been no analysis of the impact of DV and IDV courts in responding to unintended consequences associated with the implementation of zero tolerance charging and prosecution policies and the over-enforcement of child protection laws. An assessment of the impact of DV and IDV courts on those who are racialised, poor, Indigenous, or otherwise marginalised is also largely absent from the literature (Koshan, 2014). Some literature does raise potential problems with segregating domestic violence matters into specialised courts, arguing that this may result in the isolation, marginalisation and privatisation of domestic violence (Koshan & Wiegers, 2007; MacDowell, 2011; Weissman, 2000-2001).

More specific to IDV courts, concerns have been raised that increased information sharing amongst justice system and service providers may increase the likelihood that victims of domestic violence will be subject to over-zealous child protection proceedings and other adverse family law outcomes (Epstein, 1999; Levey, Steketee, & Keilitz, 2001; MacDowell, 2011). Another concern is that victims may lose control over whether to participate in criminal proceedings when they are consolidated with family law matters (Dunford-Jackson et al., 1998-1999; MacDowell, 2011). Due process concerns have also been identified with respect to the rights of the accused, given that they will appear in front of the same judge for family and criminal matters. The fear is that adverse findings made in family matters will negatively influence criminal liability, where the standard of proof should be higher (Dunford-Jackson et al., 1998-1999; MacDowell, 2011). In light of studies showing that dual charging has been one of the consequences of criminal zero tolerance policies, these due process concerns extend to women who are criminally charged in circumstances where they were resisting violence (Koshan, 2014). The shortage of lawyers with sufficient expertise in both family and criminal issues is also seen as a possible challenge for parties in IDV courts (Dunford-Jackson et al., 1998-1999; Levey et al., 2001).

Of all the specialised DV courts, IDV courts are the most likely to deal with contact disputes because of their jurisdiction over family law matters. The next section will explore the evaluations of IDV courts, focusing on how these courts have responded to and what impact they have had on disputes about contact, and more generally on their potential to protect the safety of women and children.

Evaluations of IDV courts in the United States and Canada

Manhattan IDV court

In the fall of 2011, the author undertook a qualitative study of the IDV court in Manhattan, New York. This particular court was selected because New York has been a leader in the IDV court movement, with a large number of IDV courts and evaluations in that State. New York is also the base of the Center for Court Innovation, which has been involved in the set-up and evaluation of several DV and IDV courts. The author's primary interest in pursuing this project was to evaluate the impact of the Manhattan IDV court on access to justice, defined in the literature as the 'obligation to make simple, rapid, adequate and impartial…recourses available, without discrimination, for the purpose of investigating and punishing [violence against women] and providing redress' (Inter-American Commission on Human Rights, 2007, para. 5). A further interest was to explore the extent to which IDV courts may assist in avoiding some of the unintended consequences of the criminal justice response to domestic violence, as well as the systemic impact of the court on the twin goals of victim safety and offender accountability. Contact disputes were not the focus of the study, but some of the findings are relevant to that context (Koshan, 2014).

The Manhattan IDV court has been in operation since 2007, and like most IDV courts, uses a one judge-one family model. The court has a dedicated judge, as well as specialised prosecutors, a resource coordinator, a court attorney, and victim and children's advocates. The court sits five days a week in the criminal court building in lower Manhattan, and hears non-jury criminal matters and family law matters excluding child protection cases. The study's evaluation was based on courtroom observations, as well as interviews with advocates for victims, offenders and children and with justice system and institutional personnel (not including the prosecution service or police, who did not respond to requests for interviews). The findings were also compared to the outcomes of evaluations of several other IDV courts in New York, which are discussed in the next section.

The interviewees identified several advantages that IDV courts hold over the more traditional fragmented approach to dealing with domestic violence issues. These include the avoidance of inconsistent orders; better logistical coordination and access to information for the parties and justice system actors; better communication and collaboration between the players; access to justice advantages for litigants, including less delay and repetition of evidence and more accommodation of work and other scheduling concerns; the enhanced availability of services for victims, offenders, and children; greater participation of victims and children in the proceedings, often due to the presence of advocates; better monitoring of offenders, including their compliance with batterer treatment programmes; and overall an increased sensitivity to domestic violence issues with more mindful outcomes. Most pertinent to contact disputes were the observations that the presence of independent children's advocates provided the court with a fuller picture when considering and monitoring visitation. More generally, monitoring of the offender, which is conducted by the judge on a regular basis following disposition, was seen as holding him accountable and enhancing the safety of his ex-partner and children (Koshan, 2014, pp. 1020–1021).

There were also concerns raised by the some of the interviewees about the IDV court's handling of cases including the court's minimal impact on recidivism, reporting rates, and the police response to domestic violence (including dual arrests); the court's relative lack of expertise in some areas and its failure to deal with child protection issues due to limited resources; the lack of expertise of some attorneys, particularly on family law matters; clients' lack of basic information about the process; insufficient security and privacy for litigants and their advocates; and the concern that information seepage between criminal and family matters may facilitate litigation harassment in some circumstances, or impact due process rights. It was also noted that the court is not keeping statistics that would allow an assessment of its impact on marginalised litigants; anecdotally it was said that African American and LGBTQ litigants appear to be underrepresented on the court's docket. In relation to contact disputes, the shortage of supervised visitation sites was identified as a concern, and the court was said to sometimes fail to consider domestic violence seriously as a factor relevant to limiting batterers' visitation rights. Some interviewees noted the pressure to settle issues, including visitation, but also acknowledged that the court often took a gradual approach in allowing contact, particularly when moving from supervised to non-supervised contact, with regular monitoring (Koshan, 2014, pp. 1022–1024).

In terms of recommendations, interviewees suggested more resources for intensive, ongoing training for judges, advocates, police, forensic evaluators, and supervised visitation providers; certification and better oversight of supervised visitation sites; more comprehensive services, including legal representation for protection order petitions; and more ongoing collaboration, outreach, reflection, and evaluation by and of IDV courts (Koshan, 2014, p. 1025).

Other IDV court evaluations in the United States

It has been argued that comparison of different IDV courts is challenging, as each court 'has a unique mandate' and may have different eligibility criteria and processes (Birnbaum et al., 2014, 133). Many evaluation studies use qualitative methods, and while this approach may be useful in identifying participants' experience of the process, it offers a partial perspective (Birnbaum et al., 2014; Saini, Birnbaum, & Bala, 2016). Some studies evaluate IDV courts using quantitative methods, but few have employed control groups for comparison purposes, and studies differ in the measures they choose to assess court effectiveness (Birnbaum et al., 2014). With these cautions in mind, this section will review other IDV court evaluations in the United States with a view to identifying the lessons they offer with respect to contact disputes.

A number of other evaluations of New York IDV courts have been published and confirm many of the observations made by the interviewees in the Manhattan IDV court study based on both quantitative and qualitative research methods (Cissner et al., 2011; Cissner, Picard-Fritsche, & Rempel, 2014; Katz & Rempel, 2011; Levy et al., 2008; Picard-Fritsche, 2011; Picard-Fritsche, Cissner, & Puffett, 2011). These studies support the finding that IDV courts have advantages in reducing inconsistent orders; improving access to information, communication, collaboration, and services; and some access to justice benefits. Qualitative studies show that a majority of victims believed the IDV court process was generally fair, compared to a minority of offenders, with levels of satisfaction for both groups (and their lawyers) often dependent on court outcomes. Concerns were expressed, particularly by offenders, about information sharing between family and criminal matters and the inability to judge-shop. Victims were more likely to see the advantages of the one judge-one family model, and although this was not specific to contact disputes, it seems reasonable to assume that information from criminal matters would be likely to have some impact on disallowing contact or requiring it to be supervised. In contrast, some of the quantitative studies show a higher degree of settlements in IDV courts as compared to non-IDV courts, which may have negative repercussions for contact disputes where victims feel pressured to settle. Lack of resources and the need for enhanced services were also identified as challenges for IDV courts in these studies, which may have implications for contact disputes as well (Koshan, 2014, pp. 1025–1028).

No evaluations of IDV courts in the United States directly examine the impact of these courts on contact disputes. According to a recent review of the literature by Birnbaum et al. (2017), only two studies of American IDV courts include any results on family law outcomes (Coll & Stewart, 2007; Katz & Rempel, 2011).

Coll and Stewart's report evaluates Idaho's Ada County Family Violence Court. Unlike some other IDV courts, the Ada County court's one judge-one family model includes child protection matters as well as other family law and misdemeanour criminal issues, and focuses on treatment for battering and substance abuse with court coordination and monitoring (Coll & Stewart, 2007, pp. 2–3). The evaluation used quantitative and qualitative methods, with the latter consisting of exit surveys and interviews of the participants and justice system stakeholders. It found that 71 per cent of participants reported a reduction in conflict with the other party, including a 48 per cent reduction in conflict between parents about visitation, a 25 per cent decrease in fighting during exchanges, and a 25 per cent increase in the ability to trust and reason with the other parent. Parents also believed their children were safer when they were with the other parent after the programme than pre-programme (Coll & Stewart, 2007, p. 38), which was confirmed by data showing that participants were less likely to have new criminal charges or protection orders than persons in a comparison group (Coll & Stewart, 2007, p. 45). More specifically, at intake, 67 per cent of participants had violent criminal charges, 39 per cent were subject to protection orders, 13 per cent had charges for violating no contact orders, and 10 per cent had violated protection orders. At the time of programme exit, these percentages had all dropped to zero (Coll & Stewart, 2007, p. 56). This finding is consistent with that reported by Schlueter, Wicklund, Adler, Owen, and Halvorsen (2011), who found that an IDV court in Vermont had a positive impact on recidivism for domestic violence and other violence offences. Overall, Coll and Stewart conclude that 'Case management – along with coordinated treatment programs and the involvement of the criminal justice system – may be a key strategy to help families recover from domestic violence, substance abuse, and child maltreatment issues' (2007, p. 55).

Katz and Rempel's report concerns case outcomes in nine New York IDV courts with similar jurisdiction to the Manhattan IDV court, and compares these outcomes to cases in non-IDV courts using quantitative methods. They found that family law matters took almost twice as long to resolve and involved almost twice as many court appearances in IDV courts than in comparison cases in non-IDV courts. Even discounting the time it takes to transfer cases to IDV courts, they still took longer to resolve (Katz & Rempel, 2011, p. 10). This finding is consistent with that reported by Rickard (2011), who found that protection orders took one month longer to obtain in IDV courts as compared to matrimonial civil courts in New York City's five boroughs. While these results may be explained by the fact that IDV courts prioritise criminal matters, they may still have negative implications for the safety of victims and children (Rickard, 2011, p. 13).

In Katz and Rempel's study, cases involving custody and visitation issues were less likely to be dismissed in IDV courts (4 per cent) than those in non-IDV courts (17 per cent). Moreover, cases heard in IDV courts were more likely to be settled or withdrawn than cases in non-IDV courts, with a difference of 31 per cent to 22 per cent respectively in cases involving custody and visitation (Katz & Rempel, 2011, p. 11). The authors interpret this finding as possibly showing that 'a greater percentage of IDV court litigants achieve a mutually acceptable resolution for the family without a court-imposed decision' (Katz & Rempel, 2011, p. 18). It is also possible to conclude, as I argue above, that victims may feel pressured to settle, which may have negative consequences for contact disputes. However, less than 10 per cent of parties were found to be involved in subsequent family court filings one year after their case was completed (Katz & Rempel, 2011; p. 12; see also Picard-Fritsche et al., 2011). While this result was not dependent on whether their case was resolved in an IDV or non-IDV court, it may support the interpretation that many parties negotiated a mutually satisfactory outcome. In contrast to the Idaho study, the authors found that offenders involved in IDV court proceedings in New York 'were significantly more likely than comparison defendants' to be arrested for violations of protection orders (Katz & Rempel, 2011, p. iv). They interpret this finding to mean that although IDV courts may not have an impact on re-offending *per se*, 'by forging closer relationships between victims and victim advocates or by engaging in closer judicial monitoring of the offenders, it is possible that IDV courts are particularly effective at detecting protection order violations' (Katz & Rempel, 2011, p. 16). A similar conclusion is drawn by Picard-Fritsche et al. (2011) that IDV court processes in Erie County, New York may make victims more willing to report breaches of protection orders.

In their review of many of these studies, Birnbaum et al. note that 'clearly more research is required' about the value of IDV courts, 'particularly about the effects on children and victims of domestic violence.' (2014, pp. 140–141). They make an effort to review these impacts in their evaluation of Toronto's IDV court, which I examine in the next section.

Toronto IDV court

Toronto's IDV court began operations in June 2011 as a pilot project, following consultations between judges, family and criminal lawyers, and members of the local domestic violence professional community. The court was modelled on the New York IDV courts' one judge-one family approach. It operates at the lower court level in the Ontario Court of Justice, which limits its jurisdiction to only summary criminal matters and some family law matters, excluding divorce and matrimonial property issues. Although it has jurisdiction to hear child protection issues, it does not do so at the present time. According to Birnbaum et al., the limited nature of the court's jurisdiction has an impact on the litigants who appear before it, who tend to be persons of limited financial means in predominantly non-marital relationships of relatively short length (2017, p. 624). At first, the consent of all parties was required to participate in the IDV court, but the process has evolved such that cases are now automatically scheduled for IDV court where the same parties are involved in eligible criminal and family law matters. The court has a small catchment area in downtown Toronto, and sits only once every two weeks. It operates with one of two specialised judges, and has other specialised personnel including a dedicated Crown prosecutor, criminal and family legal aid lawyers, a community resource coordinator, and victim/family support workers. Similar to other IDV courts, criminal matters are heard first, followed by family law matters, with use of more informal case conferencing between the judge and lawyers and/or parties (Birnbaum et al., 2014, 2017).

Birnbaum et al.'s evaluation of the Toronto IDV court has been built in from the court's inception. The researchers have engaged in observations of court hearings and stakeholder meetings, interviewed stakeholders and parties involved in the IDV court, and established a baseline set of data for comparison purposes, using family court files with charges related to domestic violence in families including at least one child. They compared the 160 baseline cases to 53 IDV court cases in terms of demographic information, information on criminal and family law outcomes, and variables regarding court process.

The Toronto interviews reveal many of the same perceptions as those of stakeholders and litigants in the American IDV courts. Judges, Crown prosecutors and support workers were generally positive about the value of information sharing and its potential to reveal safety concerns and provide for more thoughtful and holistic decisions, including on custody and access. Lawyers for parents were more likely to voice concerns about information sharing, especially if they represented the offender, based on fears that information that would otherwise be inadmissible would be used by the judge to decide other matters. At the same time some defence lawyers found useful information about the opposing party in family law files, and of the small number of litigants interviewed (two victims and two offenders), most appreciated the benefits of information sharing and thought the process had a positive impact on themselves and their children. Interviewees were generally supportive of the range of services available, but noted that more services for offenders were needed, legal aid and interpretation services were not always adequate, and that service providers might sometimes misuse information obtained about the litigants (e.g. by sharing it with the Crown). Litigants and professional stakeholders believed the process for hearing both criminal and family matters took too long, and noted it could be expensive in light of legal aid coverage limits. For litigants, the process was also incomplete in that child protection and other matters remained to be heard in separate proceedings (Birnbaum et al., 2014, pp. 155–167).

The quantitative data also reveal interesting results. The two samples showed no statistical differences with respect to age, education, or income of the parents, with parents in both samples most likely to have one child (average age 4.91 years). Data on ethnicity, immigration status, Aboriginality, and other factors relevant to possible marginalisation were not available, so – as is the case with American IDV courts – assessment of the impact of the Toronto IDV court on this basis is not possible. The authors indicate that the majority of offenders were male, but exact numbers are not provided (Birnbaum et al., 2017, pp. 625, 629).

In terms of the involvement of agencies and service providers, child protection agencies were more likely to be connected to cases in the IDV court (26 per cent) than in the baseline comparison sample (22 per cent). Supervised access services were also involved in more IDV court cases (8.0 per cent) than in non-IDV court cases (none), but even the IDV court numbers are low. The Office of the Children's Lawyer (OCL) provided legal representation for children in the IDV court sample more often (3.9 per cent) than in the comparison group (1.9 per cent), but both numbers are again quite low, especially in light of the Manhattan IDV court model where an independent children's lawyer is always available. The participation of offenders in a partner assault response programme (PAR) did not significantly differ between the two groups, but completion rates were higher in the IDV court group (35.7 per cent) as compared to the baseline group (2.0 per cent). The authors suggest that compliance rates may be influenced by more monitoring by the same judge in the IDV court. None of the parties in the IDV court sample were self-represented, with legal representation provided either through the parties' own counsel or legal aid criminal or family duty counsel. Duty counsel were not similarly available for litigants in the non-IDV court sample, resulting in a much lower proportion of legal representation (5.6 per cent of applicants and 30.4 per cent of respondents) (Birnbaum et al., 2017, pp. 625–626).

Turning to court procedures and outcomes, there was no significant difference in the number of appearances litigants in the two groups made for family matters, though fewer criminal court appearances were required in IDV court compared to the baseline group. The number of trips to the courthouse was also much lower for IDV court litigants, consistent with the access to justice advantages found for IDV courts in the United States. However, criminal cases in the IDV court took a longer time to disposition (12.18 months on average) than cases in non-IDV courts (9.84 months on average). There were no statistical differences in the outcome of criminal cases, and limited data available at this stage on recidivism (Birnbaum et al., 2017, pp. 627, 629).

Of particular relevance to contact disputes, there was found to be less use of no contact orders and other conditions in the IDV court: in criminal cases, fathers in IDV court proceedings were the subject of restrictive conditions in bail or probation orders in 71 per cent of cases as compared to 91.3 per cent of cases in the comparison group, and mothers had civil protection orders in place in 23.5 per cent of cases in the IDV court as compared to 46.8 per cent of cases in the baseline sample. Parenting arrangements also changed significantly over the course of IDV court proceedings as compared to baseline. In the IDV court group, mothers had sole custody of children in 84.6 per cent of cases when the proceedings commenced, but in only 66.7 per cent of cases at the close of proceedings; for the baseline group the number was steady in the mid-80 per cent range at both the beginning and end of proceedings. Conversely, joint parenting orders increased in the IDV court from 1.9 per cent initially to 13.3 per cent at the stage of the final order, compared to a change of 3.9 per cent to 6.9 per cent in non-IDV court proceedings. IDV court outcomes are thus more favourable to joint parenting orders and less favourable to sole custody for mothers (Birnbaum et al., 2017, pp. 627–628). As the authors put it, 'fathers in the IDVC group were significantly more likely to have increased involvement in their children's lives than in the comparison group' (Birnbaum et al., 2017, p. 628). They suggest that this result could be explained by closer monitoring of parents by service providers, and the possibility that case management leads to better parent-child relationships. However, they also acknowledge the possibility that domestic violence concerns are not being adequately addressed by the IDV court, particularly in terms of children's safety (Birnbaum et al., 2017, p. 629).

Based on how often the opposing party sought variation of arrangements, the study cites a 94.4 per cent compliance rate with custody orders in the IDV court, compared to 83 per cent compliance amongst baseline cases. This finding should be approached with caution, however, as there may be other reasons for not seeking variation of custody orders regardless of whether the opposing party is complying. Access arrangements were subject to much higher levels of variation applications in both groups (92.5 per cent in the IDV court and 94.4 per cent in the non-IDV court). The data also show that, similar to the findings in the United States, family matters are very likely to settle in the IDV court - in fact no family matters went to trial in IDV court during the time period covered by the study. This means that there are no reasons for decision to review in parenting disputes, making it difficult to know how past incidents of domestic violence and fears of future safety risks influenced the outcomes in the Toronto IDV court.

Conclusion: the strengths and weaknesses of IDV courts for contact disputes

Although the evaluations of IDV courts in the United States and Canada reviewed in the previous section are not focused on contact disputes, some conclusions can be drawn about the strengths and weaknesses of the IDV court model for protecting the safety of women and children.

One clear advantage of IDV courts is the fact that one judge follows the family throughout multiple proceedings, allowing for avoidance of conflicting court orders and a better appreciation of changes in the parties' circumstances - such as breach of protection orders - that might create safety issues. This is especially so in light of the monitoring component built in to most IDV courts, which requires parties to appear before the judge even subsequent to disposition, and likely leads to better outcomes in terms of compliance with batterer treatment, supervised visitation, contact, and other orders. A related advantage is the possibility of fuller information about many aspects of the case, including both criminal and family issues, as a means to more fulsome and less inconsistent decision making. This information sharing does have the associated risks of creating due process concerns and the possibility of litigation harassment or over-zealous child welfare involvement. The role of lawyers in mitigating these concerns is significant, and the Toronto model, where duty counsel are available for advice on family and criminal issues, provides an important safeguard in this respect (provided legal aid coverage is sufficient). Independent and funded legal representation for children is also a key component of IDV courts. Providing IDV courts with sufficient resources to deal with child protection matters would also help to ensure that information sharing does not inappropriately disadvantage parents, as the same judge could look at child protection issues in their broader context. Given that it is largely mothers who are poor, racialised, or otherwise marginalised who disproportionately come to the attention of child welfare authorities (see, e.g. Mosoff, Grant, Boyd, & Lindy, 2017), this is an important shortcoming of most current IDV courts. The Ada County IDV court may be a useful model for courts considering the addition of child protection matters. On the other hand, delay is already a significant concern in some IDV courts, and adding child protection matters would likely increase the time to disposition.

Although IDV court judges should have a better sense of the parties' circumstances and the existence of safety issues, the fact that settlement rates are high in these courts precludes the possibility of scrutinising the courts' reasons for decision. Legal representation may again offset the concern that parties are being pressured to settle or that domestic violence concerns are being minimised. However, given the concerns expressed about power dynamics in negotiations in the domestic violence context, vigilance over settlement proceedings is necessary (see, e.g. Beck et al., 2010; Neilson, 2014). This concern is especially evident in Toronto, where the high number of joint parenting outcomes and the low rates of protection orders and other no contact provisions, along with the limited use of supervised access – all in cases involving a history of domestic violence – may raise concerns about whether safety is being prioritised. Were domestic violence victims pressured into settling these matters in favour of the increased involvement of fathers in their children's lives? The small numbers of variation applications in the Toronto and New York studies may mitigate that concern, but as noted there are many reasons for not seeking to vary court orders, including financial and personal costs.

Another concern is the higher rate of breaches of protection orders in some jurisdictions with IDV courts. This may be explained by better monitoring and circumstances that facilitate victim disclosure rather than by a *de facto* increase in the number of breaches, and if that is the case then safety may be enhanced by the identification and prosecution of breaches. However, more research is required to investigate the implications of this outcome. The Ada County IDV court evaluation offers a useful model for such studies, as the qualitative interviews with litigants help to put the quantitative statistics into perspective in terms of women and children's perceptions of safety. The Toronto IDV court will be subject to further qualitative research with parents and children, and it is to be hoped that these interviews will shed more light on the statistical outcomes. More research is also required on the specific impact of IDV courts on parenting disputes, including disputes about contact, and the impact of IDV courts on litigants who are marginalised.

Would an IDV court have made a difference in the case of Chloe and Aubrey Berry? The family law case was unclear whether their father Andrew had been criminally charged, so the parties may have been ineligible for participation in an IDV court even if one was operating in British Columbia (Cotton v Berry, 2017 at para 33). One judge-one family models have also been recommended for family court proceedings more broadly, which may have some of the same advantages in terms of holistic decision making and monitoring of outcomes, and may be more realistic in smaller jurisdictions

(Bala et al., 2010). Jurisdictions without the resources to implement IDV courts may also wish to develop information sharing protocols to avoid inconsistent orders in different courts, while being mindful of the risks of information sharing identified here. While no one court model can ever solve all of the difficulties and risks inherent in domestic violence cases, procedures that involve dedicated and specially trained judges and other court personnel, legal representation and other support services for the parties (including children), and judicial monitoring of compliance with court orders hold some promise for better resolving parenting disputes and better protecting the safety of women and children.

Notes

1. I primarily use the term 'domestic violence' in this paper as that is the term used to refer to specialised courts in this area. My focus is on intimate partner violence, and my language is gendered in recognition of the fact that women are the primary victims and men the primary perpetrators.
2. This section of the paper draws on the literature review conducted for Koshan (2014).

Disclosure statement

No potential conflict of interest was reported by the author.

Funding

The research in this paper was funded in part by a grant from the Social Sciences and Humanities Research Council (Canada).

References

Aldrich, L., & Kluger, J. H. (2010). New York's one judge-one family response to family violence. *Juvenile & Family Court Journal*, *61*, 77–86.
Bala, N., Birnbaum, R., & Martinson, D. (2010). One judge for one family: Differentiated case management for families in continuing conflict. *Canadian Journal of Family Law*, *26*, 395–450.
Beck, C., Walsh, M. E., Ballard, R. H., Holtzworth-Munroe, A., Applegate, A. G., & Putz, J. W. (2010). Divorce mediation with or without legal representation: A focus on intimate partner violence and abuse. *Family Court Review*, *48*, 631–645.
Bennett, D. (2012). *Imagining courts that work for women survivors of violence*. Vancouver: Pivot.
Birnbaum, R., Bala, N., & Jaffe, P. (2014). Establishing Canada's first integrated domestic violence court: Exploring process, outcomes, and lessons learned. *Canadian Journal of Family Law*, *29*, 117–171.
Birnbaum, R., Saini, M., & Bala, N. (2017). Canada's first integrated domestic violence court: Examining family and criminal court outcomes at the Toronto IDVC. *Journal of Family Violence*, *32*, 621–631.

Boyd, S. B., & Lindy, R. (2016). Violence against women and the BC Family Law Act: Early jurisprudence. *Canadian Family Law Quarterly*, *35*, 101–138.

Breger, M., Elkins, L., & Fosbinder, J. (2010-2011). *New York law of domestic violence* (Vol. 1, 2nd ed.). New York: Thomson/West.

Brown, T. (2000). *Charging and prosecution policies in cases of spousal assault: A synthesis of research, academic, and judicial responses*. Ottawa: Department of Justice.

Busby, K., Koshan, J., & Wiegers, W. (2008). Civil domestic violence legislation in the Prairie Provinces: A comparative legal analysis. In J. Ursel, L. M. Tutty, & J. Lemaistre (Eds.), *What's law got to do with it? The law, specialized courts and domestic violence in Canada* (pp. 197–227). Toronto: Cormorant Books.

Calder, G., & Boyd, S. B. (2018, January 3). Comment: Connecting the dots in family-violence cases. *Times Colonist*. Retrieved from: http://www.timescolonist.com/opinion/op-ed/comment-connecting-the-dots-in-family-violence-cases-1.23134672.

Center for Court Innovation. (2005). *Key principles of domestic violence court: Accountability*. New York: Author. Retrieved from https://www.courtinnovation.org/articles/key-principles-domestic-violence-court-accountability?mode=7&type=art&url=research/7/article

Center for Court Innovation. (2009). *A national compendium of domestic violence courts*. New York: Author.

Center for Court Innovation. (2011a). Civil domestic violence courts: Key principles. Retrieved from: https://www.courtinnovation.org/sites/default/files/documents/DV_Civil_Fact_Sheet.pdf.

Center for Court Innovation. (2011b). Criminal domestic violence courts: Key principles. Retrieved from: https://www.courtinnovation.org/sites/default/files/documents/DV_Criminal_Fact_Sheet.pdf.

Center for Court Innovation. (2011c). Integrated domestic violence courts: Key principles. Retrieved from: http://www.courtinnovation.org/sites/default/files/documents/IDV_FACT_SHEET.pdf.

Cissner, A., Labriola, M., & Rempel, M. (2013). *Testing the effects of New York's domestic violence courts: A statewide impact evaluation*. New York: Center for Court Innovation.

Cissner, A., Picard-Fritsche, S., & Puffett, N. K. (2011). *The Suffolk County integrated domestic violence court: Policies, practices, and impacts*. New York: Center for Court Innovation.

Cissner, A., Picard-Fritsche, S., & Rempel, M. (2014). New York State's integrated domestic violence court model: Results from four recent studies. *Domestic Violence Report*, *19*(4), 51–54.

Cleveland, A. (2010). Specialization has the potential to lead to uneven justice: Domestic violence cases in the juvenile & domestic violence courts. *The Modern American*, *6*, 17–24.

Coker, D. (2001). Crime control and feminist law reform in domestic violence law: A critical Review. *Buffalo Criminal Law Review*, *4*, 801–860.

Coll, K., & Stewart, R. (2007). *Ada County family violence court comprehensive evaluation report*. Retrieved from: https://isc.idaho.gov/dv_courts/FVC_Comprehensive_Eval_Report.pdf.

Cotton v Berry (2017) BCSC 907.

Currie, D. (1990). Battered women and the state: From the failure of theory to a theory of failure. *Critical Criminology*, *1*(2), 77–96.

Dalley, J. (2013). One family, one judge: Towards a new model for access to justice for families facing violence in BC. *Appeal*, *18*, 3–19.

Dunford-Jackson, B. L., Frederick, L., Hart, B., & Hofford, M. (1998-1999). Unified family courts: How will they serve victims of domestic violence. *Family Law Quarterly*, *32*, 131–146.

Epstein, D. (1999). Effective intervention in domestic violence cases: Rethinking the roles of prosecutors, judges and the court system. *Yale Journal of Law & Feminism*, *11*, 3–50.

Evaluation Division, Office of Strategic Planning and Performance Management. (2009). *The unified family court summative evaluation: Final report*. Ottawa: Department of Justice Canada.

Goodmark, L. (2004). Law is the answer? Do we know that for sure? Questioning the efficacy of legal interventions for battered women. *St Louis University Public Law Review*, *23*, 7–48.

Hester, M. (2009). The contradictory legal worlds faced by domestic violence victims. In E. Stark & E. S. Buzawa (Eds.), *Violence against women in families and relationships: The family context* (Vol. 2, pp. 127–146). Denver: Praeger.

Hyman, E. M., & Aldrich, L. (2011). Rethinking access to justice: The need for a holistic response to victims of domestic violence. *Women's Rights Law Reporter, 33*, 449–462.

Inter-American Commission on Human Rights. (2007). *Access to justice for women victims of violence in the Americas.* OEA/Ser L/V/II doc 68. Washington: Organization of American States.

Jackson, M., & Martinson, D. (2015). *Risk of future harm: Family violence and information sharing between family and criminal courts.* Vancouver: FREDA Centre for Research on Violence against Women and Children.

Jaffe, P., Crooks, C., & Bala, N. (2008). Domestic violence and child custody disputes: The need for a new framework for the family court. In J. Ursel, L. M. Tutty, & J. Lemaistre (Eds.), *What's law got to do with it? The law, specialized courts and domestic violence in Canada* (pp. 254–271). Toronto: Cormorant Books.

Katz, S., & Rempel, M. (2011). *The impact of integrated domestic violence courts on case outcomes: Results for nine New York State courts.* New York: Center for Court Innovation. Retrieved from https://www.courtinnovation.org/sites/default/files/documents/Nine_IDV.pdf

Keilitz, S., Guerrero, R., Jones, A. M., & Rubio, D. M. (2000). *Specialization of domestic violence case management in courts: A national survey.* Williamsburg: National Center for State Courts.

Koshan, J. (2014). Investigating integrated domestic violence courts: Lessons from New York. *Osgoode Hall Law Journal, 51*, 989–1036.

Koshan, J., & Wiegers, W. (2007). Theorizing civil domestic violence legislation in the context of restructuring: A tale of two Provinces. *Canadian Journal of Women & the Law, 19*, 145–178.

Labriola, M., Bradley, S., O'Sullivan, C. S., Rempel, M., & Moore, S. (2009). *A national portrait of domestic violence courts.* New York: Center for Court Innovation.

Levey, L., Steketee, M. W., & Keilitz, S. L. (2001). *Lessons learned in implementing an integrated domestic violence court: The District of Columbia experience.* Williamsburg, VA: National Center for State Courts.

Levy, F., Ross, T., & Guthrie, P. (2008). *Enhancing safety and justice for victims of domestic violence: Voices of women in the Queen's integrated domestic violence court.* New York: Vera Institute of Justice.

MacDowell, E. (2011). When courts collide: Integrated domestic violence courts and court pluralism. *Texas Journal of Women & the Law, 20*, 95–130.

Martinson, D. (2012). *Judicial coordination of concurrent proceedings in domestic violence cases.* Vancouver: The FREDA Centre for Research on Violence against Women and Children.

Mazur, R., & Aldrich, L. (2003). What makes a domestic violence court work? Lessons from New York. *Judges Journal, 42*, 5–42.

Moore, S. (2009). *Two decades of specialized domestic violence courts: A review of the literature.* New York: Center for Court Innovation.

Mosher, J. (2015). Grounding access to justice theory and practice in the experiences of women abused by their intimate partners. *Windsor Yearbook of Access to Justice, 32*, 149–179.

Mosoff, J., Grant, I., Boyd, S. B., & Lindy, R. (2017). Intersecting challenges: Mothers and child protection law in BC. *University of British Columbia Law Review, 50*, 435–504.

Neilson, L. (2012). *Enhancing safety: When domestic violence cases are in multiple legal systems (criminal, family, child protection).* London, ON: Centre for Research & Education on Violence against Women and Children.

Neilson, L. (2014). At cliff's edge: Judicial dispute resolution in domestic violence cases. *Family Court Review, 52*, 529–563.

Neilson, L. (2015). *Enhancing civil protection in domestic violence cases: Cross Canada checkup.* Fredericton: Muriel McQueen Fergusson Centre for Family Violence Research.

Nixon, K., Tutty, L., Weaver-Dunlop, G., & Walsh, C. (2007). Do good intentions beget good policy? A review of child protection policies to address intimate partner violence. *Children and Youth Services Review, 29*, 1469–1486.

Ontario, C. C. (2015). *Domestic violence death review committee 2013-14 annual report*. Toronto: Ministry of Community Safety & Correctional Services.

Ontario Court of Justice. (n.d.). Integrated domestic violence courts: Overview. Retrieved from: Ontario Court of Justice, http://www.ontariocourts.ca/ocj/integrated-domestic-violence-court/overview/.

Picard-Fritsche, S. (2011). *Litigant perspectives in an integrated domestic violence court*. New York: Center for Court Innovation.

Picard-Fritsche, S., Cissner, A. B., & Puffett, N. K. (2011). *The Erie County integrated domestic violence court: Policies, practices, and impacts*. New York: Center for Court Innovation.

Quann, N. (2006). *Offender profile and recidivism among domestic violence offenders in Ontario, Canada*. Ottawa: Department of Justice. Retrieved from http://www.justice.gc.ca/eng/rp-pr/csj-sjc/crime/rr06_fv3-rr06_vf3/rr06_fv3.pdf

Rickard, E. (2011). Civil protective orders in integrated domestic violence court: An empirical study. Retrieved from: https://ssrn.com/abstract=1782212.

Sack, E. (2002). *Creating a domestic violence court: Guidelines and best practices*. San Francisco: Family Violence Prevention Fund.

Sack, E. (2004). Battered women and the state: The struggle for the future of domestic violence policy. *Wisconsin Law Review, 2004*, 1657–1739.

Saini, M., Birnbaum, R., & Bala, N. (2016). Access to justice in Ontario's family courts: The parents' perspective. *Windsor Review of Legal & Social Issues, 37*, 1–25.

Schlueter, M., Wicklund, P., Adler, R., Owen, J., & Halvorsen, T. (2011). *Bennington County integrated domestic violence docket project: Outcome evaluation - final report*. Northfield Falls: Vermont Center For Justice Research.

Schneider, E. (2000). *Battered women and feminist lawmaking*. New Haven: Yale University Press.

Shaffer, C. (2004). Therapeutic domestic violence courts: An efficient approach to adjudication? *Seattle University Law Review, 27*, 981–997.

Shelton, D. (2007). *The current state of domestic violence courts in the United States, 2007*. Williamsburg: National Center for State Courts.

Tsai, B. (2000). The trend toward specialized domestic violence courts: Improvements on an effective innovation. *Fordham Law Review, 68*, 1285–1327.

Turpel-Lafond, M. E. (2009). *Honouring Christian Lee – No private matter: Protecting children living with domestic violence*. Victoria: BC Representative for Children and Youth.

Turpel-Lafond, M. E. (2012). *Honouring Kaitlynne, Max and Cordon: Make their voices heard now*. Victoria: BC Representative for Children and Youth.

Tutty, L., Ursel, J., & Douglas, F. (2008). Specialized domestic violence courts: A comparison of models. In J. Ursel, L. M. Tutty, & J. Lemaistre (Eds.), *What's law got to do with it? The law, specialized courts and domestic violence in Canada* (pp. 69–94). Toronto: Cormorant Books.

Tutty, L., Ursel, J., & Lemaistre, J. (2008). The verdict on specialized justice responses to domestic violence. In J. Ursel, L. M. Tutty, & J. Lemaistre (Eds.), *What's law got to do with it? The law, specialized courts and domestic violence in Canada* (pp. 272–278). Toronto: Cormorant Books.

Tutty, L., & Koshan, J. (2013). Calgary's specialized domestic violence court: An evaluation of a unique model. *Alberta Law Review, 50*, 731–755.

Ursel, J., Tutty, L., & Lemaistre, J. (2008). The justice system response to domestic violence: Debates, discussions and dialogues. In J. Ursel, L. M. Tutty, & J. Lemaistre (Eds.), *What's law got to do with it? The law, specialized courts and domestic violence in Canada* (pp. 1–17). Toronto: Cormorant Books.

Vollens, A. (2010). *Court-related abuse and harassment*. Vancouver: YWCA.Retrieved from

Weber, J. (2000). Courts responding to communities: Domestic violence courts: Components and considerations. *Journal of the Center for Families, Children & Courts, 2*, 23–139.

Weissman, D. (2000-2001). Gender-based violence as judicial anomaly: Between 'the truly national and the truly local'. *Boston College Law Review, 42*, 1081–1159.

Wolf, R., Aldrich, L., & Moore, S. (2004). *Planning a domestic violence court: The New York State experience*. New York: Center for Court Innovation.

Specialist domestic violence courts for child arrangement cases: safer courtrooms and safer outcomes?

Mandy Burton

ABSTRACT
Child arrangement cases in England and Wales are dealt with in the ordinary family courts. Whilst a special practice direction is applicable to child arrangement proceedings where there are allegations of domestic abuse, there is no specialist domestic violence court in the family justice setting. However, court specialisation is a feature of the criminal justice system and has been demonstrated to have success in domestic violence cases. Some of the potential benefits of specialisation, such as the provision of safer courtrooms, might be transferable to the family justice setting. Given the well documented problems of ordinary courts dealing with child arrangements in domestic violence cases, this article considers whether court specialisation could provide victims with safer courtrooms and safer outcomes in child arrangement cases.

Introduction

Specialist domestic violence courts (SDVCs) dealing exclusively with domestic violence matters, usually through a method of clustering such cases together, have been operating in England and Wales for almost two decades. They operate only in the criminal justice setting and, apart from an experiment with an integrated SDVC in one location, there have been no attempts to introduce SDVCs into the family justice setting. However, whilst the overall goals of the criminal courts may be very different to those of the family courts, some of the issues that arise with domestic violence cases in the criminal justice setting also arise in the family courts. The need for professionals to be aware of the dynamics of domestic abuse, to keep victims safe within the court proceedings and to contribute to longer term safety through case outcomes, are just as applicable to the family courts as they are to the criminal courts. This article will consider whether the introduction of SDVCs in the family justice setting to deal with child arrangement cases could contribute to safer courtrooms and safer outcomes for the child and adult victims of domestic abuse. It will do this by examining the benefits of specialisation in the criminal justice context and evaluating whether these could be replicated in child arrangement cases involving domestic abuse.

The development and evaluation of sdvcs in the criminal justice setting

The first SDVC in England and Wales was set up in Leeds in 1999. It was closely followed by specialist courts in Cardiff, West London, Wolverhampton and Derby. The history of SDVCs is one of rapid expansion in the criminal justice system around the turn of the last century, followed by more recent contraction due to the magistrates' court closure programme and resourcing issues (Bettinson, 2016). SDVCs are now sometimes referred to as specialist domestic abuse courts (SDACs) to reflect the broader definition of domestic violence, which includes non-physical abuse in addition to physical violence. The terms domestic violence and domestic abuse are often used interchangeably, however there has been a shift towards recognising non-physical abuse in the criminal law through the creation of a new offence of coercive and controlling behaviour under s. 76 of the Serious Crime Act 2015. Whether this will result in the practices of the criminal justice agencies changing significantly, or create fresh issues, is a matter of debate (Bettinson & Bishop, 2015, 2018). Broader definitions do not always result in immediate changes to the practices or cultures of professionals responsible for responding to domestic abuse (Barnett, 2017). Before this new offence was enacted, prosecutors only had the general offences against the person and other established offences to select for domestic violence prosecutions. It is likely that these general offences will still form the bulk of domestic violence prosecutions despite the new offence. The limitations of the general criminal law for domestic violence cases have been well documented, not least in relation to the difficulty in evidencing recognisable psychiatric injury for the purposes of assault (Burton, 2010; Munro & Shah, 2010). SDVCs were therefore introduced in a context where the substantive criminal law offered little in the way of tailored redress. However, the idea behind court specialisation was to make the processes work better in domestic violence cases, even though the law itself was not domestic violence specific.

The expansion of SDVCs in England and Wales was mainly driven by a policy initiative, led by the Crown Prosecution Service (CPS), to try to overcome some of the traditional obstacles to successfully prosecuting domestic violence. For many years both the police and the CPS had been accused of failing victims of domestic violence (Burton, 2008, ch. 6). The CPS traditionally relied very heavily on the evidence of victims and would often drop cases where victims withdrew their complaints rather than consider alternatives (Cretney & Davis, 1997). At a time when police officers were being encouraged to improve their evidence gathering to support prosecutions without victims (Ellison, 2002), the CPS became interested in specialist courts, which it hoped might be a way of decreasing victim retractions and increasing convictions. As such it commissioned an evaluation of the first five courts (Cook, Burton, Robinson, & Vallely, 2004) and subsequently set up a pilot of two further courts operating in Croydon and Gwent (Vallely, Robinson, Burton, & Tredigda, 2005).

Prior to Cook et al.'s (2004) evaluation, all of the first five SDVCs, with the exception of Derby SDVC, had been subject to their own separate reviews. There were reports on Leeds SDVC (Grundy, 2000), West London SDVC (Standing Together, 2002, 2003), Wolverhampton SDVC (Cook, 2003) and Cardiff SDVC (Robinson, 2003), highlighting features that were working well and areas for improvement. However, Cook et al. (2004) were able to compare the operations of the five courts, identifying similarities and differences. In addition they carried out quantitative analysis of a sample of 216 cases dealt with by all five courts in total over the same time period at the end of 2003. All of the courts, apart from Cardiff which had a fast track system into the Crown Court (Robinson, 2003), operated in the magistrates' courts only. Although the five courts had different models of specialisation, most shared the features of clustering cases to a particular day of the week. A significant feature of most of the courts, facilitated by clustering, was the presence of an independent domestic violence advocate (IDVA) to support the victim of abuse (Cook et al., 2004).

Cook et al. (2004) found that the success of the courts was heavily dependent upon effective multi-agency working and specialist training for all the practitioners to achieve a better understanding of the dynamics of domestic abuse and the needs of victims. Many of the courts had specialist domestic violence police officers who attended and the aim was also to use only prosecutors or magistrates who had specialist training. However, one of the main reasons why victims felt better supported in the SDVC than in the non-specialist courts, was the presence of a lay advocate, or IDVA, who could keep them informed and be a source of support within the court proceedings and outside. The role of the IDVA has developed over time. Their involvement in Multi Agency Risk Assessment Conferences (MARACs) helping high risk victims of domestic abuse to access support is now well known. For example, Robinson and Payton (2016) observe that lay advocates working in a multi-agency partnership can access support for victims which they may not have had the capacity to achieve alone. They can also bring about positive change in the policies and practices of agencies they are working with. In the first five courts, lay advocate support was at different stages of development at each site (Cook et al., 2004, p. 81). In three of the courts, Leeds, West London and Cardiff, lay advocacy support was well integrated. In Cardiff support was provided through the Women's Safety Unit (Robinson, 2003), in Leeds through the Help and Advice Law Team (HALT) (Grundy, 2000) and in West London through ADVANCE and Eaves (Standing Together, 2003). In the other two courts lay advocacy was not so well embedded; perhaps in Derby this was partly attributable to the fact that the court itself had not been running long at the time of the evaluation. In the early days Derby SDVC was struggling to identify a funded stream of lay advocates, relying on a rota of volunteers from various agencies with an idea to possibly recruit students. This was not ideal given that Cook et al. (2004, p. 82) noted that lay advocates were seen by the victim and criminal justice agencies 'as the trusted links into the system' and that victims felt more confident in attending the SDVC with the support of an IDVA. As Bettinson (2016) has more recently observed, the IDVA is central to a 'victim-centred court', yet identifying and maintaining a funding stream for IDVAs has always been an issue. She concludes that 'it is essential that austerity cuts do not remove the IDVA's presence from the legal process' (Bettinson, 2016, p. 89); a conclusion which is supported by the first five courts evaluation and also by the evaluation of the SDVC pilots at Croydon and Gwent (Vallely et al., 2005). The withdrawal of IDVAs from the Croydon Family Justice Centre (FJC) from attending the SDVC at Croydon, which was due at least in part to funding issues, was a feature which threatened to undermine what in many other ways was a 'successful' SDVC pilot (Vallely et al., 2005).

Looking at more traditional measures of 'success' within the criminal justice system, the first five courts and two pilots were evaluated according to their ability to 'narrow the justice gap' and bring more perpetrators to justice, as well as their ability to speed up the processing of cases and reduce the number of hearings. Whilst some SDVCs were able to speed up the process, this was not always the case and defence lawyers were often blamed for frustrating this objective (Cook et al., 2004, pp. 69–71). One of the rationales of speeding up cases is to try to reduce victim withdrawal; the longer a case goes on and the more hearings there are, the more likely it is thought that the victim will retract. Quantitative evaluation of the cases going through the SDVCs found that victim retraction was not reduced. Approximately half of all victims in the case file sample retracted their complaint at some point in proceedings, supporting the views of practitioners interviewed in the study that specialisation had no impact on victim withdrawal.

However, it has been argued that victim retraction is not an appropriate measure of success for SDVCs (Robinson & Cook, 2006) and that more attention should be paid to whether the victim is appropriately supported through that retraction process. It could also be argued that the focus on maintaining the victim as a witness is misguided, especially given the enhanced evidence policies that the police are supposed to implement to ensure that case files contain other sources of evidence. At the time of the first five courts' evaluation, there was little evidence of implementation of enhanced evidence gathering in SDVC cases. For example, less than half the cases in the case file sample where there were recorded injuries included photographic evidence, even though this was the main type of additional evidence on file (Cook et al., 2004, p. 115). These findings suggest that court specialisation itself is not enough to stimulate better evidence gathering. However, the introduction of the pilot SDVC at Croydon did seem to have a positive impact on evidence gathering. Vallely et al. (2005) found that the proportion of cases with case exhibits and medical evidence almost doubled after the SDVC was introduced. The impact of enhanced evidence gathering was reflected in a rise in the proportion of defendants convicted in Croydon SDVC following a not guilty plea and trial. Thus, whilst SDVCs do have the potential to demonstrate success according to traditional criminal measures, caution must be exercised regarding the impact of court specialisation on the police investigation process. There is more recent evidence to suggest that the police continue to miss significant opportunities to gather evidence in domestic violence cases (Her Majesty's Inspectorate of Constabulary, 2014).

If the measures of success of the first SDVCs had rested solely on 'narrowing the justice gap' through reducing retractions and increasing convictions, it is doubtful whether the case outcomes in the five courts or the two further pilots would have provided a strong case for expansion. However, the drive for expansion also rested on evaluating the experiences of victims using the courts. It was because victims of domestic abuse felt safer and better supported within the specialist court setting that the case for expanding SDVCs was made (Cook et al., 2004; Vallely et al., 2005). On the back of this a court specialisation programme and a National Resource Manual for SDVCs was introduced. A review of the first 23 SDVCs within the specialist court programme was carried out with a view to understanding the components to success of SDVCs and keeping the manual up to date (CPS, Her Majesty's Court Service (HMCS), & Home Office, 2008, 2011). The SDVC resource manual is due to be updated following a recent CPS 'deep dive' to identify best practice in the newly termed specialist domestic abuse courts (CPS, 2017). According to the Manual there are 12 components of a successful SDVC. Some of these components are linked to greater levels of success in achieving the traditional criminal justice target of bringing offenders to justice. Other components are more strongly linked with success in support and safety of the victim. Success in achieving criminal justice targets is strongly linked to effective multi-agency working, correct identification of cases, IDVA support within the court, specially trained and dedicated personnel, court listing to facilitate clustering and ways of managing perpetrators (through appropriate perpetrator programmes for example) to reduce repeat victimisation. Success in supporting the victim and victim safety is more strongly linked to SDVCs where there are safe court facilities and where IDVAs are engaging with victims more generally (as opposed to being focused on court proceedings), including through MARACs, where there is a focus on safety planning (CPS, HMCS, & Home Office, 2011). It will be interesting to see whether the latest CPS 'deep dive' exercise into SDACs supports these earlier findings. It would be surprising if safe court facilities were not an essential component of best practice for all SDACs.

Going to court should not pose a danger to the victim of domestic abuse or her children, yet many victims have stated that going to court is fraught with possibilities of intimidation and abuse. Many court buildings have a single entrance which is used by all the parties in the case. They also often have one waiting area which is shared by all the parties. If the victim of abuse arrives and leaves by the same door as the perpetrator the potential for abuse within the court building or immediate surroundings is heightened. The victim may also be followed by the perpetrator if she leaves the courthouse at the same time. Court specialisation has the potential to improve victim safety in the court building and courtroom, although in the first five SDVCs progress with improving facilities was initially slow (Cook et al., 2004).

Cook et al. (2004) found large variations in the court facilities in the first five SDVCs; at best there were not separate entrances but there were separate waiting rooms, some of which had secured entry, for example with access by a PIN. Once inside the courtroom, again the facilities across the five courts varied. Some had secure docks, others did not; those which did were regarded as offering a higher standard of protection. However, a secure dock in itself does not necessarily prevent the victim feeling intimidated; courtroom layout is another factor to be considered. At West London SDVC there was a secure dock in the courtroom used for domestic violence cases but it was in very close proximity to the witness box and the victim had to walk right in front of the dock in order to get into the witness box. Witnesses reported feeling intimidated by the defendant (Standing Together, 2003) and were advised to turn their body away and face the magistrates as they walked past the dock (Cook et al., 2004 p. 62).

The issue of witness intimidation in the courtroom can be addressed, at least partly, by the use of special measures, such as screening the victim or giving evidence by video link from another room in the court or a remotely linked location. The remote link has the additional advantage that the victim does not have to attend the court building, avoiding the potential to be followed on exiting. Most of the first five SDVCs courts had facilities for special measures such as screening of the witness and video links (Cook et al., 2004). However, at the time of the evaluation, now 15 years ago, these measures were only just being rolled out in England and Wales and so were not being fully utilised. Victims stated that they would have benefited from them. As special measures have become more embedded in the criminal justice system, those SDVCs which utilise those measures have been identified as examples of best practice (Crown Prosecution Service, Her Majesty's Court Service, & Home Office, 2011).

Recent independent reviews of SDVCs in England and Wales are somewhat sparse. A snapshot review of SDVCs in 2013 noted that 'There is evidence that courts are being made to feel safer for victims of domestic violence' (New Economics Foundation, 2014) However, the report observed that, although the majority of those surveyed thought special measures were being effectively provided, a significant minority did not and commented that the process of obtaining special measures was too 'laborious'. Bettinson (2016), who carried out her own small scale empirical study of an SDVC, highlights the potential impact of magistrates' court closures on the provision of safe court facilities for victims of domestic abuse. Commenting on the court closure programme, she notes that the Ministry of Justice has maintained a commitment to providing alternative venues for magistrates' courts, possibly using other civic buildings. But these locations will not necessarily have the facilities, such as separate entrances and waiting areas that are core to victim safety (Bettinson, 2016, p. 95). Her research also highlights that correct case identification is an ongoing issue in some SDVCs, with non-domestic cases incorrectly being listed into the SDVC and a valuable resource being wasted. As Bettinson observes, in times of 'austerity' SDVCs are under threat, however it is vital that this resource is preserved. A cost-benefit analysis of SDVCs in the criminal justice setting suggests that they are well worth the investment (Cook et al., 2004).

Integrated domestic violence courts: bridging the gap between criminal and family proceedings

Part of the original inspiration for SDVCs in England and Wales came from looking to other jurisdictions for models of court specialisation, in particular the US (Plotnikoff & Woolfson, 2005). The US provided insights into an alternative 'problem solving' approach (Mazur & Aldrich, 2002), which is used not only for domestic violence but other types of offending that may benefit from more holistic intervention (Donoghue, 2014). Whilst in the domestic violence context nearly all of the court specialisation in England and Wales has focused on criminal matters, Croydon was innovative. Not only did Croydon SDVC attempt to bridge the gap between criminal and family proceedings, it also attempted to adopt elements of the 'problem solving' approach. Whilst still operating only as a criminal court, Croydon SDVC started to hold 'compliance hearings' where convicted perpetrators were brought back three months after their sentence to review progress and provide appropriate encouragement or admonishment (Burton, 2006). Vallely et al. (2005) noted that the introduction of compliance hearings was a significant feature and benefit of the court. It was a feature which Croydon tried to maintain when it introduced an integrated court although there was some concern about the legal basis for the compliance hearing and whether defendants understood their attendance was voluntary (Hester, Pearce, & Westmarland, 2008).

Whilst Croydon SDVC started life dealing with criminal matters only, it was always intended that the SDVC would be a forerunner of an integrated domestic violence court (IDVC). IDVCs are courts where multiple legal proceedings in different jurisdictions but all relating to domestic violence in the same family can be heard in one specialist court. Domestic violence can involve proceedings in the criminal, civil and family courts simultaneously. This can cause problems because the professionals in each jurisdiction are working in isolation; a problem which Hester (2011) has described as 'three planets', where no one has much idea of what is happening on the other planets and each operates with its own history, culture, laws and professionals. There are obvious limitations to the separate planets, not least the potential for conflicting orders which undermines the ability to achieve coherent and effective remedies for victims of domestic abuse (Burton, 2004). Hester (2011) comments that the tensions and contradictions in the professional discourses on the criminal justice, child protection and child contact planets makes tackling domestic violence more difficult. In some jurisdictions an IDVC approach is preferred, but although Hester (2011) calls for a more 'unified approach' with 'much closer and coherent practices across the three areas of work', she does not explicitly call for an IDVC (Hester, 2011, p. 850).

Croydon SDVC made the evolution from a court operating only in the criminal setting to an IDVC in 2006. The aim of the court was to bring together domestic violence cases in the criminal setting with concurrent proceedings under the Children Act 1989 or civil injunctions under the Family Law Act 1996. The approach of the IDVC was broadly speaking to be the 'one family, one judge' model found in some IDVCs in other countries. The setting up of the IDVC in Croydon was not straightforward as there was concern about human rights legislation preventing criminal matters being heard by the same judge when civil findings have been made (Hester et al., 2008). There was also a question of perceived bias if the criminal trial was held by the same judge who had, for example, granted a non-molestation order or restricted contact with children based on findings of domestic abuse. Eventually it was decided that, at least in the early days, instead of using lay magistrates as in the SDVC, a professional judge (Deputy District Judge) would be authorised to hear cases in both the criminal and civil jurisdiction and undertake the appropriate training and maintain the experience to do so. The judge was to hear the criminal case first, up to the point of acquittal or conviction, before considering the family law matters. It was originally intended that Croydon IDVC would be supported by an independent lay advocacy service. However, for funding reasons, the FJC which was providing IDVAs for in-court support in the SDVC, cut back on their involvement. This withdrawal of lay advocate presence in the SDVC continued and worsened once the IDVC was introduced, impacting on both (Hester et al., 2008, p. 17).

Hester et al. note that 'the detachment of the advocacy service was a critical disappointment' for those involved in the integrated court at Croydon (2008, p. 18). It might be expected that given the significance of independent advocates for the success of SDVCs, at least in terms of victim satisfaction and safety, the results of the IDVC pilot would be disappointing. However, on top of the lay advocacy issue, the court faced another 'huge disappointment' in that very few cases materialised during its first year of operations (Hester et al., 2008, p. 31). It had been anticipated that there would be at least one case a week but in fact only five cases went through the IDVC during the evaluation period. The research team evaluating the IDVC observed that the reasons for the low caseload were not entirely clear; it may be that there were more cases with overlapping proceedings but they had not been correctly identified as involving domestic violence in the relevant jurisdiction (Hester et al., 2008, p. 32). In any event, the low numbers prevented the research team from doing any quantitative analysis on case progression or outcomes. Some qualitative analysis was done on the five cases that did go through the court. Only one of these five cases involved criminal proceedings overlapping with child arrangement proceedings. The researchers observed: 'the situation where a father has become detached from his family by bail conditions and then makes application for child contact might be expected as a typical scenario and it is surprising that more such cases did not occur' (Hester et al., 2008, p. 34).

It impossible to evaluate whether integration was a success or a failure on the basis of the small caseload going through the Croydon IDVC. However, the qualitative analysis suggested that there were issues which had the potential to limit the impact of the court, even if more cases were identified. A number of interviewees were concerned about the heightening of tensions where criminal and family proceedings were being held together (Hester et al., 2008, p. 16). The importance of victims feeling safe in the court building and courtroom was considered in the planning for the IDVC. The IDVC courtroom had a lockable dock and provision for witness screening. Although the court building had a single entrance, there were separate waiting areas. Some of the interviewees felt the facilities were as good as they could be within financial and court building constraints. They believed that safety issues could be dealt with on a case by case basis. The research team observed some situations where the court staff did have to intervene; once when there was an 'altercation' in the foyer and on another occasion when the victim became distressed when the perpetrator 'made overtures' as she was leaving the courtroom. The court staff were observed to be 'vigilant, prepared and effective in handling potentially threatening situations where these arose' (Hester et al., 2008, p. 16).

Hester et al. (2008) observed that special measures were readily granted in two of the five cases that were heard in the IDVC during the evaluation period. In both of these cases the victims benefited from screening during the criminal component of the proceedings and were escorted into the courtroom by the witness service by an entrance which avoided the perpetrator and his supporters in the waiting area. However, one of the victims who was assisted and screened during criminal proceedings, was then left to sit at the back of the court on her own when the civil part of the case was being heard (Hester et al., 2008, p. 19). The fact that the protections afforded during the criminal proceedings ended before the whole case was heard is clearly a 'failure' from a victim safety perspective.

None of the five cases that went through the IDVC offered scope to test the issue of bias or perceived breaches of human rights of defendants where the same judge decides criminal and civil matters. There were no cases where the judge found a defendant guilty following criminal trial and then proceeded to civil or family matters. Hester et al. (2008) noted the disappointment of some interviewees that these issues had not been resolved by a test case. They cite the case of *Hammerton v Hammerton* [2007] EWCA Civ 248, where there was criticism of a judge who heard child arrangement matters together with committal proceedings for breach of an undertaking and a non-molestation order at the same hearing. They observe that the case does not say this should never happen (Hester et al., 2008, p. 21), however it does not bode well. In *Hammerton v Hammerton* the appeal court decided that hearing criminal matters for contempt of court at the same time as child arrangement proceedings placed the defendant in an impossible position.

The defendant has a right to silence in criminal proceedings which may be inconsistent with the need to give evidence to support an application for contact with children of the relationship. This point has since been confirmed in the case of *Morris v Morris* [2016] EWCA Civ 812, where it was held that the judge had erred in hearing a judgment summons for a debt relating to unpaid maintenance (a criminal matter) with an application for variation of maintenance (a civil matter). The Court of Appeal decided that 'wrongly' hearing the criminal matters along with the civil matters deprived the defendant of his procedural rights, notably the right to silence in criminal proceedings. Procedural fairness and perceptions of bias might still therefore present an issue for IDVCs in England and Wales should they adopt a 'one family, one judge' approach. There is certainly scope for legal challenges where a judge has made comments on one issue that suggest that they have closed their mind to further evidence or argument when it comes to deciding other matters (Heaton, 2015).

Leaving aside the specific challenges in integrating domestic violence proceedings faced by Croydon IDVC, not everyone believes that integrated domestic violence courts are a good idea. They have been critiqued not only from a practical but also from a normative perspective. MacDowell has argued that the value of court pluralism is often overlooked and 'court fragmentation can be an opportunity' for victims, not least because integration may compromise the 'autonomy enhancing' elements of the civil courts (MacDowell, 2011, p. 96). In arguing this she is not blind to the critiques of the civil justice system in responding to domestic violence but points out that the criminal courts are mainly concerned with the normative functions of the criminal law (holding the perpetrator to account for the benefit of society) rather than the individual needs of the victim. MacDowell also argues that just as court separation is not the source of the problems of lack of information sharing and conflicting orders, integration is not the solution. The problems can be dealt with in other ways. As noted above, one of the traditional concerns about integration has been ensuring fairness to the defendant and avoiding perceptions of bias against the perpetrator but, as MacDowell points out, victims may also perceive that judges are biased against them in an IDVC. She argues that if the judge decides the criminal matters in favour of the defendant (acquitting him or finding the case not proven), the victim may perceive that the judge is predisposed to the defendant in civil and family matters. In this situation another forum for the non-criminal matters may be preferred by the victim. There is also the issue of victims potentially being directed to unwanted services in the IDVC and feeling compelled to take them for fear of being judged negatively in relation to child protection and child arrangement matters. The empirical evidence on IDVCs in other jurisdictions suggests that integration might make matters worse rather than better, resulting in delays in obtaining civil protection orders and perhaps even pressure to agree to contact when it is not safe. The findings of these evaluations of IDVCs in the USA and Canada are dealt with by Koshan in her article in this issue. There is room for different interpretations of some of the data but, as yet, the empirical evidence does not yet make a convincing case for integration.

It has been suggested that, instead of aiming for integration, efforts should be focused on improving how each jurisdiction deals with domestic violence to ensure that victims receive 'multi-layer' protection (MacDowell, 2011). It may well be that if each 'planet', to return to Hester's analogy, could be reformed it would be preferable to keep them separate but orbiting in a way that keeps victims safe. A better alternative to developing IDVCs in England and Wales might be to aim for specialisation in the family justice setting to run alongside specialisation in the criminal justice setting. If there were improved information exchange between the two specialised systems it would then not be necessary to fully combine proceedings to ensure the best protection for victims.

The case for specialisation in child arrangement cases?

There are special rules for how the family courts should deal with allegations of domestic abuse contained in Practice Direction 12J (PD12J), as discussed in the Introduction to this special issue. The rules have been recently reviewed to take into account concerns expressed by Women's Aid and others that judges in family law cases are failing adequately to protect women and children in child arrangement cases involving allegations of domestic abuse (Cobb, 2017). The failures relate both to safety at court and unsafe case outcomes, as the Women's Aid review of child homicides in domestic violence cases where there was court ordered contact demonstrates (Women's Aid, 2016).

Evidence to the All Party Parliamentary Group on Domestic Violence (APPG) (APPG & Women's Aid, 2016) suggested that many victims of domestic abuse are being subjected to further abuse in the family court setting as the courts do not have appropriate facilities or use special measures to protect them. Responses to a Women's Aid survey in 2015 showed that 55% of women who had been to the family courts had no access to any special measures and 39% were physically abused by their former partner in the family court. Mr Justice Cobb recommended that paragraph 10 of PD12J be amended 'for the courts to consider more carefully the waiting arrangements at court prior to the hearing, and arrangements for entering and exiting the court building' (Cobb, 2017, p. 4). In her foreword to the APPG report, the Chair of the APPG (Jess Phillips MP), noted that over the past 20 years the criminal courts have made 'huge strides' in improving the experiences of victims of domestic abuse through SDVCs and special measures, but that family courts had 'not moved with the times' (APPG & Women's Aid, 2016). The APPG heard evidence that requests for separate waiting rooms were refused and women were frequently forced to enter and leave the courts by the same route and at the same time as their abusive ex-partners, resulting in 'women commonly being followed, stalked, harassed and further traumatised after leaving court' (Cobb, 2017, p. 4). The APPG observed there should be 'no family court that forces a survivor of domestic abuse to wait in the same room as their perpetrator' or go through the ordeal of leaving the court at the same time in the same way (APPG & Women's Aid, 2016, p. 16). As the family courts have let victims down so badly in terms of ensuring safety at court, there is a case for specialisation. Court specialisation could provide the impetus for providing safer court facilities and ensuring victims have access to special measures, in the same way that is has in the criminal courts.

An urgent problem with the family courts in child arrangement cases involving domestic violence is that they do not appear to be putting the safety of children first. It has been suggested, as documented elsewhere in this issue, that there is a culture of contact at any cost (e.g. Barnett, 2014). This seems to be at least partly based on misunderstandings of the nature of domestic abuse; family judges are wrongly assuming that domestic abuse towards the mother does not impact on the children and wrongly assuming that, once the relationship ends, so does the abuse. These misconceptions are contributing to unsafe outcomes and in extreme cases children are, as Women's Aid (2016) has highlighted, being killed. If judges, and all the professionals, including solicitors and barristers, in child arrangement cases were specially trained this could help to ensure that family justice professionals have a good understanding of the dynamics of domestic abuse. Specialist courts in the criminal setting have, as a matter of best practice, specially trained and dedicated personnel. This has contributed towards achieving safer outcomes, for example on bail conditions (Vallely et al., 2005), although the impact of this is undermined if a family court orders contact in contradiction to a criminal court which has issued bail with no contact conditions. Better information exchange and trained specialists in the family courts could avoid these conflicts. If only trained specialists could deal with child arrangement cases involving allegations of domestic abuse, then awareness of the PD12J would increase. The APPG heard that there is variable awareness of the Practice Direction throughout the family court judiciary (APPG & Women's Aid, 2016, p. 17), and yet the view is that if it were properly implemented it would provide a sound framework for keeping women and children safe.

In criminal SDVCs, where there is adequate resourcing, the voice of the victim is heard through the IDVA. In the family justice setting, in theory, the victim has her own legal representation. The issue in civil and family justice has been how to fund that representation as legal aid for victims of domestic violence has been under attack. Reforms to legal aid under the Legal Aid Sentencing and Punishment of Offenders Act 2012 (LAPSO), preserved legal aid for victims of domestic abuse in child arrangement cases and those seeking non-molestation orders under the Family Law Act 1996, but only if they could provide specific documentary evidence of domestic violence. Research showed that many victims of domestic abuse had difficulty meeting the evidential requirements (Hunter, 2014; Rights of Women, 2013). Rights of Women brought a successful legal challenge against the rules (*R (on the application of Rights of Women) v Secretary of State for Justice* [2016] EWCA Civ 91), and the rules have been amended so that new types of evidence, including that of refuge workers, will now be accepted. These reforms will perhaps go some way to ensuring that victims of domestic abuse do have legal representation in child arrangement proceedings, although it should be acknowledged that many victims will still struggle to satisfy the new third party evidence rules and/or to find a suitable legal aid provider. Restrictions in legal aid have resulted in a growth in litigants in person and it has been convincingly argued that the unavailability of legal aid breaches human rights (Choudhry & Herring, 2017). The difficulties and dangers of direct cross examination by the perpetrator have been highlighted in child arrangement cases involving allegations of domestic abuse (e.g. *Re J* [2018] EWCA Civ 115). It is to be hoped that the possibility of direct cross examination of the victim by the perpetrator will be stopped, with or without specialisation. This was to be addressed, at least partially, by a clause in the Prison and Courts Bill 2017, but the Bill lapsed due to the election called in 2017. At the time of writing no effective steps have been taken to end the practice through legislation. However, leaving aside the problems of securing legal aid and litigants in person, the potential gains to be made from specialisation in family proceedings go beyond due process in the courtroom.

Specialisation in the family justice system could facilitate the provision of IDVAs, which might help victims of domestic abuse both in and outside the courtroom. Inside the courtroom they could help to ensure that victims of domestic abuse are heard and not intimidated in child arrangement proceedings. The impact that the presence of lay advocates might have on outcomes is speculative. In evidence to the APPG it was suggested that Croydon is an example of good practice in so far as the implementation of PD12J is concerned, due to the existence of the FJC and the links it has with the family courts (APPG and Women's Aid, 2016, p. 16). This might seem at odds with the research findings discussed above, that the SDVC and IDVC in Croydon struggled to support victims as well as they might have due to the withdrawal of independent advocates working with the FJC. Although the aspiration was that the advocacy services would have an in court presence in the IDVC every time that it sat, this did not happen. The FJC decided that IDVAs would only attended the SDVC and IDVCs with victims they were already supporting, which meant that only one of the five cases in the IDVC had IDVA support. However, a daily in-court service continued to be provided in the county court. The FJC reported that it prioritised provision in the county court because it considered it more cost effective. Furthermore, its stated aims as a 'one stop shop' were to support all victims, not just those engaging with the legal system (Hester et al., 2008, p. 17). It may be that although the withdrawal of IDVAs from the SDVC and IDVCs was detrimental for the criminal justice response (Hester et al., 2008; Vallely et al., 2005), there were some benefits in the civil justice system as a result of the independent advocacy resource being deployed there. If the presence of IDVAs can stimulate better implementation of Practice Direction 12J, as the evidence to the APPG suggests, then specialisation in the family court setting to facilitate that provision is arguably worthwhile. Of course there would have to be a funding stream to support IDVAs, otherwise the same problems as occurred in the criminal courts in Croydon would occur in the family justice setting. However, if a properly funded IDVA service is maintained, in addition to potentially stimulating better implementation of PD12J, victims can be directed to a range of support accessible through services not wholly focused on the legal system. Victims should have the option of whether to take up these services. Specialisation within the family justice setting should aim to preserve the autonomy of victims and the choices they make about the services they use in safety planning for themselves and their children.

Conclusion

The development of SDVCs in the criminal courts in England and Wales was driven by the prosecuting authorities and their desire to improve the way that domestic violence cases were handled using criminal justice measures of success, such as reducing victim retractions and increasing convictions. Whilst the first SDVCs showed that prosecutions were not necessarily improved by reference to traditional measures of success, the benefits in terms of victim safety in the courtroom and victim satisfaction with the level of support received, made the case for expansion convincing. Although resources for

SDVCs in the criminal context in recent years have been dwindling, there are lessons to be learned about the benefits of specialisation which, it has been argued here, are applicable to the family justice setting. No victim of domestic abuse attending the family courts in child arrangement proceedings should feel unsafe inside the courtroom. Just as importantly, all the professionals dealing with child arrangement proceedings where domestic abuse is an issue, ought to be aware of the complex nature of the problem and how to help victims plan for a safe future for themselves and their children. Victims of domestic abuse need to have an effective voice in legal proceedings so that their experiences and concerns can be heard. At the moment, the traditional family courts are struggling to meet the safety needs of domestic abuse victims in child arrangement cases.

It seems unlikely that the introduction of IDVCs would provide a solution to the problems in family law cases. Firstly, there may be difficulties in identifying cases where there are overlapping proceedings in the criminal, civil and family courts. Secondly, there are likely to be cases in the family courts where there are no overlapping criminal proceedings, either because these matters have already been concluded, or because the criminal justice agencies or victims have decided not to seek redress in this sphere. The limited empirical evidence from England suggests that an IDVC has practical limitations which mean it is not going to be entirely effective for child arrangement disputes. The empirical evidence on IDVCs in other jurisdictions does not yet make a strong case for this approach to be adopted to resolve difficulties in child arrangement cases involving domestic abuse in England and Wales. However, that does not mean that the idea of a specialisation for child arrangement cases should be abandoned. A model of specialisation within each of the criminal and family justice systems, with improved information exchange between the two, could work to provide victims of domestic abuse with better multi-layered protection. Specialisation in the family court setting might enable the family courts to deal with child arrangement cases involving domestic violence more effectively; providing access to safer courtrooms and, through fuller implementation of PD12J, safer outcomes.

Disclosure statement

No potential conflict of interest was reported by the author.

References

All Party Parliamentary Group on Domestic Violence (APPG) & Women's Aid. (2016). *Domestic abuse, child contact and the family courts: Parliamentary briefing*. London: APPG and Women's Aid.

Barnett, A. (2014). Contact at all costs? Domestic violence and children's welfare. *Child and Family Law Quarterly*, *26*, 439–462.

Barnett, A. (2017). 'Greater than the sum of its parts': Coercive control and the question of proof. *Child and Family Law Quarterly*, *29*, 379–400.

Bettinson, V. (2016). Surviving times of austerity: Preserving the specialist domestic violence court provision. In S. Hilder & V. Bettinson (Eds.), *Domestic violence: Interdisciplinary perspectives on protection, prevention and intervention* (pp. 81–103). London: Palgrave-Macmillan.

Bettinson, V., & Bishop, C. (2015). Is the creation of a discrete offence of coercive control necessary to combat domestic violence? *Northern Ireland Legal Quarterly*, *66*, 179–197.

Bettinson, V., & Bishop, C. (2018). Evidencing domestic violence, including the behaviour that falls under the new offence of 'controlling and coercive behaviour'. *International Journal of Evidence and Proof*, *22*, 3–19.

Burton, M. (2004). *Lomas v Parle* – Coherent and effective remedies for victims of domestic violence: Time for an integrated domestic violence court? *Child and Family Law Quarterly*, *16*, 317–329.

Burton, M. (2006). Judicial monitoring of compliance: Introducing 'problem solving' approaches to domestic violence courts in England and Wales. *International Journal of Law, Policy and Family*, *20*, 366–378.

Burton, M. (2008). *Legal responses to domestic violence*. London: Routledge.

Burton, M. (2010). Commentary on *R v Dhaliwal*. In R. Hunter, C. McGlynn, & E. Rackley (Eds.), *Feminist judgments: From theory to practice* (pp. 255–260). Oxford: Hart Publishing.

Choudhry, S., & Herring, J. (2017). A human right to legal aid: The implications of changes to the legal aid scheme for victims of domestic abuse. *Journal of Social Welfare and Family Law*, *39*, 152–167.

Cobb, M. J. (2017). *Review of Practice Direction 12J FPR 2010: Child arrangement and contact orders: Domestic violence and harm. Report to the President of the Family Division*. Retrieved from https://www.judiciary.gov.uk/wp-content/uploads/2017/01/PD12J-child-arrangement-domestic-violence-and-harm-report-and-revision.pdf.

Cook, D. (2003). Evaluation of Wolverhampton Specialist Domestic Violence Court, RRI, University of Wolverhampton.

Cook, D., Burton, M., Robinson, V., & Vallely, C. (2004). *Evaluation of specialist domestic violence courts/fast track systems*. London: Crown Prosecution Service and Department for Constitutional Affairs.

Cretney, S., & Davis, A. (1997). Prosecuting domestic assault: Victims failing courts or courts failing victims? *Howard Journal of Criminal Justice*, *32*, 146–157.

Crown Prosecution Service. (2017). *Violence against women report 2016-7*. London: CPS.

Crown Prosecution Service, Her Majesty's Court Service, & Home Office. (2008). *Safety with justice*. London: CPS, HMCS and Home Office.

Crown Prosecution Service, Her Majesty's Court Service, & Home Office. (2011). *Domestic Violence Courts national resource manual, revised*. London: CPS, HMCS and Home Office.

Donoghue, J. (2014). *Transforming criminal justice? Problem-solving and court specialisation*. London: Routledge.

Ellison, L. (2002). Prosecuting domestic violence without victim participation. *Modern Law Review*, *65*, 834–858.

Grundy, M. (2000). *Final evaluation report of leeds domestic violence cluster court*. Huddersfield: University of Huddersfield.

Heaton, D. (2015). Bias and previous determinations: Four recent cases in the court of appeal and privy council. *Civil Justice Quarterly*, *34*, 138–154.

Her Majesty's Inspectorate of Constabulary. (2014). *Everyone's business: Improving the police response to domestic violence*. London: HMIC.

Hester, M. (2011). The three planet model: Towards an understanding of contradictions in approaches to women and children's safety in the contexts of domestic violence. *British Journal of Social Work*, *41*, 837–853.

Hester, M., Pearce, P., & Westmarland, N. (2008). *Early evaluation of the integrated domestic violence court, Croydon. London*: Ministry of Justice,

Hunter, R. (2014). Exploring the 'LASPO Gap'. *Family Law*, *44*, 660–663.

MacDowell, E. (2011). When courts collide: Integrated domestic violence courts and court pluralism. *Texas Journal of Women and the Law*, *20*(2), 97–130.

Mazur, A., & Aldrich, L. (2002). *What makes a domestic violence court work?* New York: Center for Court Innovation.

Munro, V., & Shah, S. (2010). *R v Dhaliwal* Judgment. In R. Hunter, C. McGlynn, & E. Rackley (Eds.), *Feminist judgments: From theory to practice* (pp. 261–272). Oxford: Hart Publishing.

New Economics Foundation. (2014). *Better courts: A snapshot of domestic violence courts in 2013.* London: Centre for Justice Innovation.

Plotnikoff, J., & Woolfson, R. (2005). *Review of the effectiveness of specialist courts in other jurisdictions*. London: Department for Constitutional Affairs.

Rights of Women. (2013). *Evidencing domestic violence: A barrier to family law legal aid.* London: Author.

Robinson, A. (2003). *The Cardiff Women's Safety Unit: A multi-agency approach to domestic violence.* Cardiff: Cardiff University, School of Social Sciences.

Robinson, A., & Payton, J. (2016). Independent advocacy and multi-agency responses to domestic violence. In S. Hilder & V. Bettinson (Eds.), *Domestic violence: Interdisciplinary perspectives on protection, prevention and intervention* (pp. 249–271). London: Palgrave-Macmillan.

Robinson, A., & Cook, D. (2006). Understanding victim retraction in cases of domestic violence: Specialist courts, government policy and victim-centred justice. *Contemporary Justice Review*, *9*, 189–213.

Standing Together. (2002). *First soundings from a specialist domestic violence court.* London: Author.

Standing Together. (2003). *Heard not judged: Consultation with survivors of domestic violence in the London Borough of Hammersmith and Fulham 2002-2003.* London: Author.

Vallely, C., Robinson, A., Burton, M., & Tredigda, J. (2005). *Evaluation of domestic violence pilot sites at Caerphilly (Gwent) and Croydon.* London: Crown Prosecution Service.

Women's Aid. (2016). *Nineteen child homicides.* Bristol: Author.

Conclusion: international best practices

Rosemary Hunter and Shazia Choudhry

ABSTRACT

Three approaches presented at the International Symposium on Contact Disputes and Allegations of Domestic Violence – Identifying Best Practices offered the possibility of overcoming the limitations identified in the preceding papers in this special issue. A human rights framework, trauma-informed practice and integrated services taking a whole-of-family approach can all help to achieve cultural change in contact proceedings and to ensure the availability of the resources needed to address the issue of domestic abuse holistically. Four Australian initiatives are described as examples of trauma-informed practice and integrated services: Legally Assisted Family Dispute Resolution (LAFDR), the Family Safety Model (FSM), the Family Violence Courts Division of the Victorian Magistrates Court (FVCD), and the Family Advocacy and Support Service (FASS). FSM and LAFDR are out-of-court initiatives which aim to address a family's abuse-related needs before they get to a court. The FVCD and FASS pick up families whose cases have entered the court system, and at that stage attempt to offer a wrap-around service which addresses both legal and non-legal needs. Lastly, the article describes the European human rights framework, which is designed to operate in cases which are ultimately adjudicated by a court.

Introduction

The articles in this special issue have documented the limitations and failures of a range of approaches adopted internationally to the issue of domestic abuse allegations in child arrangements cases. The common themes running through these articles are that the ability to prioritise safety and healing from trauma is inevitably compromised and undermined in any family justice system in which there remains a fundamental commitment to contact at all costs (England and Wales, the USA, New Zealand, Spain, Sweden, Scotland, Ireland) and/or in which inadequate resourcing and excessive focus on the internal requirements of the legal system result in the extra-legal needs of some (or all) family members being neglected (England and Wales, New Zealand, integrated domestic violence courts, judicial education).

Three approaches presented at the International Symposium on Contact Disputes and Allegations of Domestic Violence – Identifying Best Practices offered the possibility of avoiding these twin traps. A human rights framework, trauma-informed practice and integrated services taking a whole-of-family approach can all help to achieve cultural change and to ensure the availability of the resources needed to address the issue of domestic abuse holistically. Three Australian initiatives were described as examples of trauma-informed practice and integrated services: Legally Assisted Family Dispute Resolution (LAFDR), the Family Safety Model (FSM) and the Family Violence Courts Division of the Victorian Magistrates Court (FVCD). A fourth initiative subsequently rolled out in Australian family courts, the Family Advocacy and Support Service (FASS), provides another example of an integrated service and trauma-informed practice. What is striking about each of these models is that rather than treating allegations of domestic abuse as a problem for the legal system and one that needs to be contained and managed, they treat allegations of abuse as a problem for the family, and the family's encounter with the legal system as an opportunity for that problem to be addressed comprehensively. The European human rights framework similarly focuses attention on the rights of all family members, and provides a clear hierarchy of rights, in which the right to be free from torture or inhuman or degrading treatment (Article 3) takes priority over all others.

These various models of good practice operate at different stages of proceedings. FSM and LAFDR are out-of-court initiatives located in mediation services. Their aim is to address a family's abuse-related needs before they get to a court, and in the case of LAFDR, specifically to help families remain out of court by assisting them to make safe arrangements for children through out-of-court dispute resolution. The FVCD and FASS pick up families whose cases have entered the court system, and at that stage attempt to offer a wrap-around service which addresses both legal and non-legal needs. A human rights framework is designed to operate in cases which are ultimately adjudicated by a court. This article follows the order just outlined, beginning with the Australian out-of-court models and ending with a discussion of the application of European human rights to family law proceedings involving allegations of domestic abuse.

The Australian models

Trauma-informed practice

The concept of trauma-informed practice underpins all four of the Australian models. The principles underpinning trauma-informed practice include:

- understanding the prevalence and nature of trauma arising from interpersonal violence and its impacts on other areas of life and functioning;
- ensuring that organisational, operational and clinical practice protect the physical and emotional safety of consumers/survivors;
- creating service cultures and practices that empower consumers in their recovery by emphasising autonomy, collaboration and strength-based approaches;
- recognising the...gender, race, culture and ethnicity of consumers, which shape both their needs as well as recovery and healing pathways; and
- recognising the relational nature of both trauma and healing. (Family Law Council, 2016, p. 95, citing Quadara, 2015)

Trauma-informed practice requires the delivery of services with an awareness of the client's past and current experiences of abuse, an understanding of the neurological effects of trauma on parents and children and the coping strategies they develop, and a commitment to promote healing from trauma and to avoid re-traumatising clients. This includes avoiding replicating the power and control experienced in abusive relationships (Family Law Council, 2016, pp. 77, 95). Mindful of people's vulnerability and the damage already caused by abuse, it also includes a duty of care to guard against the escalation of conflict or any other actions which could exacerbate trauma. In relation to children, it involves looking not just at recent and imminent risks to a child's safety but at the cumulative impact of trauma on the child over time. Compounded experiences of multiple episodes of abuse diminish a child's sense of safety, stability and wellbeing and affect their development, and this needs to be understood and addressed (Family Law Council, 2016, p. 32).

The Family Safety Model

The FSM was developed by the Victorian branch of Relationships Australia (RAV), which runs a range of community-based services for separated families, including family dispute resolution/mediation and a men's behaviour change programme (domestic violence perpetrator programme). The FSM was originally attached to the men's behaviour change programme and was designed actively to prioritise the safety of the (former) partners and children of the men participating in the programme (Family Law Council, 2016, p. 85). It was subsequently trialled within the mediation service as well, with the evaluation of this pilot scheme due to be delivered in mid-2018.

In the mediation context, any potential client assessed at initial intake as affected by family violence is referred to an in-house Family Safety Practitioner (FSP). The model then involves three steps (see generally Family Law Council, 2016, pp. 33–34, 85–86; Relationships Australia, 2017). First, the FSP undertakes a comprehensive psycho-social assessment of all family members, including a risk assessment, needs assessment and history of legal interventions and breaches of domestic violence protection orders. On the basis of these assessments the FSP, in collaboration with the clients, develops an overall case plan incorporating safety plans and therapeutic and legal interventions. This may or may not include mediation – the service for which the client originally approached RAV. Even if they are screened out of mediation because they are not ready to mediate or mediation cannot safely occur, they will still receive assistance focused on the underlying issues of domestic abuse affecting their family.

Secondly, the FSP makes referrals to relevant in-house or external services and agencies to meet each family member's ongoing safety, support and trauma recovery needs. These are warm referrals (that is, the FSP personally introduces clients to the other services) based on the FSP's contacts and networks. They also support transitions between services, to ensure that no-one falls through the gaps. Thirdly, the FSP tracks the family's engagement with support services for up to a year, which may include updated risk assessments and revisions to the case plan, until the case meets the formal criteria for closure.

In summary, the FSM offers a trauma-informed, whole-of-family, integrated and coordinated approach to safety from domestic abuse. The FSP co-ordinates the provision of and engagement with a range of services for abusive and non-abusive parents and their children. In the process, the overall responsiveness of the service system to the family's multiple needs is enhanced (Family Law Council, 2016, p. 85). Rather than just providing a one-off service and leaving other agencies to do the same, the central organisation takes broader responsibility for the welfare of the clients who walk through their doors, together with their children and (ex-)partners.

Legally Assisted Family Dispute Resolution

LAFDR's aim is not so holistic, but it too adopts a trauma-informed, whole-of-family approach which takes proactive responsibility for client safety. Its objectives also explicitly include access to justice.[1]

LAFDR is based on a partnership between Victoria Legal Aid (VLA)'s Family Dispute Resolution Service and Women's Legal Service of Victoria (WLS) to provide access to justice for vulnerable parties who would otherwise be screened out of mediation. In Australia, parties are required to attempt family dispute resolution before proceeding to court (subject to exceptions), and VLA runs a family dispute resolution service which is available where at least one of the parties is legally aided. The legally aided party is assigned an in-house legal aid lawyer, but if the other party is not legally aided and cannot afford their own lawyer, they can attend the conference without a lawyer. Where there was a history of domestic abuse, or the other party was otherwise particularly vulnerable, cases were screened out of mediation if the other party did not have a lawyer, as the power imbalance between the legally-aided and non-legally aided party rendered mediation inappropriate. The only alternative for the non-legally-aided party in these circumstances, however, was to proceed to court as a litigant in person, a situation in which they would also be vulnerable and have difficulty advocating for themselves and achieving a safe outcome.

The partnership between VLA and WLS (which for the purposes of LAFDR trades as Family Law Legal Service (FLLS) and represents both women and men) enables both parties to have a lawyer, and thus enables mediation to be conducted more fairly and safely, resulting in fewer cases being screened out.[2] Specialised personnel are key to the scheme. The lawyers involved on both sides are trained and must be experienced in family law, have a good understanding of the dynamics of domestic abuse and the principles of family dispute resolution, and must be willing to take a trauma-informed, child-focused and non-adversarial approach to the process. The LAFDR model has also been adopted by two other mediation services (the Family Mediation Centre, and the Melbourne Family Relationships Centre), in each case in partnership with FLLS and another community legal service.

An initial, detailed risk assessment by the mediation service identifies the need for legal assistance, and lawyers from the separate participating legal services are assigned. Prior to the first mediation session, each of the lawyers consults with their client by telephone to provide information and advice, discuss options, manage expectations and take instructions. The mediation service in conjunction with the lawyers also undertakes safety planning for the mediation session. The session itself takes a shuttle format with each party in a separate room supported by their lawyer, who assists in maintaining focus on children's welfare and containing conflict, ensures their client has a voice and is able to address all the issues important to them, and reality tests proposals. Lawyers can work through issues with their clients while the mediator is with the other party and their lawyer, and sessions often include a time during which the two lawyers meet with the mediator to negotiate directly. Parties may also be accompanied by a family member or friend if they request it and all participants agree. Empowerment of vulnerable clients is seen as a crucial precondition to reaching safe, child-focused arrangements, and this often involves small steps, putting in place and testing interim arrangements and then returning if necessary. If no agreement is reached, the lawyer does not continue to act but clients are given advice about options, including whether to go to court, and referred to other sources of legal and non-legal support.

Family Advocacy and Support Service

The Family Advocacy and Support Service is a new service being piloted in Australian family courts in 2017–18, based on recommendations made by the Family Law Council (2016, pp. 12, 120–121). FASS is an integrated duty lawyer and domestic violence support service for litigants in person. People arriving at court without a lawyer are seen by a coordinator who conducts an initial risk identification, and then makes warm referrals to the duty lawyer and/or the men's or women's DV support worker. Duty lawyers do not undertake representation in court, but can help with information about court processes, how the court approaches family violence, how to obtain and use evidence, and the availability of special measures for giving evidence; information about making safe arrangements for children; legal advice; coaching for court appearances; obtaining urgent orders; and completing and amending documents (House of Representatives Standing Committee, 2017, pp. 144–147). In some of the pilot locations, the duty lawyer roles are staffed by two separate legal services so that legal assistance can be available to both parties where both are unrepresented. Support workers offer a trauma-informed approach to identifying and addressing non-legal needs, including full risk assessments, safety planning, dealing with housing or homelessness issues, and linking parties to counselling and drug and alcohol services via identified contacts (House of Representatives Standing Committee on Social Policy and Legal Affairs, 2017, pp. 144–145). Thus, from the parties' perspective, the court is transformed from being simply a place where litigation occurs to a place where they receive information, advice and help with navigating services. Stakeholders have identified 'clear improvements to the safety of families affected by family violence as a result of the service' (House of Representatives Standing Committee on Social Policy and Legal Affairs, 2017, p. 145), both through risk identification and safety planning, and the making of safer orders, whether by consent or judicial determination. A formal evaluation of the service is due to be published in 2019.

Family Violence Courts Division

Victoria's FVCD is an integrated domestic violence court which is able to deal with multiple legal issues relating to family violence, including civil protection orders, family law parenting matters,[3] criminal law, child protection, and victims of crime compensation, on the model of 'one judge, one family' (Family Law Council, 2015, pp. 81, 101). Its aims include:

- making access to court easier
- promoting the safety of victims of family violence
- increasing the accountability of perpetrators of family violence and encouraging them to change their behaviour
- increasing the protection of children exposed to family violence
- ensuring support services are available to improve victims' safety and assist in overcoming trauma caused by family violence
- minimising the need for parties to attend multiple courts, the proliferation of hearings and the repetition of evidence and assessments. (Family Law Council, 2015, pp. 81, 102)

The FVCD is located within the Victorian Magistrates Court. This is the jurisdiction which makes civil protection orders, and is thus very often the first court encountered by victims of domestic abuse (Family Law Council, 2015, p. 77). All court personnel are trained specialists, including the registrar/court clerk, magistrates, prosecutors, legal services and victim and perpetrator support workers. The inclusion of support workers enables parties' legal and non-legal needs to be addressed simultaneously, and also enables a coordinated approach. When making a final civil protection order, for example, a magistrate may mandate participation by the respondent in a men's behaviour change programme, which can then be monitored through the subsequent court process (Royal Commission into Family Violence, 2016, Vol. III, p. 128). The 'one judge, one family' model also helps to avoid systems abuse by perpetrators, who are unable to exploit the fragmentation of the court system to bring multiple proceedings in different courts and over time as a means of controlling and harassing their former partners.

The recent Victoria Royal Commission into Family Violence (2016) noted that although the FVCD has not been formally evaluated, there are 'compelling indications' of its effectiveness (Vol. III, p. 160). The Royal Commission further recommended that there should generally be a transition from reactive and piecemeal approaches to managing family violence to a court culture and practice that supports positive and effective interventions for affected family members and perpetrators. The therapeutic features of the FVCD and the ability to deal with all related legal issues should be available in all courts where civil protection order applications are heard (2016, Vol. III, p. 158).

Evaluating the models

As noted above, while these four models of practice appear very promising and have garnered praise from external observers (Family Law Council, 2015, 2016; House of Representatives Standing Committee on Social Policy and Legal Affairs, 2017), three of the four have not yet been formally evaluated. The LAFDR scheme operated by VLA and FLLS in 2011–14 has been subjected to limited evaluation, involving consultation with professional stakeholders but not with clients. The evaluation was very positive, with participants perceiving benefits for parties and their children, as well as for the legal aid system in terms of cost savings. Settlement rates were high, with around 90% of cases achieving full or partial settlement, including sometimes quite complex issues.[4] Anecdotal evidence from WLS suggests that the process can be very empowering for women, who are given the ability to assert their views and an opportunity to be heard and to exercise some control in a context where this would otherwise be lacking. It can also work well for men who tend to find the process less threatening than court and are given something of an opportunity to save face.[5] In its recent submission to the parliamentary inquiry into 'A Better Family Justice System to Support and Protect those Affected by Family Violence', Women's Legal Services Australia argued that 'a well-supported and safe mediation process, with expert lawyers and mediators who have a sound understanding of family violence and family law, can be an empowering process for a victim', whereas '[s]imply referring a matter into a complex court system rarely results in a good outcome for victims' (Women's Legal Services Australia, 2017, p. 25).

In light of the articles by Jennifer Koshan and Mandy Burton in this special issue, questions for the evaluation of the FVCD in particular might include whether the combination of civil and criminal proceedings raises due process concerns for alleged perpetrators of abuse, whether child contact disputes are settled at a problematically high rate and/or with problematic outcomes, whether a higher rate of compliance with orders (including orders to attend men's behaviour change programmes) is achieved, and whether the court sees a higher rate of breaches of protection orders (and if so, why this might be the case). On the other hand, features which international evaluations have rated positively include having a single judge dealing with the range of legal issues raised by domestic abuse; having dedicated and specially trained judges and other court personnel, legal representation and support services for parties and children; and specific attention to victim safety and protection from further abuse and intimidation at court. What the Australian models add to international experience is the explicit commitment to trauma-informed practice and a whole-of-family approach, and the extension of specialist domestic abuse provision to out-of-court dispute resolution processes.

The European human rights framework

Finally, we return to the issue of legal doctrine and the approach taken by courts in determining contested child arrangements cases. UK courts are required to act compatibly with the rights set out in the European Convention on Human Rights (Human Rights Act 1998 (HRA), s 6), and there are a number of Convention rights which are germane when dealing with applications for contact by perpetrators of domestic abuse. However, in England and Wales, it is clear that this rights-based approach is under-utilised. When human rights are addressed in child arrangement cases it is invariably in relation to the right to family life under Article 8; other relevant articles such as Article 2 (the right to life) or Article 3 (the right to freedom from torture and inhuman or degrading treatment) have not been addressed at all (Birchall & Choudhry, 2018). Moreover s 1 of the Children Act 1989 (CA), which makes the child's welfare the paramount consideration when deciding child arrangements cases, has been interpreted to mean the welfare of the child is to be the single deciding factor (*J v C* [1970] AC 668), that is, not simply paramount over, but in fact displacing, all other considerations. Elevating the welfare of children is, of course, laudable but becomes problematic under a system in which paramountcy is taken to mean exclusivity, which results in adults arguing their interests under the guise of child welfare because they cannot be argued separately and transparently (see Herring, 2001; pp. 164–6; Reece, 1996). Arguably, the courts' focus on the best interests of children as the only consideration and their failure to take the rights of all participants separately into account amounts to a breach of the judiciary's obligations under the HRA (see Choudhry & Herring, 2010, pp. 235–7).

In addition to the requirement to act compatibly with Convention rights under s 6 of the HRA, courts also have a duty under s 2 of the HRA to take Convention jurisprudence into account,[6] and an obligation under s 3 of the HRA to interpret legislation in a way which is compatible with Convention rights so far as it is possible to do so. This allows for an alternative approach to be taken to s 1 of the CA by reinterpreting the meaning of the term 'paramount' in line with the approach of the European Court of Human Rights (ECtHR). This approach would involve a detailed, case by case, consideration of what is the best outcome for all the parties concerned. The welfare of the child is certainly given priority by the ECtHR, but this priority will only be accorded after a detailed consideration of all the rights of the parties involved. Crucially, the ECtHR does not elevate children's welfare to the status of exclusive consideration (see Choudhry, 2003; Choudhry & Fenwick, 2005; Herring, 1999). This difference in approach has a number of distinct advantages in comparison to that employed currently under the CA. First, it allows for a better risk assessment by focusing on the differing rights involved, as opposed to the current approach which insufficiently captures the differing rights of family members by focusing solely on child welfare. Second, it allows for a consideration of all of the parties' rights and interests on an equal footing before the welfare of the child is considered and given priority (Choudhry, 2012; Choudhry & Herring, 2006a, 2010; pp. 261–2). Finally, the ECtHR approach has the added advantage of being consistent with Article 3(1) of the UN Convention on the Rights of the Child (CRC), under which the rights of children are to be a 'primary' consideration of the court rather than the paramount consideration. The CRC has been ratified by the UK, and although it is not yet incorporated into law in England and Wales, it is invoked in judgments and legal arguments in other contexts.[7]

Article 8 of the ECHR

Among the Convention rights which have direct relevance to situations of domestic abuse and child arrangements, Articles 2 and 3 are 'absolute' rights and thus cannot be balanced against the rights of others or the needs of society. On the other hand, Article 8 on the right to private and family life is a 'qualified' right and thus may be interfered with in order to protect the rights of another or the wider public interest. It is clear, for example, that the ECHR does allow for a proportionate interference with the Article 8 right to family life of a perpetrator of domestic abuse as long as the interference satisfies the process of qualification within Article 8(2).[8] Further, due to the number of Article 8 claims at play in a contact dispute that involves domestic abuse - that is, the Article 8 claims of the abusive parent, the non-abusive parent and the child - the parallel analysis will also need to be employed (Choudhry & Fenwick, 2005). In other words, all three Article 8 rights must be considered as possible exceptions to the others, by applying the tests within Article 8(2). The court should also acknowledge that the rights of the child or children involved should be of particular importance.

The key consideration in such a case will therefore be whether the state has taken all the necessary steps to facilitate contact between the abusive parent and the children as can reasonably be demanded in the circumstances of the case. It may be that in striking a fair balance between the competing rights of the family members involved, the nature and extent of the abuse is considered too great to grant a request for any form of contact where such contact could interfere with other family members' rights. However, it may also be the case that allowing supervised or unsupervised contact may, according to the individual facts of a case, be the more proportionate response bearing in mind the positive obligations that are owed to parents under Article 8 to facilitate contact with their children if possible. What is also important to bear in mind is the recent acknowledgement by the ECtHR of the detrimental effects that witnessing domestic abuse may have on a child and therefore on *their* right to family life (see *Bevacqua and S v Bulgaria*, no 71127/01, [2008] ECHR 498). It may follow that a cautious approach, such as the implementation of a presumption against contact where domestic abuse has been proved, would not be regarded as disproportionate under Article 8 (Choudhry & Fenwick, 2005).

However, it should be recalled that whilst certainly pertinent, Article 8 is not the only right that falls to be considered in such cases and that as a qualified right it cannot 'trump' claims made under the absolute rights of Articles 2 and 3. Given the lack of judicial attention accorded to these rights in England and Wales and the contrasting approach found at the ECtHR, the focus of this discussion will be on the right most likely to be relevant in child arrangement cases involving allegations of domestic abuse, that is, the right to remain free from inhuman or degrading treatment under Article 3.

Article 3 of the ECHR

Article 3 of the ECHR states: 'No one shall be subject to torture or to inhuman or degrading treatment or punishment.' The phrase 'ill treatment' is the umbrella term used when the court assesses whether the treatment referred to in the case is sufficient to fall within the scope of Article 3. The ECtHR has established that ill treatment includes actual bodily harm or intense physical or mental suffering (see *Ireland v UK* [1978] ECHR 1). 'Degrading treatment' includes conduct that humiliates or debases an individual, shows a lack of respect for, or diminishes human dignity. It also includes conduct that arouses feelings of fear, anguish or inferiority capable of breaking an individual's moral and physical resistance (see, e.g. *Price v UK* [2011] ECHR 2270, paras. 24–30; *Valasinas v Lithuania* [2001] ECHR 483, para. 117). In considering whether treatment is 'degrading' the court will have regard to whether its object was to humiliate and debase the victim as well as the effect on the victim. Article 3 not only prohibits the State from inflicting torture or inhuman or degrading treatment on its citizens, it also requires the State to protect one citizen from torture or inhuman or degrading treatment at the hands of another (*A v UK* [1998] ECHR 85; *E v UK* [2002] ECHR 769). A State will infringe an individual's right under Article 3 if it is aware that she or he is suffering the necessary degree of abuse at the hands of another and fails to take reasonable, adequate or effective steps to protect that individual (*A v UK* [1998] ECHR 85, para. 24; *Z v UK* [2001] ECHR 333, para. 73; *E v UK* [2002] ECHR 769). There is a particular obligation on the State to protect the Article 3 rights of vulnerable people, such as children and arguably victims of domestic abuse. The obligations imposed on the State include ensuring that there is an effective legal deterrent to protect victims from abuse; to ensure that there is proper legal investigation and prosecution of any infringement of the individual's rights; and where necessary to intervene and remove a victim from a position where she or he is suffering conduct which is prohibited by Article 3. Hence States have been found to infringe Article 3 when they have been aware that children are being abused but have not taken steps to protect them (*E v UK* [2002] ECHR 769), where the law on sexual assault required proof that the victim had physically resisted the sexual assault, and where the police failed to properly investigate or take steps to prosecute men alleged to have committed sexual assaults (*MC v Bulgaria* [2003] ECHR 651).

The right under Article 3 is an absolute one. Unlike many of the other rights mentioned in the ECHR there are no circumstances in which it is permissible for the State to infringe this right. This makes it clear that the rights of another party cannot justify an infringement of someone's Article 3 rights. So, for example, it cannot be successfully argued that a family's right of privacy justifies non-intervention by the State if that non-intervention infringes one family member's Article 3 rights. In other words, the State cannot justify its failure to protect a victim's Article 3 rights in a child arrangements case by referring to that person's right to respect for private and family life under Article 8.

Research on the effects upon children and adults of witnessing or experiencing domestic abuse has demonstrated that those effects will often be sufficiently intense to engage Article 3. Physical abuse is likely to fall within Article 3, unless the physical injuries are of a minor kind. Emotional abuse, intimidation or debasement can also fall within Article 3 as 'degrading treatment', particularly when these aspects of the practice are intended to humiliate and demean the victim (see, e.g. Edwards, 1996, pp. 180–91).

The application of Article 3 to a child victim of domestic abuse has recently been addressed by the ECtHR.[9] In *DMD v Romania* [2017] ECHR 815, proceedings that lasted over eight years were brought by a son (DMD) against his father and ended in the father's conviction for physically and mentally abusing his child. DMD, the applicant, complained that those proceedings had been ineffective and that he had not been awarded damages. The ECtHR held, unanimously, that there had been a violation of Article 3 because the investigation into the allegations of abuse had lasted too long and had been marred by other serious shortcomings. The Court also recalled that Member States should strive expressly and comprehensively to protect children's dignity, which requires an adequate legal framework affording protection to children against domestic violence. This should also include effective deterrence against such serious breaches of personal integrity, reasonable steps to prevent ill-treatment of which the authorities have, or ought to have, knowledge, and effective official investigations where an individual raises an arguable claim of ill-treatment. Several points were made as to the inadequacy of the proceedings but of particular note was the observation that the domestic courts' approach in this case to the issue of domestic abuse, apparently suggesting that 'isolated and random' acts of violence could be tolerated within the family, was not compatible either with domestic law or with the Convention.

The application of Article 3 to domestic abuse against adult victims was directly addressed by the ECtHR for the first time in its highly significant decision in *Opuz v*

Turkey [2009] ECHR 870, in which the applicant, a victim of domestic abuse, alleged that the injuries and anguish she had suffered as a result of the violence inflicted upon her by her husband had amounted to torture within the meaning of Article 3. Furthermore, by consistently failing to take any action to protect her from his violence in response to her repeated requests for help, the State had made her feel debased, hopeless and vulnerable. The ECtHR agreed, coming to this conclusion by a straightforward application of the principles that it had developed in relation to Article 3 discussed above. Of particular relevance was the principle that children and other vulnerable individuals, in particular, are entitled to State protection, in the form of effective deterrence, against serious breaches of personal integrity. The Court thus considered, as had been predicted (see Choudhry & Herring, 2006a, 2006b), that the applicant and therefore other victims of domestic abuse could fall within the group of 'vulnerable individuals' entitled to State protection that was referred to in *A v UK* [1998] ECHR 85. Relevant factors in coming to this conclusion that were cited by the Court were: the violence suffered by the applicant in the past, the threats issued by her husband following his release from prison and her fear of further violence. Importantly, the Court also acknowledged that domestic abuse which is non-physical can also come within Article 3: 'The Court observes also that the violence suffered by the applicant, in the form of physical injuries *and psychological pressure*, were sufficiently serious to amount to ill-treatment within the meaning of Article 3 of the Convention' (*Opuz v Turkey* [2009] EHCR 870, para. 161, emphasis added).

The Court then turned to the question of whether the national authorities had taken all reasonable measures to prevent the recurrence of violent attacks against the applicant's physical integrity. After reviewing the response of the authorities in some detail, the Court considered that they had not. Although the authorities had responded each time a complaint had been made, the reliance upon the applicant's continued complaints for further action and the general inadequacy of the measures taken against her husband meant that the local authorities had failed to demonstrate the required diligence to prevent the recurrence of violent attacks against the applicant (paras. 166–75).

The potential significance of this decision for *all* victims of domestic abuse cannot be underestimated. The case was notable for the Court's reference throughout to principles established by international institutions and courts regarding the nature of violence against women, gender-based discrimination and human rights, such as the Convention on the Elimination of All Forms of Discrimination against Women, the UN Commission on Human Rights (predecessor to the Human Rights Council), the Belém do Pará Convention and the Inter-American Commission on Human Rights (paras. 72–86). This demonstrates the acceptance and application by the ECtHR of the establishment of a number of legal norms created by a variety of international instruments and decisions in relation to domestic violence. These norms will also have application to victims of domestic abuse within private family law proceedings as part of the positive obligations of member States created under the ECHR.

The case also demonstrates that the State's obligations under Article 3 cannot be satisfied by the passing of appropriate legislation alone. What is also required to be demonstrated is that the legislation is reasonably *effective*. The decision thus underlines the need to fully implement and carefully monitor the effectiveness of domestic abuse policy and legislation. Finally, with information provided by NGOs, the Court concluded that domestic violence was disproportionately suffered by women in Turkey and there was evidence of a difference in the treatment by the courts and by law enforcement agencies of this issue compared with other criminal offences. As a result, the ECtHR recognised that there was a 'general and discriminatory judicial passivity in Turkey' that denied women equal protection under the law (para. 198). The Court's willingness to refer to the reports provided by NGOs and advocacy groups means that such evidence will be of considerable importance when it comes to any future assessment by the Court of a State's performance of its obligations in this regard. Research conducted domestically by such organisations in relation to the gendered experiences of women victims of domestic abuse in the family courts could thus prove to be crucial when assessing whether the courts are complying with their obligations to undertake effective investigations and risk assessments in order to protect victims from further abuse (see Birchall & Choudhry, 2018). The *Opuz* decision has been followed in a number of subsequent ECtHR decisions concerning domestic abuse.[10]

In summary therefore, the ECtHR has established that particular regard will be given to children and vulnerable adults when considering the extent of the positive obligations that are to be imposed on member States towards them, notwithstanding that the 'treatment' at issue is being meted out by private individuals. Liability under Article 3 will be incurred if the following criteria are met:

- the treatment concerned comes within the definition established under Article 3;
- the State had or ought to have had knowledge that such treatment was occurring; and
- the State failed to take reasonably available measures that could have mitigated the resulting harm.

Thus, although Article 3 is drafted in absolute terms, the duties imposed by it on States are not. When an assessment is undertaken of the conduct of the State in relation to Article 3 cases the real issue is whether the police, local authorities and/or courts were properly to be regarded as responsible for the conduct that was prohibited by Article 3. Nevertheless, the fact that government policies against domestic abuse exist is not sufficient. The actual implementation of such policies must be closely monitored in order to ensure that State obligations are really being fulfilled. In practical terms, this could mean that in child arrangements cases a failure by the family court to provide protection to a vulnerable child and/or adult against direct contact with an abusive parent where Article 3 type treatment or the risk of it can be evidenced may lead to a breach of that child's and/or adult's rights under Article 3, and also a breach of the court's obligations under section 6 of the HRA.

Cases in which domestic abuse reaches the level of Article 3 type treatment of a child are usually dealt with in England and Wales via child protection proceedings under the Children Act 1989 and, if relevant, criminal proceedings. However, as noted above, the Article 3 rights of both children and adult victims of domestic abuse are rarely considered in private family law proceedings. Where Article 3 applies in such cases, the denial of direct contact should be a relatively straightforward exercise in judicial reasoning for, according to the terms of the Article itself, the balancing of the rights and interests of others is not required. If Article 3 type treatment or the risk of it is proved then that is the end of the matter. The refusal to award direct contact to an applicant who has meted out such treatment or is judged to be at risk of doing so to a child can easily be legally justified. Any competing claims under Article 8 as a qualified article (or any other justifications) should not override a finding that Article 3 as an absolute article has been breached. Where the abuse does not meet the threshold for Article 3, however, the applicability of Article 8 and the competing claims that will arise under it must be considered.

Conclusion

As the articles in this special issue demonstrate, the International Symposium on Contact Disputes and Allegations of Domestic Violence – Identifying Best Practices succeeded in identifying more poor practices than best practices. Moreover, while poor practices may easily be identified in day to day operation in many jurisdictions, best practices tend to remain theoretical, inchoate or novel. Despite the resultant difficulty in certifying best practices, the lessons learnt from experiments with SDVCs and IDVCs as explained by Koshan and Burton, from judicial education as explained by Jaffe et al., and from the views of children who have experienced and witnessed domestic abuse as explained by Holt and Mackay, together with the approaches discussed in this concluding article, appear to contain the greatest promise for future development. They certainly provide an agenda which may enable the family justice system in England and Wales to transcend the 'cycle of failure' experienced with PD12J. They also suggest that what is needed is not more or different legislation but practices informed by an expert understanding of the dynamics and effects of domestic abuse, which address the legal and non-legal needs of both children and adults, and which prioritise safety from, ending of, and recovery from abuse.

Notes

1. The following section is largely based on conversations held by Rosemary Hunter in Melbourne with Professor Helen Rhoades, former Chair of the Family Law Council of Australia, 11 December 2017 and Henrietta Barclay, Director, Legal and Policy, Women's Legal Service Victoria, 14 December 2017, together with an unpublished, undated evaluation of LAFDR 2011–2014 conducted by Emma Pritchard, on file with Rosemary Hunter.
2. Cases are still screened out if they involve child sexual abuse or severe family violence, including e.g. breaches of protection orders or imprisonment for domestic violence offences.
3. Current limits on the FVDC's family law jurisdiction in the Australian federal context include the ability only to make interim and final consent orders in parenting matters and little effective scope to deal with financial matters.
4. See above n 1.
5. Ibid.
6. Where that jurisprudence is clear and consistent it should be treated as binding: see *R (on the application of Alconbury Developments Ltd) v Secretary of State for the Environment* [2001] 2 WLR 1389 [26] (Lord Slynn).
7. The CRC is often referred to in immigration, education and other cases concerning children. For references in the specific context of family law see, for example, *In re M (Children) (Abduction: Rights of Custody)* [2007] UKHL 55; *Re E (Children)* [2011] UKSC

27; *Re B (A Child)* [2013] UKSC 33, para. 73 (Lord Neuberger); *Re D (A Child) (International Recognition)* [2016] EWCA Civ 12; *Re F (Children)* [2016] EWCA Civ 546; *Re M (Children)* [2017] EWCA Civ 891, para. 20; *Re C (Children)* [2017] EWCA Civ 980, para. 101.

8. Limitations on Article 8 rights must be 'in accordance with the law' and 'necessary in a democratic society' (i.e. must meet a pressing social need and be proportionate) and be related to one or more of the permissible aims, in this case the protection of the rights and freedoms of others.
9. This question had come up in the case of *Bevacqua and S v Bulgaria* (Application no. 71127/01, 12 June 2008) but the Court declined to consider Article 3, opting instead to consider the complaint under Article 8 alone.
10. See amongst others: *E and S v Slovakia* [2009] ECHR 1282; *Eremia and Others v the Republic of Moldova* [2013] ECHR 453; *Talpis v Italy* [2017] ECHR 224.

Disclosure statement

No potential conflict of interest was reported by the authors.

References

Birchall, J., & Choudhry, S. (2018). *"What about my right not to be abused?" Domestic abuse, human rights and the family courts*. Bristol: Women's Aid.

Choudhry, S. (2003). The Adoption and Children Act 2002, the welfare principle and the Human Rights Act 1998: A missed opportunity. *Child and Family Law Quarterly, 15*, 119–137.

Choudhry, S. (2012). Contact, domestic violence and the ECHR. In M. Freeman (Ed.), *Law and childhood studies: Current legal issues Vol 14* (pp. 339–356). Oxford: Oxford University Press.

Choudhry, S., & Fenwick, H. (2005). Taking the rights of parents and children seriously: Confronting the welfare principle under the Human Rights Act. *Oxford Journal of Legal Studies, 25*, 453–492.

Choudhry, S., & Herring, J. (2006a). Domestic violence and the Human Rights Act 1998: A new means of legal intervention. *Public Law, 2006*, 752–784.

Choudhry, S., & Herring, J. (2006b). Righting domestic violence. *International Journal of Law, Policy and the Family, 20*, 95–119.

Choudhry, S., & Herring, J. (2010). *European human rights and family law*. Oxford: Hart Publishing.

Edwards, S. (1996). *Sex, gender and the legal process*. London: Blackstone.

Family Law Council. (2015). *Families with complex needs and the intersection of the family law and child protection systems: Interim report – June 2015 (Terms 1 and 2)*. Canberra, Commonwealth Attorney-General's Department.

Family Law Council. (2016). *Families with complex needs and the intersection of the family law and child protection systems: Final report – June 2016 (Terms 3, 4 and 5)*. Canberra, Commonwealth Attorney-General's Department.

Herring, J. (1999). The Human Rights Act and the welfare principle in family law. *Child and Family Law Quarterly, 11*, 223–235.

Herring, J. (2001). *Family law: Issues, debates and policy*. Cullumpton: Willan.

House of Representatives Standing Committee on Social Policy and Legal Affairs. (2017). *A better family law system to support and protect those affected by family violence*. Canberra: Parliament of the Commonwealth of Australia.

Quadara, A. (2015). *Implementing trauma-informed systems of care in health settings: The WITH study* (Landscapes: State of knowledge paper). Sydney: ANROWS.

Reece, H. (1996). The paramountcy principle: Consensus or construct? *Current Legal Problems, 49*, 267–304.

Relationships Australia. (2017). Submission no 55 to the Parliamentary inquiry into a better family law system to support and protect those affected by family violence. Retrieved from the inquiry website at: https://www.aph.gov.au/Parliamentary_Business/Committees/House/Social_Policy_and_Legal_Affairs/FVlawreform/Submissions.

Royal Commission into Family Violence (Victoria). (2016). *Report and Recommendations*. Melbourne: Victorian Government Printer.

Women's Legal Services Australia. (2017). Submission no 6 to the Parliamentary inquiry into a better family law system to support and protect those affected by family violence. Retrieved from the inquiry website at: https://www.aph.gov.au/Parliamentary_Business/Committees/House/Social_Policy_and_Legal_Affairs/FVlawreform/Submissions.

Index

Note: **Bold** page numbers refer to tables; *italic* page numbers refer to figures and page numbers followed by "n" denote endnotes.